HINDU
AND
JUNGIAN PSYCHOLOGY

OTHER BOOKS BY J. MARVIN SPIEGELMAN, PH.D.

- The Tree — Tales in Psychomythology
- The Knight
- The Quest — Further Tales in the Unconscious
- The Nymphomaniac
- The Modern Jew in Search of a Soul, with Dr. Jacobson
- Buddhism and Jungian Psychology, with Dr. Miyuki
- Mysticism, Psychology and Oedipus, with Drs. Regardie and Hyatt

Inquiries into the availability of these books are welcomed by Falcon Press.

HINDUISM
AND
JUNGIAN PSYCHOLOGY

By
J. Marvin Spiegelman, Ph.D.
and
Arwind U. Vasavada, D. Litt.

1987
FALCON PRESS
PHOENIX, ARIZONA, U.S.A.

International Standard Book Number: 0-941404-44-7
Library of Congress Catalog Card Number: 87-080326

First Edition 1987

Typesetting Design — Cate Mugasis

Cover Design — Clara Cohan

Editing and Production Consultation — Christopher S. Hyatt, Ph.D.

Illustrations for *Maya, The Yogini* — Martin Mondrus

Chakra Drawings © TIMELESS BOOKS

Falcon Press
3660 N. 3rd Street
Phoenix, Arizona 85012, U.S.A.
(602) 246-3546

Manufactured in the United States of America

TABLE OF CONTENTS

Foreword — by J. Marvin Spiegelman   i

PART ONE: Hinduism and Jungian Psychology from a Personal Point of View

India and Jungian Psychology: A Personal Perspective (1985)
by J. Marvin Spiegelman   3

India and Jungian Psychology: A Personal Experience (1985)
by Arwind U. Vasavada   14

PART TWO: Kundalini Yoga

A Psychological Commentary on Kundalini Yoga (1985)
by J. Marvin Spiegelman   27

Comments
by Arwind U. Vasavada   63

Maya, the Yogini — A Fictional Tale of Kundalini (1967)
by J. Marvin Spiegelman   69

PART THREE: Aspects of Hinduism and Jungian Psychology
by Arwind U. Vasavada, with Comments by J. Marvin Spiegelman

Yogic Basis of Psychoanalysis (1941)   113

The Process of Individuation and Self-Realisation
A Comparison (1957)   120

Alchemy and Catatonic Depression (1960)   130

A Reflection on Jung's Autobiography (1964)   135

Philosophical Roots of the Psychotherapies of the West (1965)   140

The Unconscious and the Myth of the Divine Mother (1971)   152

Dr. Jung, a Psychologist or a Guru? (1971)   163

Fee-Less Practice and "Soul Work" (1980)   177

Meeting Jung   186

Afterword — A Letter from C.G. Jung   191

ILLUSTRATIONS

Muladhara: The First Chakra   195
Svadhisthana: The Second Chakra   196
Manipura: The Third Chakra   197
Anahata: The Fourth Chakra   198
Vishuddha: The Fifth Chakra   199
Ajna: The Sixth Chakra   200
Sahasrara: The Seventh Chakra   201

Maya, The Yogini

Whipping Men   202
The Tree   203
Holding up the Goat's Eye   204
Dance of the Moon Goddess   205
Books of Lives   206
Six Headed Goddess   207

ACKNOWLEDGEMENTS

The authors are grateful to the following publishers for reprinting some papers or quoting parts of others. Every effort was made to obtain written permission, most of which were received by the time of publication.

Narayana Burukula, Srinivasapuram P.O., Varkala, Herala, India
Bharatiya Vidya, Journal of the Bharatiya Vidya Bhavan, Bombay India
 Philosophical Congress
Rascher Verlag, Zurich, and *Spectrum Psychologia*
Spring Publications (for quotes from Jung's Kundalini Papers)
Ganesh & Co., Madras, India (for quotes from Avalon's *Serpent Power*)
Falcon Press, Phoenix, Arizona, for republishing "Maya, the Yogini" (from
 The Tree, 1982)
Drawings of the chakras are reprinted by permission of Timeless Books, Porthill, ID.

Foreword

Hinduism and Jungian Psychology is the third in a series of books which aim at bringing into relationship the attitude and findings of Jungian psychology together with various religious traditions and also other branches of the human spirit, such as the sciences and literature.

The first book in this series, *Buddhism and Jungian Psychology*, written by Dr. Mokusen Miyuki and myself, appeared in May of 1985 (8). The second, *A Modern Jew in Search of a Soul*, which I edited along with Dr. Abraham Jacobson, contained the contributions of twenty-seven people, many of whom were Jungian analysts or had undergone Jungian analysis, appeared in May of 1986 (9). This third book, written by Dr. Vasavada and myself, conforms more to the pattern set out in the first one, in that various scholarly chapters are combined with personal ones. Most importantly, the work is written by two people steeped in Jungian analysis, so that there is a relationship among the fields at an inner level, as well as at an outer one.

It was with this distinction in mind that I approached the book *Jung and Eastern Thought* (2) written by Harold Coward, Professor of Religious Studies at the University of Calgary, along with contributions by two other scholars, J. Borelli and J.F.T. Jordens. I had rather expected that this work -- which came into my hands in October, 1985 after most of our work was completed -- would accomplish what I had set out to do in the Foreword to the Buddhism book, namely to present Jung's general views on the field in a clear manner. My expectations were more than fulfilled, since the work does, indeed, present the views of Jung in a most complete and scholarly fashion, as well as compare some Hindu concepts, such as Prana, Prajna and Purusha, to the Jungian ideas of libido, consciousness, and self. I therefore recommend that book to the reader of this one as a useful companion to it. The overlap, as one might expect -- given the distinction between therapists writing from the personal/transpersonal perspective in contrast to that of the scholar -- is not great. Yet the differences in attitude are relevant and make the dialogue we are both attending to, more precise. I intend, then, to devote some attention to this difference here.

Professor Coward notes (p. 16) the central difference between Jung and the Hindu conception by stating that Jung does not believe, on scientific grounds, that there can be consciousness without an ego. Coward says, quite rightly, that Jung was of the view that there can be no life at all without the experience of the tension of the opposites. He selected a very

i

germane excerpt from one of Jung's Letters (3, p. 247), which is worth quoting again here, since it is so precise and vivid:

> It is certainly desirable to liberate oneself from the operation of the opposites but one can only do it to a certain extent because no sooner do you get out of the conflict than you get out of life altogether. So that liberation can only be a very partial one. It can be the construction of a consciousness just beyond the opposites. Your head may be liberated, your feet remain entangled. Complete liberation means death.

This colorful image of liberated head and entangled feet has just the sort of concreteness that we therapists continually have to use to help our patients maintain a connection with their bodies. We in the West, unfortunately, do not have the kind of union of spirit and flesh which has so long been a mainstay of the East. Whereas Jung says that the East is pre-Kantian in their scientific development, we in the West are often "pre-whole" in our body-soul.

In my own chapter on Kundalini in the present book, I devote some time to this issue, which fundamentally states that insofar as we try to be scientific, we must remain with what Jung affirms: we are empirical. It is quite possible for us to have had experiences which transcend this condition, but we can only assert it, not prove it to be true. This is the case for anyone, including those Christians who believe that *only* Jesus is savior.

An unproven assertion, I regret to say, is made by Professor Jordens, in his chapter in Coward's book, on "Prakriti and the Collective Unconscious: Purusa and Self." Jordens states that "the purusa, final goal of yogic samadhi, remains beyond his (Jung's) reach" (p. 165). Is that so? On what grounds? I am afraid that this distinction between what is asserted as true and can be demonstrated *scientifically*, as against what is asserted as true *religiously* or is revelatory from the divine, is not seen so clearly by many people, including scholars. This, I think, is because the psychological point of view of Jung is hard come by. It involves a simultaneous experiencing and carrying of the opposites of objectivity and subjectivity, resolved in the conception of *psychic reality*, which knows its own limits. It is for this reason that the dialogue needs to be extended to those who understand experientially, as in analysis, and in knowledge, as in scholarship. Unfortunately, we are all limited in both of these, so that these delicate questions become confused.

Professor Jordens valuably points out, however, in another chapter ("Prana and Libido: Prajna and Consciousness") that Jung was quite wrong when he asserted that he had no metaphysical claims in his psychology (p. 182). Of course we all have a metaphysical basis for what we proclaim as our ground or viewpoint; it is the psyche itself, as Jung was ever demonstrating. It is our *unconscious* assumptions which drive us, even when we claim to be Hindu or scientific or whatever, and it is for this reason that we analyze ourselves to discover what our "metaphysical assumptions" (read "unconscious assumptions") are. Once we have made these conscious, we can then try to harmonize the conflicts. Jung's conscious metaphysics was that of science, and, even more so, empiricism. He insisted on the demonstrability of the facts which led to the concepts that he put forward about the psyche. It may well be -- seen from the perspective of his "guru" dream late in life -- that he had an "unconscious" assumption closer to the Hindu, to be revealed to him later. All the same, as shown in his *Memories, Dreams, Reflections* (4), he remained true to his western and scientific view that ego and self need each other, and that final transcendence is not to be achieved while we are mortal.

One indication of the strength of Jung's commitment to maintaining a connection with his mortal existence is to be found in the chapter of his autobiography in which he describes his confrontation with the unconscious. After stating that "The unconscious contents could have driven me out of my wits," he acknowledges the value of his family and profession to keeping him grounded, unlike that which happened to Nietzsche. Such irreality was a horror for him since (4, p. 189):

> I aimed, after all, at *this* world and *this* life. No matter how deeply absorbed or how blown about I was, I always knew that everything I was experiencing was ultimately directed at this real life of mine. I meant to meet its obligations and fulfill its meanings.

When we realize that Jung wrote these words and this autobiography in the last years of his life, after he experienced his "guru dream," we can rest assured that his fundamental viewpoint of ego and self, expressed above, remained unchanged, despite the differences and softenings which occurred between his initial presentations on Hindu thought in the 1930's and his "later thoughts" in the late 1950's.

We can agree, however, that the transcendence that is being referred to can be achieved only for certain periods of time. Surely Jung, as have others of us, experienced this transcendence and freedom from opposites for moments, but we quickly return to the opposites in some form. Jung's assertion that an ego is always needed in such experiences must be questioned further.

Professor Jordens, once more very valuably, (pp. 178-184), shows that Jung's conceptions are more similar to the early Upanishads, such as the Kausitaki, which are more psychological in nature, and different from the absolutist claims of the later works, such as is found in Vedanta. Are we not faced with a continuing pair of opposites in this discussion? I think so. I would formulate it as follows: Jung's conception is closer to the primitive psyche and thus is similar to the "early" Hindu, when we consider the *experience* being described. The "later" Hindu, as in Vedanta, or even Patanjali, is, indeed, still "pre-Kantian" in *formulation*, whereas Jung, with his very advanced psychological conception which is both scientific and based on subjective conditions, is "post-Kantian." In essence, this means that each conception is primitive in one way and advanced in another.

This is rather like the discussion Jung undertakes in his description of Kundalini in the 1932 seminars which I discuss in considerable detail later on. In one way, we in the west are "advanced" and think with our heads at *ajna*. In another way, however, we are not there at all, and our consciousness is very much at *muladhara*. The Hindu is in the reverse position. (See: "A Psychological Commentary on Kundalini Yoga.")

In addition to the paradoxical differences already discussed, we may also consider where Jungian psychology reaches its limits when dealing with "larger wholes", such as that described or asserted here in Hindu thought, but also when considering the idea that there is "group consciousness" transcending the individual. The latter, for example, is central to groups which find their basis in the work of Alice Bailey and her guru (1). They assert that "group work" on a conscious level can not only be done, but must be done to continue the evolution of consciousness on the planet.

The "absolute knowledge" spoken of by the Hindus who have achieved Samadhi or even *Pranaprajnatman* (the metaphysical absolute), and even the "group consciousness" of the spiritual groups, seem to go beyond Jung's claims. He would not deny them, he would merely assert that they have to prove it, and probably can't (forgive the pun on Kant!). Yet the claims of the "absolutists" and the "groupists" can not be denied. It seems to me that it remains a work for the latter to demonstrate their findings to a larger psychological or scientifically inclined audience, and for us who are psychological to penetrate more deeply into what these people are intending. It is true that they seem to violate Jungian tenets. The "absolutists" do this by violating what we know as scientific limits and the nature of "psychic reality".

The "groupists" violate our psychological viewpoint by claiming that consciousness can reside in a "group soul" or in an inner guide who leads many at one time, as they exist together in relationship. It is better for us to say that this may be possible and we should, perhaps, try to experience this rather than simply be "fundamentalistic" ourselves and deny it. Our condition is still that of trying hard to maintain the value of the *individual* in the collective, or the atman or self in the individual psyche, when that is continually being either denied or raised beyond what we can know scientifically. So, the tension between these opposites continues.

Professor Coward, in the conclusion to his book, gracefully accepts this continuing duality, and appreciates Henderson's statement in the introduction, that the aim of the healer is different than that of the scholar, although both need each other. I can only add my own appreciation of this, and aver that this dialogue, indeed, is part of the ongoing encounter of East and West. This will continue until we integrate our differences in such as a way that a true wholeness emerges.

Our present book, *Hinduism and Jungian Psychology*, is, on a small scale, a continuing dialogue on the same themes, although here we have two people who are themselves Jungian analysts, both having graduated from the C.G. Jung Institute, Zurich. Our work is presented in both a personal and impersonal way, as is right for therapists, but we also come to conceptual differences, since we are, indeed, West and East. A feature of this book is the commentary that each of us has written about some of the work of the other. In this, perhaps, the reader will find a further insight into how these grand opposites work out in the small scale of the individual human endeavor.

As in the Buddhism book, there is a Foreword, outlining Jung's views (here taking up problems presented by the Coward book which has already done this for us), followed by a section of personal experience (Part I). Here Vasavada and I both tell how Jung and Hinduism have found their representation in our psyches.

Dr. Vasavada's paper, his most recent work, was written at the co-author's invitation for another book, one in which a number of Jungian Analysts -- all of whom had some contact with Jung -- write about their own approach to therapy. It is also included in this book, since it, too, is a clear presentation of the mutual impact of Jungian Psychology and Indian thought. In it, we see Dr. Vasavada at work on this process within himself. He follows the way of the Guru *and* the way of Jung, understanding both clearly, using each as is necessary.

As a reader of his most recent paper, I sense his calm, his serenity, and his resolution of the conflict of years. For me, the ultimate in this struggle appears in the 1980 paper on "Fee-Less Practice," in which both Guru and Jung reached their ultimate and then "died" as his center, to be superceded by the discovery of his Self. This Self is apparent in the latest paper, and we can see how this singular personality, the only one to come from India to the West and take on the work of Jungian psychology, has manifested.

Part II is taken up with my psychological study of Kundalini. There is an essay which examines basic texts, and includes Jung's views as well as my own. Following this, I present a fictional account of that process -- a story of a woman undergoing Kundalini Yoga by herself. I wrote this tale -- as part of a larger work of ten people from as many traditions on their own individuation voyage -- in *The Tree: Tales in Psychomythology* (5) and its sequels *The Quest* (6) and *The Love* (7).

Part III is devoted to a series of papers by Dr. Vasavada, in which his development as psychologist, healer and Hindu disciple is portrayed in vivid fashion. Although some of these papers show a deep connection between Jungian "gnosis" and the ancient Hindu tradition, others reveal Dr. Vasavada's understanding and struggles with Western psychology in general. The authors recognize that though some readers have a strong background in this area and may find some of it redundant, their significance becomes more apparent as we see the development of this most interesting "Hindu-Jungian" mind. Unfortunately, we were forced to delete two other papers of Dr. Vasavada because of space limitations.

I hope the reader will be as pleased with his work as I have been. I have kept my comments brief with one exception, and trust that this will enhance his contribution. As with the Buddhism book, an Afterword concludes the discussion. This final word, appropriately, is a letter from C.G. Jung.

It is a great privilege for me to be involved with this series of books. It provides me with the opportunity of realizing my own ecumenical myth, and I am grateful to Falcon Press for having the courage to support this endeavor. I am aware that I am not alone in this quest. Our whole planet is slowly and painfully reaching toward that larger synthesis we all long for, in which the individual and the group are both valued and, in turn, find a meaningful connection with the larger societies, the world, and, finally, the cosmos itself.

> J. Marvin Spiegelman
> Studio City, California
> Winter 1985-1986

REFERENCES

1. Bailey, Alice A. *A Treatise on Cosmic Fire*, Lucis Publishing Company, New York, 1950. Original 1925, and Collected works.

2. Coward, Harold. *Jung and Eastern Thought*, State University of New York Press, Albany, New York, 1985.

3. Jung, C.G. Collected Letters of C.G. Jung, edited by Gerhard Adler, Vol. I, Princeton University Press, 1973.

4. Jung, C.G. *Memories, Dreams, Reflections*, Random House, New York, 1961.

5. Spiegelman, J. Marvin, *The Tree: Tales in Psycho-mythology*, Falcon Press, Phoenix, AZ, 1982 (original 1974).

6. Spiegelman, J. Marvin, *The Quest: Further Tales in Psycho-mythology*, Falcon Press, Phoenix, AZ, 1984.

7. Spiegelman, J. Marvin, *The Love* (not yet published).

8. Spiegelman, J. Marvin and Miyuki, Mokusen, *Buddhism and Jungian Psychology*, Falcon Press, Phoenix, AZ, 1985.

9. Spiegelman, J. Marvin and Jacobson, Abraham, *A Modern Jew in Search of a Soul*, Falcon Press, Phoenix, AZ, 1986.

PART ONE

HINDUISM AND JUNGIAN PSYCHOLOGY
from a Personal Point of View

India and Jungian Psychology: A Personal Perspective — 1985
by J. Marvin Spiegelman

India and Jungian Psychology: A Personal Experience — 1985
by Arwind U. Vasavada

INDIA AND JUNGIAN PSYCHOLOGY:
A PERSONAL PERSPECTIVE (1985)

by

J. Marvin Spiegelman

In these days of the increasing interpenetration of East and West, it seems important to me that those who try to address the issues arising from that encounter, particularly the spiritual dimension of it, should give some hint of their personal experience of this interchange. In the literature pertaining to the learning of Eastern spirituality by Western seekers, or in books about Western science and technology, what is common to both is the attempt at universality, at the general level of "truth" as it is achieved by the chief practitioners of both civilizations.

In the East, it is the inner, spiritual truth that is presented, along with the way of achieving it, via the technical methods of Yoga. In the West, it is the outer, material truth, achieved by the technical methods of science and engineering. Both claim objectivity, but both leave out the individual, by and large. The East, it is true, shows a path for that individual to achieve enlightenment and self-realization, but his particular experience is usually to be corrected and conformed to general methods in order to achieve his longed-for goal. The West, of course, is interested in the individual only in the abstract, but its goals are to improve his material and intellectual well-being also.

In short, the individual, personal dimension is lacking in both of these, and it is precisely in depth psychology, particularly Jungian psychology, that this dimension is emphasized. Analytical psychotherapy is an art based on science, whose "subject" constitutes individuals pursuing a personal journey, accompanied by an analyst whose own predilections, character and experience effect the outcome. It is exactly from this work that the symbols and experiences which have long occupied center stage in Eastern spirituality have emerged in the psyches of Western people. This was the startling finding of Jung, which made possible the ultimate union of Eastern and Western viewpoints.

Jung also found that one could become "lost" in the fascination with the

3

opposite of one's own tradition, whether that resides in Eastern spirituality or the unconscious itself. Since he both discovered and valued the Individuation process, it was important that the person pursuing such a path in his own psyche not lose track of who he was and what he came from. His personal ego was just as important as his Self, and the union of the two was an empirical matter rather than a question of what was proper.

Jung longed to be understood by his fellow scientists and aimed at the presentation of general principles in most of his writing. He is therefore quite objective and transpersonal. His greatest writing, however, in my opinion, lies precisely in those documents wherein he tries to be both personal and transpersonal, *viz. Answer to Job* (1) and his autobiographical *Memories, Dreams, Reflections* (2). As a pioneer in the encounter between East and West, indeed as its chief explorer, he shows us the possibility of embracing the "other," yet not losing our own standpoint. As I mention in the foreword to this book and in the foreword to its sister book, *Buddhism and Jungian Psychology*, (7) Jung was especially leery of an uncritical acceptance of Eastern spirituality, just as he was less than ecstatic over the achievements of Western civilization. He shows us the importance of the individual. I would say that this has been achieved and that the next step is for the many who are embarked on such a path of individuation to report on the results of their work. This, so to speak, can constitute further evidence, from which another advance in the hoped-for scientific-spiritual union can take place. Just as the "personal equation" has become of central importance, if not significance, in Western scientific observation, just so is that "personal equation" important for those attending to Eastern methods.

With these considerations in mind, I have asked my colleague, Professor Arwind Vasavada, to give us some hints of how East and West have encountered each other in his own soul. I also pursued this tack in my previous book on *Buddhism and Jungian Psychology*, written with Professor Mokusen Miyuki, my Buddhist friend and colleague. I felt it important to continue this path for myself in my contribution to the sequel to that book, *A Modern Jew in Search of a Soul*, (8), and continue that policy here. In so doing, not only will the reader be able to gain some inkling of the "personal equation" of the writer, but also the latter (myself) will have the possibility of reflecting on just that particularity and thus gain further consciousness of his own process.

Explanation and *apologia* completed, I will now relate how India and its philosophy entered into my psyche and gradually required an encounter at the various levels of my being.

At the beginning of high school, before I was fourteen years old, about the same time that my Eastern *anima* was touched by experiencing Japanese classmates, I began to learn something about India and its philosophical riches. A friend had joined an occult group of Rosicrucians, headquartered in my native state of California, and was both attending lectures and reading books. I went along with him to a lecture or two and felt critical of the presentation, since I was intent on keeping a scientific attitude toward such things. I remember, particularly, being very deeply struck when the concept of reincarnation was presented. I felt as if a dim knowledge was awakened in me, but I argued -- rather amateurishly, I imagine -- with the speaker about it (the usual criticisms of population increase, etc.) since it was not scientific. At the next lecture, a demonstration was given, in which the aura was produced in the lecturer and his two assistants. Despite my reservations, I could clearly see a purple-bluish color around the lecturer and one assistant, not the other, and there was no apparent way that this could be faked. I did not know what to make of this, and wondered whether the music presented earlier -- romantic and mysterious -- might not have hypnotized me into it. But no; what I saw, I saw. Of my two friends present, one also saw one aura, the other saw nothing.

I then began to read some of the books of this Rosicrucian order, including one called *Mansions of the Soul* by H. Spencer Lewis (3), and another on Lemuria (4). These, combined with travel and adventure books by Richard Halliburton and various sailors who undertook voyages on small boats, brought out a longing in me to visit the East. I also undertook some of the experiments mentioned by that Rosicrucian order, such as sitting in darkness before a mirror illuminated only by two candles and staring deeply at one's own reflection for some time. After some minutes, two images presented themselves sequentially. The first was of a young man of the early 19th century who seemed to be a poet, and the second was of an older man, European, who was something of a philosopher. A little frightened by these visions, I left off the experimental angle and resumed my reading, but in many fields besides religion and the occult.

My present consciousness is satisfied that my initial visions in the mirror presented me with the archetypes of the *puer eternus* and the *wise old man*, which were both certainly constellated by that religious longing and have since been fleshed out by my own spiritual, therapeutic and literary endeavors. I must add, however, that six years later, when, as a sailor in the Merchant Marine, I was on the first allied ship to enter Copenhagen, Denmark at the end of World War II, I had an experience that made me tremble and reminded me of my vision of the wise old man.

I was touring the city with a Danish friend I had met. He brought me to an old castle and we were about to open a door leading into a main room. I stopped my friend and said that I had an uncanny experience at that moment. I "saw" inside the room and knew that a throne was present therein with two lions on either side. I had been there, I said, as a kind of philosopher. My friend was astonished, since he was aware that my description of the room was accurate, as I discovered myself when we entered. This encounter with history was my first experience of Europe, and like my first experience of Asia -- in India, as I will relate in a moment -- it was a highly numinous one. In a sense, the two constituted my first outward experience of East and West and both touched me deeply, though there was nothing of a union in them, except in their impact.

To return to the earlier time, I can say that the Indian spirit did not again enter my consciousness -- except in my voracious reading -- until somewhat before my nineteenth birthday, in early 1945. I had completed many months of preliminary training as a Cadet-Midshipman in the Merchant Marine Cadet Corps, and was now assigned to a ship to both continue my training practically and to enter the "real war." The ship, the S.S. Texarkana Victory, was destined to leave California and sail around the world. It was a very adventurous time for me, since I was now fulfilling an earlier dream of world travel, and was going on a "voyage" in Jack London's sense. I even started a diary, with the intention of writing a book.

One month after sailing, with a one night's docking in Melbourne, Australia, our ship steamed up the Hooghly River, a tributary of the Ganges, to arrive in Calcutta. It had been an adventurous crossing, all right, both because of the usual initiation of sailors who cross the international dateline (hazing, really), and the two torpedoes which were launched at us but failed to hit us. All of that and the adventure at sea were as nothing compared to the experience of Calcutta. From the moment I stepped ashore until we left a month later, I walked and saw, as if in a dream.

I recall Jung's paper, entitled "The Dreamlike World of India," and I can attest that it was so for me. Not only the throngs of people, the deep poverty contrasted with great beauty and wealth, but the heat, the smells, the intensity of colors, all contributed to this overwhelming sense of so much reality that it was irreality. From my present perspective, I can understand Jung's experience when he ran away and hid his head behind a tree, grasping the Indian's need to deny the outer world. I can also understand, in my fashion, the Indian preoccupation with the opposites, since the world there seemed so laden with it in every way, from cows wandering in the bazarres, to proper British Victorian structures, ancient Hindu and Jain temples, Sikhs making their presence known, and every variety of material and spiritual existence. But all is under this dream-like quality that any westerner who has been there will agree.

The crucial spiritual experiences for me during that month, however, had to do with both art and religion. That haunting and hypnotic music, accompanying the dramatic movements of the masked dancers, not only overwhelmed me but put me into a trance from which I did not want to recover. I had heard Indian music before, but this fresh and first-hand experience of ritual music and ragas, of meditative and concert music, made me emotional in a manner unknown by me before. I also enjoyed the popular music and got several records of the current female star, Manta Santi. Even the popular music carried a spiritual quality in its longing and wailing.

This deeply religious quality to Indian sound was compounded for me when I spent many hours at the temple of Kali in the Kalighat section of Calcutta. This place of worship of the Great Goddess was built, the legend says, to house the toe that fell to earth at this spot when she was dismembered in the heavens. And it was certainly, for me, a taste of heaven and earth when I listened endlessly to the praying and chanting of the epic poem, the *Mahabharata*, by those spiritual men accompanied by musical instruments. To merely be in that spot was enough to give proof of the Indian vision, the spirituality which encompasses everything and rejects nothing, even while it rejects the ego-centric attachment to existence. I watched in awe to see, in this so spiritual and so advanced a context, an example of animal sacrifice, and looked long at that goat's eye which looked back at me. I tried to record this experience and its significance in a story I wrote thirty-two years later, called *The Arab*, and appearing, with nine other stories of individuation, in a book called *The Tree: Tales in Psycho-mythology* (6). This "Arab" travelled the world as a sailor, in order to know and transform his animal desires, while he nourished his spiritual nature by visiting all the holy places in his travels. And so it was for me, too, as a youth; I am ever-indebted to the Goddess Kali for Her gift to me of transcendence, of highest and lowest in one spiritual/material place. Calcutta, like Nazareth and my birthplace, Los Angeles, are generally not held in high esteem as spiritual centers, but there, too, is where the divine is born.

There were to be no more experiences of India or the East, for the remainder of the war, nor even very much when I returned to my home and resumed my studies at the University. I continued to read, of course, but my attention became focussed on a career, and psychology seemed the thing to do, when my writing did not result in publication.

It was only when I began my own analysis, in 1950, that the East came up once more, in the form of dreams and visions. I have already mentioned, in *Buddhism and Jungian Psychology*, that the first Christmas after I had begun this work I had a dream and vision in which a divine child was being born, attended by three new wise men, a Jewish rabbi, a Christian priest and a Buddhist priest. Notably, there was no Hindu nor any other Indian present, among others also left out. It was Buddhism and Japan that called to me.

Nonetheless, I had one dream, during the next year, in which a Hindu wise-man appeared. I was in India, amongst a large group of people, some of whom were listening avidly to this guru. I was ambivalent about him, not knowing why, when he pointed to me angrily and said words which I could not comprehend. I understood this dream only years later, when I read Jung and discovered his ambivalence toward Indian spirituality as well. This has to do, I believe, with the attraction to that same spirituality, but one's unwillingness to submit to a guru, to a prescribed path. The guru of my dream was chastising me, I believe, because I was unwilling to accept him as my teacher. But more about that in a moment, when I bring matters up to the present.

During those years between the war and my studies in Zurich, I felt warmly toward things Indian and Eastern, often listening to Indian music, on records and in concert. I sometimes attended lectures on Indian topics, or heard gurus who were beginning to appear in California, but was, at best, unimpressed. I did like Krishnamurti, however, and even took my wife-to-be to hear him in Ojai on an early date. Early in my analysis, I had an intense auditory dream in which a powerful voice (like the Old Testament) spoke in blank verse. One of the verses said:

> Holy man, hollow man
> Solo man, Solomon.

I concluded that all holy men were hollow in two senses, that they were in touch with the Void, but that they were only general guides for collective spiritual paths, thus "empty." For me, the "wisest" path was that of going my own way. That, too, I suppose, is what contributed to the mutual suspicion in my dream of the Indian guru.

It was a loss for me, I fear, in that I did not take the opportunity to study with Yogananda, who had come to Los Angeles not long before my graduate school days. My subsequent reading and experience with other gurus, however, even the best of them, always turned me away, on the same grounds. Many are great, often kind, certainly wise and spiritual, but there was always that matter of "submission," which I, like Jung, had difficulty doing with any outer authority.

Not long ago, no more than a couple of years, I was invited to attend a guest week-end at a center embracing the viewpoint of Rajneesh. I had read several volumes of his *Book of Secrets* (5) and was greatly impressed with his knowledge of paths East and West, his spirituality, his good sense, and his capacity to embrace so much. I also enjoyed the meditation and the original ways of overcoming western "nervousness" that I practiced on that week-end. After a time, however, when discussions took place with the leaders (Western ones, to be sure, but very much in the Eastern spirit), it was clear that submission was the key, that no true enlightenment could occur without this commitment. For me, I had long since committed myself to my own process, to the Self as manifested within, so I could not do this. Once more, this is clearly a loss, but my experience of patients who have undergone various schools of spirituality and their rampant authoritarianism also convince me that this path has been right for my own soul.

I return, now, to my experiences in Zurich, and the re-opening of the East for me. Since this was largely in connection with Buddhism and Japan, I have already recounted that in the chapter "East and West: A Personal Statement" in the *Buddhism and Jungian Psychology* book, mentioned earlier. India was not without its effect, however. During my first semester at the C.G. Jung Institute, in 1956, and even living in the same *pension* on *Plattenstrasse* as my wife and myself, I met a fellow student who hailed from India, my co-author of the present book, Dr. Arwind Vasavada.

Dr. Vasavada was finishing up his studies at that time, preparing to return to his teaching and practice in India, and I was in the midst of getting established, learning my way around, etc., so we did not get to speak to each other as much as I would have liked. All the same, I was very impressed with his knowledge and, particularly, his courage to leave his work and family, and to come all the way to Zurich to pursue his own path of reconciling East and West. As far as I saw, he managed rather well, even able to handle the criticism of one faculty person at the Institute who was doubtful that he should be a Jungian Analyst, since he was so "contained in his religion." This sounds a bit insulting, and I believe it to be too narrow in itself, but the thought behind it is not as ridiculous as it sounds. The view of the faculty person was that those who are fully absorbed in their religion are already at one with the archetypes, and do not need nor can they cope with a conscious individuation process, which usually becomes activated just when one can no longer believe in or be fully "contained" in the religion of one's origin. This is surely the case with most Jungians, but it is also clear that, in the modern day, there are many people, even clergy, who can be loyal to their faith, and embark upon a psychological direction as well.

For me, this demand of the faculty person was similar to what I understood that gurus — and most religious teachers of the West — were demanding, namely, submission to one point-of-view. It is the great gift of Jungian psychology, in my opinion, to free us all to follow our own paths as our spirits direct us, from within, and thus be adherents or not.

After the Zurich days, I heard from Dr. Vasavada once more, asking me to come to India and teach the Rorschach Technique there, among other things. I was on the faculty at UCLA at the time, doing just that. Unfortunately, there was no funding available at that time, and I, with my wife and two small children, was in no position to avail myself of that marvellous opportunity. So, once more, there was a barrier between me and the possibility of deepening my connection with the spirituality of India.

Many years were to pass before my contact with Dr. Vasavada was to be resumed. This was in 1980, at the International Congress of Analytical (Jungian) Psychology in San Francisco. I had only then re-connected with the "Jungian collective," since my resignation from my local society in 1966. I had been invited to give a paper and this led to a renewal of ties at the institutional level. In the meantime, Dr. Vasavada had come to the United States some years before and had been practicing in Chicago. Once more, our personal connection was brief, due to the multitude of events and concerns at a convention, and such a renewal of ties for me. All the same, I was deeply moved by his paper on Money and the profound way in which this spiritual man of tremendous integrity struggled within his own soul to be true to his tradition in the midst of the Western temptations to be otherwise. That paper appears in this volume, and I am sure it will be received with the appreciation that it merits.

In 1983, I proposed a volume on East and West, Buddhism and Jungian Psychology, to my publisher at Falcon Press and he avidly consented to it. My friend and colleague, Dr. Mokusen Miyuki, and I, worked on that and when it appeared in May of 1985, it was very well received. At that same time (and now I return to the "present" and the old dream that I mentioned earlier), I had a dream and a fantasy of the guru who had appeared judgementally so many years before. Now this wise man was very friendly to me, warm and supportive. I was given to understand that what I had done all these years was the correct path for me, and that now he returned to do whatever seemed right. I immediately had the idea of doing a work similar to the Buddhism book, but one now involving Hinduism and the religious thought of India, along with Jungian Psychology. I thought at once of Dr. Vasavada and wrote to him asking if he would be willing to share authorship with me in this task. He graciously answered at once, declaring full pleasure in engaging in such a mutual work, sending several of his papers, both published and unpublished, in which he had taken up this theme.

On my side, there was only the format of the previous book, my own experience, desire, and deep interest. Foremost among these was my encounter with Kundalini Yoga, as I mention in my work on that topic in the present volume. I was introduced to this topic and those remarkable pictures at a lecture given in Zurich by my analyst, Dr. C.A. Meier, and was as profoundly effected by them as I was earlier by my experience at the Temple of Kali in Calcutta, and was later to be by the Zen Ox-Herding Pictures.

In my Zurich days, I purchased the classic volume on the topic, *The Serpent Power*, by Sir John Woodroffe (Arthur Avalon as pseudonym), (9), but was able to read and study it intensively only years later when I wrote my story of "Maya, the Yogini" which appeared, as did the aforementioned "Arab," in the psychological fiction of *The Tree: Tales in Psycho-mythology* (6). In that story, also appearing in the present volume, an Indian woman follows an inner guru through the path of the Kundalini pictures on the way to her own individuation and enlightenment.

And now, with the reappearance of the inner-guru-who-rejected-me, as I rejected him, I am pleased to present our mutual labors in the present volume. Indeed, it is an act of fulfillment, and, as in the Buddhism book, a chance to round out what was begun in my boyhood, enriched in my youth, and nourished in my adulthood.

What remains, now, is to try to understand what the psyche is doing, generally, in such East-West encounters. My own experience of this effect began early, to be sure, and I am fortunate to have had a classic path of early adventure and travel, followed by inner work and depth, but this cross-fertilization is not unique. I have had a number of patients who have been profoundly effected by Eastern religions and paths, and who have been compelled to reconcile these two orientations in their own souls. Besides that kind of person, who often seeks Jungian therapists as people who might understand their dilemma and struggle, there are great numbers of westerners who have happily (or unhappily, at times), embarked upon the various Eastern paths with alacrity and with profit. This is to say nothing of the myriad persons who engage in the forms of yoga to a greater or lesser extent.

From the Eastern viewpoint, what we in the West have to offer seems to be our science and technology. This, rather than our religions, is what the adventurers from Asia want from us. That, I suppose, is as it should be, when one considers the enormous poverty, lack of freedom and of material possessions one encounters outside of the democratic Western countries. Yet, some few, such as Professors Vasavada and Mokusen Miyuki (of the Buddhism book), have found their way into Western spirituality, via Jung, as well. Their numbers, now, are beginning to increase -- at least in Japan -- and one hopes for a significant contribution from that side.

The Western traditional religions -- Judaism, Christianity and Islam -- have not lost their vitality, however, and there is certainly adequate membership in the latter two of these faiths in the East. One can guess that a syncretism, parallel with that happening in the Near East in the centuries just before and after the advent of the present Piscean Aeon, is taking place.

If we consider that science and technology are the extraverted spiritual equivalent of yoga and meditation in the East, in terms of value, then we are probably on the right track. This is not to discount the religions of the West, since science is truly a daughter of the Western spirit of enquiry and conquest.

In my opinion, Jungian psychology provides a finer marriage of the best in East and West, spiritually, but it does so on its own terms and by following its own inner path, without denying any of the other methods of quest. It is important, therefore, in my opinion, that as many men and women of spirit from the East undergo this particular psychological discipline, in order to continue this path of study and realization in a "universally" creative way. Miyuki and Vasavada, as well as Kawai and others, are surely showing the way for this. This, it seems to me, with its essential demand that the person be true to his own inner teacher, is a necessary compensation to all the outer changes -- in science and technology and religious conversion -- that is taking place around us.

My own winding and ecumenical path has brought me most valuable friends, East and West, and our synchronistic encounters must surely have some significance in the larger exchanges taking place. I like to think that it is the emphasis on the value of the individual and his/her inner process that is being served and emphasized. This is, indeed, a worthwhile compensation for all the outer collective exchanges and events taking place.

REFERENCES

1. Jung, C.G. *Answer to Job* in Collected Works, Volume 11.

2. Jung, C.G. *Memories, Dreams, Reflections*, Pantheon Books, Random House, New York, 1961.

3. Lewis, H. Spencer, *Mansions of the Soul: The Cosmic Conception*, Rosicrucian Press, San Jose, California, 1938.

4. Lewis, H. Spencer, *Lemuria, The Lost Continent of the Pacific*, Rosicrucian Press, San Jose, California, 1935.

5. Rajneesh, Shree, *The Book of The Secrets*, 5 Vol. Harper & Row, New York, 1977. (Lectures 1972-73).

6. Spiegelman, J. Marvin, *The Tree: Tales in Psycho-mythology*, Falcon Press, Phoenix, Arizona, 1982 (original 1974).

7. Spiegelman, J. Marvin & Miyuki, Mokusen, *Buddhism and Jungian Psychology*, Falcon Press, Phoenix, Arizona, 1985.

8. Spiegelman, J. Marvin and Jacobson, Abraham, *A Modern Jew in Search of a Soul*, Falcon Press, Phoenix, Arizona, 1985.

9. Woodroffe, Sir John (Arthur Avalon), *The Serpent Power*, Ganesh & Co., Madras, India, 1953 (original 1918).

INDIA AND JUNGIAN PSYCHOLOGY:
A PERSONAL EXPERIENCE (1985)

by

Arwind Vasavada

As a fresh graduate from the Jung Institute, working in mental hospitals at Jaipur and Jodhpur, successes and failures with patients made me feel I was doing therapy. The results affected me. I was happy with successes, and unhappy with failures. Much later, when I was in Chicago and had learned from success and failure, I began to feel that therapy was happening. Success and failure did not affect me. It did not mean I was indifferent and insensitive to the clients, their feelings, and their depressions. I was with them in their confusion, situations of stalemate, or breakthroughs. I was with them in the spontaneity of the situation. I was flowing with them. We both were facing the Unknown and the Unpredictable. I was content to be with whatever was happening. Most of the time, I had to let the client learn to stay with what Is and let them feel It as It Is. It was clear for me now that I was not *doing* therapy. I did nothing. Whatever was happening in a situation was happening as it had to.

The therapy situation, the sacred place, includes me and the client, and we both are in the process. We both are facing and experiencing the Unknown. Inability to find any direction when it happened became a humbling experience before the Unknown; an experience of my limitation before It, and acceptance of my nothingness, which at times was a religious experience. This is borne out very well by Dr. Meiers' book, *Ancient Incubation and Modern Psychotherapy*[1] and also by Jung. Reality of what they wrote and experienced became reality for me.

It seems to me, as Jung also often said, that we all are guided by fate, the Unknown. It takes us through the tortuous journey of our life to our Individuation -- to Wholeness. We may refuse this guidance at our own cost. Truly, we cannot even refuse it for long. It is more powerful than our will.

The western science of psychotherapy, in terms of Freud in the beginning and Jung later, intrigued me while I was studying, earlier on in

14

India, for my master's degree. It fascinated me. Dreams and their interpretations clearly can bare many hidden processes of the mind. It was totally a new dimension to me. I saw how Freudian interpretation of dreams uncovered mental processes. During this period, I was closely following a case of a relation who had become paranoid schizophrenic. Whatever Freud wrote about such cases was confirmed by the life history of this person. He was dominated by his powerful mother and behaved like a child before her at the age of 30. Even though he was married, he had strong homosexual tendencies. How to help him? Books could not teach the psychoanalytic technique. It had to be learned by living experience. Here was a meeting ground between East and West. Spiritual tradition has to be learned from a guru, a master. There was none to teach Freudian technique.

Experience and work at a Spiritual Healing center in Central India made me wonder at some of the successes. I learned that faith could heal, but my curiosity to know how remained unsatisfied. I wanted to understand how the mind goes wrong, and with what technique it can be set right. I wished to understand both the processes experientially: the process of the disturbed mind, and the steps taken to help. The frustration with Spiritual Healing intensified my search to find the way. There was no possibility to go West to learn it. I had no means for it. I fell back on the study of the Yoga Sutras of Patanjali. Again the study of books seemed unhelpful. I saw the similarity between Freud's method of free association and meditation, but how to use meditation to understand the process of helping the disturbed mind to balance, was the question which had no answer. It also became clear that going back to the past and uncovering the repressions released tension and brought about balance temporarily. However, old habits -- conditioning or the Samskaras -- repeated themselves, and one fell back into the old habits. It was the problem of really deconditioning the mind totally from unhealthy patterns. The therapy of Freud and Adler helped bring patients to social adjustment -- so-called normality. That did not mean enough, however. I saw within me that though I was fairly well-adjusted in society, I was neither happy nor contented. I was still a disturbed person, "freaking out" here and there, often confused and in conflict, stuck in many situations of life. There was no spontaneity in life. Traditional and social morality is also a conditioning -- conditioning by collective consciousness. I did not know myself clearly. I was not able to guide my life without conflict. The psychoanalytic way was not the answer. I needed to discover more, understand more of my own Self before I could see clearly the processes of mind within me and others. One recurrent saying of the Upanishads haunted me: "One who

knows the Self, knows all: Unheard becomes heard. Unknown known."[2]
The Yoga Sutras also said a similar thing in a different way.[3] The fully
deconditioned mind sees everything clearly. Psychological healing was
possible only by going through this process of Self knowledge. Who
would teach me that?

In 1938, I had an opportunity to go to Europe and learn what I wanted.
In 1939, I wrote to Dr. Freud that I desired to learn psychoanalysis. Many
months after that, I received a letter from Anna Freud, saying that due to
turmoil in Europe they had moved to London. Although Dr. Freud was
too old to undertake training, she would be willing to train me. But this
opportunity passed away, unavailed, because of World War II.

Some time after this, a friend and a long-term devotee of Shri Meher
Baba arranged a meeting for me with the saint. I asked him if he would
assist me in helping mentally disturbed persons. He spelled out on the
alphabetical board (since he did not speak), "One should first know
whether the person needed help. A help at the wrong time can be an
interference with the natural process of healing already going on. One has
to know the Self first in order to help others. I will help you." I was not told
what to do. I had only the assurance of his help. I had to begin my work
within on my own.

Whatever I had learned from books and felt correct within, I wrote out
in a paper, "Yogic Basis of Psychoanalysis," and I presented it to the Indian
Science Congress Session 1940 in Benares. Despite writing this paper and
intellectually understanding the link between yoga and psychoanalysis, I
was struggling and fumbling. There was a deep void I felt within. Nothing
came to fill it.

Years rolled on, and in about 1945-46, I wrote to Dr. Jung about my
desire to learn from him. He replied that he did not train anybody then as
he was growing old, but recommended me to Dr. Meier. I wrote to Dr.
Meier. He wrote back, telling me that he could train me if I came over to
Zurich. But where was the money for all this? And the Indian political
situation was in transition by 1947.

By then, I was teaching philosophy and psychology in Kota. In social
contact with friends and students, I expressed the desire to learn the
ancient wisdom of Self-Realization, if there were someone to teach it.
One day a student friend told me that he would arrange such a meeting
with one who lived and knew this wisdom.

A few months after this, the friend asked me to accompany him to his
home to meet this person. The first question that I asked of this teacher
was whether it was necessary for me to have a guru. This was because I
had heard all sorts of stories about so-called gurus. He asked me, in return,

a question, "What do you do professionally?" I told him that I was a professor and taught philosophy and psychology to students. "So, those who want to learn philosophy and psychology have to come to you, is that not so?" he said. "Yes," I replied. "Then you have come to me if you wish to learn the ancient wisdom."

Later, he came to my apartment in the evening and gave a discourse; and after a dialogue between us, he brought home to me experientially that senses, intellect, and such apparatuses available to man need the light of the Self to know things out there. They are blind without the light of the Self. The Self is the light. It was a mystic experience which remained with me for three days, during which I did not know what I taught and did. It convinced me that this person, though a householder, knew and lived what he taught. This contact remained until I went to Zurich. Many summers we lived together and I had the opportunity to see him in all the situations of life. He lived what he taught.

During this period, I came across *Modern Man in Search of Soul* and another book of essays by Jung. I could see now that Jung was a very different kind of psychologist. He taught from a different level than that of Freud. He talked of Self-Realization, something never heard in the textbooks of Western psychology. His way seemed different from that of my guru. It appeared more like the Tantric way. The way to Self lay in understanding the relationship between man and woman. Each man has Anima within and woman her Animus, which he or she projects upon a person outside. Only by going through this experience does one come upon the Self. Anima or Animus are the guardians of the unconscious -- the Self. In this manner, he was talking about Shiva and Shakti within us, and their eternal union within. I was reminded of the story of Shiva and Parvati from Shiva-Purana. Parvati, as Sati in her first birth, after marrying Shiva, burned herself into ashes with anger towards her father when he insulted her and her husband. The fire transformed her, and in her next birth, she as Parvati married Shiva. But this happened only after the death of Kama, the god of Desire -- who was burned to death by the fire from the third eye of Shiva.

All this made me aware of my strong fascination for my wife. As friends studying together in Bombay, we became very close to each other. But the economical and social distance between us made her unattainable as a partner in life. This realization brought intense suffering. The pain of separation, having reached its intensity, transformed into a mystic experience of Oneness with the Universe. I felt as if the whole Universe, the trees and flowers in the garden (this happened in a garden on a full moon night) were in tears with me. The desire of attaining her dissolved.

We remained friends from a long distance, until fate arranged the marriage. Yet this union in marriage never felt complete as I began to realize in the course of years.

My guru read all this in our relationship, my attachment to her which imprisoned us. He started working on it. The mystic joy of earlier and a few later meetings turned into pain and suffering. I had become aware of this imprisonment in attachment to my wife. I knew I had to face it and get free from it, but was never prepared to go this way. I felt my way was to completely dissolve myself in union with her and transcend the separation. Being with him during this period was a torture. I was feeling as if I were being baked alive. My wife felt differently from me. She realized the value of what was happening in accepting the way of my guru. The process of dissolution remained incomplete.

I felt Jung's way of going along with the fascination -- and accepting the naturalness of fascination -- perhaps was leading to the same goal of Self-realizaton, Eternal Union. I had to go his way.

It was now 1952-53. India was free from British rule. Scholarships to go abroad were available. Luckily, my professor Dr. S. Radhakrishnan was Vice-President of India then. I ran up to him in New Delhi and spoke to him to help me get a scholarship to study with Jung. He was kind enough to call the Education Secretary to give me a scholarship. Now I could make my pilgrimage. The fascination to learn Jung's way seemed even greater than fascination for my wife. How I could leave her back home, I wonder even now!

Coming over to Zurich, I started to work with Dr. Meier and Dr. L. Frey, as it was impossible to work with either Dr. Jung or Mrs. Jung. I had, however, the good fortune of meeting Dr. Jung professionally and a few other times at critical periods of my analysis. I learned a great deal from what he had to say and his presence.

The analytical work, with dream interpretation, made me see the experience I had undergone with my guru in India in a new way. I was learning a new language of identifying psychological processes. Ego, persona, shadow were distinguished as the vestures of personality. Indian Psychology did not analyze the contents of Psyche that way. The analysis further emphasized attention to whatever was going on in daily life and dealt with that. This was again a difference from the guru's way. The main focus in the guru's way was toward learning to be a spectator of the psychic drama. According to guru's way, ego-involvement, the conditioned ego, creates the problem. Learning to be a spectator helps free the ego from involvement with happenings. Ego involvement is attachment to objective situations. An object being a part of the process of Prakrti changes into its opposite and thus one involved goes through the see-saw of opposites -- gets into imbalance like the swings of a pendulum. A pendulum allowed to go through its momentum balances itself naturally. Here I saw the meeting ground between Indian Psychology and Jung. Jung also said that psyche is in constant motion of change into opposites -- the principle of Enantiodromia. Identification with any pole creates the conflict. Jung, through the analytical process, led man to see and experience these swings -- the tension. The experience of close proximity of the poles brought tension to its extreme stretch. If one could stay with it, the third factor -- the transcendent function -- appeared. Thus an insight was gained and a new outlook changed one's attitude toward the earlier situation.[4] Again, in this manner, Jung's way confirmed for me the understanding of the traditional Indian wisdom that psychological problems cannot be solved on that level. Transcending that level, rising to the level of spirit, the Light, the Self, dissolved the tension, because it begins to be seen from the standpoint of wholeness, the Self, where all is included in harmony. This understanding helped me to use either of the approaches with a client according to the situation and the need of the moment. Living the whole gamut of swings or learning to be a spectator of the drama both helped to decondition the mind -- the ego. The moments of deconditioned mind are moments of Eternity -- Pure Light. One then sees clearly in that moment.

Deepest involvement happens in relationship with the opposite sex. As I said earlier, I had understood Jung in this respect in my own fanciful way. Somehow Jung's way helped to dissolve the feeling of separation, or in other words, helped one to experience the union, by accepting the projection and working it out. That is how I had understood it while I was in India. Experience of Anima projection in Zurich intensified the yearning for union. It did not dissolve the sense of separation. I learned the same, but in another way. One has to withdraw the projection -- situations naturally happen when the image breaks and a sense of desolation comes about. Staying with this alone helps the withdrawal, and then one can find one's other half within. Jung was as much right in this area as my guru. The approaches, however, were different. I feel both the approaches are important. Different people need different medicine.

It became clear to me during my analysis that confrontation with the Anima or different images depended upon my attitude and the "hook" within me towards persons. Becoming aware of the inner images or "hook," and working on it changed the image. It also changed the relationship to that person. Something similar happened with the archetype of Self. I was fascinated by experiencing alternatively the archetype of the Wise Old Man or the Divine Mother, and the Black Magician or the Witch. I became aware of my identification with the archetype of the Wise Old Man and dependence upon the Divine Mother. It was an interesting discovery as to how dreams, rightly understood, can be helpful in the journey to Selfhood. Here was the meeting ground between the two wisdoms: individuation of Jung and the tradition of gurus. Archetypal images continue to appear in dreams or continue to be projected until one is totally aware or in other words, free from the "hooks" within — becomes totally deconditioned. What is that experience of totally deconditioned mind or ego -- the experience of Wholeness? It has to be one free from images, a kind of emptiness and thought-free space. The tradition of the gurus spoke about it. Jung was silent on this point. From the very beginning, when I met Jung to pay my respect to him as my guru, and later a few times at critical stages of my analysis, I had felt Jung knew That which IS. I could experience profound depth within, as I did with my guru. Why was he silent about it? Why did his writings stop at the archetypal images of Self? One feels tremendous energy in experiencing such archetypes. What is behind the image? What is the source of this energy like? Once, when he came to greet Dr. Lilliane Frey on her birthday, I was with her. I got a few minutes with him then. I asked him what is behind the archetype of Self? He was silent. His silence intrigued me and remained with me for years in India. In the course of time, I got some satisfactory answer which I brought out in my paper published in the *Journal of Analytical Psychology*, London.[5] I could feel the situation with Jung. Though a scientist, he was called mystic by the scientists. Jung, a psychologist, came upon the realm of the divine beyond psychology. He led some of those who came for counselling to experience the realm of the spirit -- Self. Jung's way thus led to religious experience beyond dogma for anyone, whatever faith he belonged to. Men of established religions thought he was trespassing on their domain. But this is what a guru does. Perhaps Jung felt that men in the West were not yet ready for such direct experience and its pronouncement. The way for the Western mind lay through exploration of archetypes -- a demonstrable experience only, at this point of time. Direct confrontation of the divine brings total annihilation of the conditioned ego or mind (Fana in Sufi terms) at first; it is then the door to grace (Baka in Sufi terms).

I happened to be in Zurich before Jung passed away. I met Mrs. Aniela Jaffe, who knew of my correspondence with Jung. She told me, "Professor Vasavada, we will soon find the answer to your question to Jung." She was referring to *Memories, Dreams, and Reflections..*[6] I was satisfied when later I read that book and came upon his words on page 353. It was more than clear how Jung experienced the divine. It is the realm beyond knowledge. It is the realm of Eros -- its incalculable paradoxes, experiencing of which one felt humble. Knowledge gives way to experiencing the divine in all its manifestations.

For this paper, I had to write all this autobiographical stuff. Writing all this once again, I went through two traditional processes: the guru's and Jung's, and came to realize what I have been doing with myself and others. The way of the guru or of Jung happens to be taken as the need arises. It seems to be my fate to speak about Jung through Eastern eyes, and also to speak about Eastern tradition through Jung's eyes. I am here and there and no-where. The way of gurus gave the clarity of the goal to which we all are being naturally led. Jung called it the individuation process. There is not the slightest difference in this between the East and Jung. For both the traditions, it is the highest value.[7] It is wholeness, holiness -- it is neither my wholeness nor yours. It includes all. We all are contained in it. It is that state of being which is pure and unconditioned. It is thought-free open space. Mind or ego, on the way to deconditioning itself of samskaras, or false vestures, experiences this Light -- the Self.[8]

Thus, the processes of deconditioning can be many. The guru's way of learning to be a spectator -- not caring about happenings personally, or Jung's way of going through current relationships, experiencing the swings of opposites and learning to be a spectator -- brings one face to face with the transcendent function. Staying with whatever the situation is objectively, in a relationship or the subjective situation of depression, stalemate, or confusion; or an archetypal situation in a dream, allowing its total impact on the organism; or what Dr. Gendlin would call focusing on it, is the way. Beyond the words or feelings that describe the situation is the Unknown. We have to experience its quality and let it speak. Both the analyst and the client have to wait and watch for what comes next from the Unconscious, the Unknown. There need not be an "Aha!" experience always. They are not frequent. If we do not expect and hope, we begin to see many different faces of the divine -- the Unknown. Knowing this, we are content to be with what IS -- the Indescribable and Unspeakable. We begin to accept the tortuous journey to individuation, which has its own natural rhythm. Spontaneity begins to come in life off and on.

It seems clear to me that archetypes and archetypal situations cannot be understood. There is no end to their varied manifestations because the energy behind them is incalculable. All that one does is to experience them, feel their nuances of feelings, which may begin to hit the right spot within. Or it may not. The more puzzling the archetypes, the nearer are we to the Unknown, because it is telling us something important: stop knowing. Enter into the Source, and be It. All the archetypes have their origin in the same Source. The Source is important.

Therapy thus becomes, once again, undertaking a journey to Selfhood, with each person who gives us this opportunity to explore the Unknown along with him. Because of what we have undergone earlier, it becomes easier to be patient, knowing the rhythm of the client. Whatever happens on the road is quite important, and yet not important, because the whole scene or outlook changes when *That* happens.

It is also easier to encounter projections of the Wise Old Man or Healer on us, because in depth we know that the Healer is doing its things to us and the client. The client, in projecting the archetype of the Healer or Wise Old Man, is experiencing something within. He is becoming aware of that within him. Maybe, later on he will see that it was always there. The problems of Transference and Counter-transference become minimal. From all these experiences, I feel the role of analyst or healer or guru can not be put on as a persona. If it is put on, one knows very well from the beginning years of practice, that it is a big burden and a great hindrance in one's journey to Individuation. Wholeness, holiness, can not be put on as a role, as a persona. It is always there, because individuation is natural, it is there right from the beginning. We become aware of it in due course. Light shines in the heart of every man and is guiding the path. The alchemical situation of analyst and client coming together begins to do its work of illuminating the dark corners within.

Jung's way is the way of Enlightenment. It is not a technique, it is a way of life. It cannot be taught, but can be lived. It cannot be narrowed to train therapists only. Everyone needs Enlightenment, everyone feels the call of the Divine within, whatever his profession. Jung's way is not the way of specialization. It is an open road, each one with intense yearning to be his Self can follow and live it, doing whatever he is called to do in this world. This is the way of the gurus. The guru is available to anyone, whosoever comes: how long he comes, and what he does with the wisdom received, is not the concern of the guru. He is merely an instrument of the Divine. Whatever happens through him, happens.

I have thus to follow two different paths and they have become useful to help those who came to me. Following either of the two, the journey ends and the doors of the Divine open and a new journey begins, of which no one can talk. It is unspeakable. If entering the door happens, it will radiate. That which IS is the highest value; all paths lead there and end there. That which IS is indifferent to paths because all belong there; they are included. In this manner, the label of a particular school is no longer divisive and distinguishing, but connotes a pilgrim following the same journey's end with others. He is a part of the community of seekers -- a pilgrim. (This paper was written in 1985.)

REFERENCES

1. C.A. Meier. *Ancient Incubation and Modern Psychotherapy*, Northwestern University Press, 1967.

2. BRIHADARAYNAKA UPANISHAD, 2.4. and 3.8.

3. PATANJALI. YOGA SUTRAS I.48. *The Textbook of Yoga Psychology*, R. Misra, Julian Press, New York, 1963, p. 163.

4. "The transcendent function does not procede without aim and purpose, but leads to the revelation of the essential man. It is in the first place a purely natural process, which may in some cases pursue its course without the knowledge or assistance of the individual, and can sometimes forcibly accomplish itself in the face of the opposition. The meaning and purpose of the process is realization, in all its aspects, of the personality originally hidden away in the embryonic germ plasm; the production and unfolding of the original potential wholeness." Collected works, Volume 7, p. 186.

5. *The Analytical Psychology of C.G. Jung and Eastern Wisdom*, 1967.

6. *Memories, Dreams, and Reflections*, C.G. Jung, Pantheon Books, New York, 1973, p. 353.

7. " . . . so always the inner experience of individuation has been appreciated as the most valuable and important thing in life. It is the only thing that brings any lasting satisfaction to a man. Power, glory, wealth are external and futile. The really important things are within. It is a more important thing to me that I am happy than that I have the external reasons for happiness. Rich people should be happy but often they are not, they are bored to death; therefore it is so much better for man to work to produce an inner condition that gives him an inner happiness. Experience shows that there are certain psychological conditions in which man gets eternal results. They have something of the quality of eternity, of timelessness, they have the quality of reaching beyond man. They have a divine quality and yield all that satisfaction which man-made things do not." *Dream Seminars*, Volume 1, p. 210.

8. "The aim of individuation is nothing less than to divest the self of the

false wrappings of the persona on one hand and of the suggestive power of primordial images on the other." Collected works, Volume 7, p. 260. See also: "But the more we become conscious of ourselves through self-knowledge, and act accordingly, the more the layers of the personal unconscious that is superimposed on the Collective Unconscious will be diminished. In this way there arises a consciousness which is no longer imprisoned in the petty, oversensitive, personal world of the ego, but participates freely in the wider world of objective interests. The widened consciousness is no longer that touchy, egotistical bundle of personal wishes, fears, hopes, and ambitions which always has to be compensated or corrected by unconscious counter-tendencies; instead it is a function of relationship to the world of objects bringing the individual into absolute, binding, and indissoluble communion with the world at large." Ibid. p. 275.

PART TWO

KUNDALINI YOGA

A Psychological Commentary on Kundalini Yoga — 1985
by J. Marvin Spiegelman

Comments, by Arwind U. Vasavada

Reply, by J. Marvin Spiegelman

Maya, the Yogini — A Fictional Tale of Kundalini — 1967
by J. Marvin Spiegelman

A PSYCHOLOGICAL COMMENTARY
ON KUNDALINI YOGA (1985)

by

J. Marvin Spiegelman

Preliminary

To enter into the world of Indian spirituality, particularly the Tantric tradition — of which Kundalini Yoga is a branch — is to find onself luxuriating in riches of imagery and concept, in words and sounds and movements whose effect is trance-inducing and ecstatic. If one listens for several hours to Indian religious music, or chants the Sanskrit language, or watches the magical performance of dance, one knows that here is an ancient and wise culture, alive with the opposites and paradox. There is a simultaneous awareness of the all-embracing One and the endless variety of the Many, whether of God and Goddess or condition of the soul, along with the realization that the ultimate truth lies within -- it is there from the beginning, but must be achieved.

There are words and God-names for every imaginable condition of consciousness, each subtly different from the other. Like the Eskimo, with his twenty-nine names for kinds of snow, the Indian spirit has as many words for awareness.

Where can one begin one's plunge into the riches of the Upanishads and the thousands of years of India's development? Which gate opens the understanding of this vast jungle and sea and sky? The "sea of the Talmud" comes to mind, where no one can navigate it all, except, perhaps, after a lifetime (lifetimes?) of total immersion. One can see how this efflorescence was just too rich for Jung, -- as he describes in a letter when asked his reaction to the *Autobiography of a Yogi*, by Yogananda[2]. It was like coconut oil for him, just too rich. Yet Jung's psychology, with its principle of opposites, its differentiation into concrete reality (Sthula) and image or soul reality (subtle body, Sukshma) and archetype (causal body), is so similar to the Indian perspective. Indeed, one can understand Jung's dream, late in life, wherein he finds himself as a guru meditating in a temple and comes away not knowing if he is dreamed by this yogi or

27

dreams him.[7] Jung, it seems to me, includes much of Indian thought in his work, although it is expressed in western, scientific language. How could it be otherwise, since both aim to describe the psyche as it is and how it can develop itself? One can also understand how Buddhism sprang from such a rich and overwhelming tree. A new appreciation arises for the Gautama, who finally sat under that Tree, was assaulted by all the myriad gods and goddesses, yet affirmed the negation, sat perfectly still, and attained Enlightenment via simplicity. The austerity of Buddhism in some of its forms (say Zen, in contrast to Tibetan), becomes quite clear as a compensation to all that variety.

This becomes apparent visually when we look at the pictures which are used to illustrate the path to Enlightenment. Compare the Zen Ox-Herding pictures with the God-filled images of Kundalini: no wonder that some Hindus think of Buddhists as atheists! No gods or goddesses for the Zen meditator, nor is there an aim of ultimate liberation (Mukti) from this world. Yet the spirit of meditation, or concentrating within, with the goal of transformation and enlightenment, of ego being encompassed in the Self, is the same for both.

When we go further afield and compare these pictures with western alchemy, as in the *Rosarium Philosophorum* series utilized by Jung in his *Transference* book[5], we are once more amazed at the differences and similarities. The opposites (King and Queen), are central in the latter, just as they are in Tantric work, but true to the western embrace of monotheism, these are Royalty, not Gods. The East understands too well that Oneness, or monotheism, is something to be achieved, and is no more real or irreal than polytheism.

Yet all these sets of pictures, Zen and Kundalini and Alchemy, were completed at about the same time, historically, roughly in the period referred to in the West as the Renaissance. Was this, synchronistically, a world-wide renewal of the spirit, expressing a similar content, but in the context of different traditions? So it seems to me. When one adds that the Jewish tradition was astonishingly enriched at this time (e.g. Moses de Leon and the *Zohar*)[11], and that the magical version of Kabbalah was using the Tarot pictures, then there is strong evidence of the earth-wide development of the spirit.

Just such comparisons should be made one day, but we have yet to produce people who can do justice to it. Jung has already provided us with keys to enter these rich domains and others are showing us ways to understand and appreciate them individually.

Our present effort, the more modest one of trying to understand

Kundalini Yoga from the Jungian perspective, is aided -- nay, buttressed --
by two sources. One, of course, is the commentary by Jung on the various
Chakras or centers of consciousness described in Kundalini[3] ,[4], and the
other is the outstanding achievement of Arthur Avalon[1] (Sir John
Woodroffe) who has presented us with a basic three-hundred page,
succinct introduction to the theory and practice of this yoga, in addition to
a translation of the Sanskrit texts used. His "big red books" are a treasure!
Having neither the scholarship of Avalon, nor the capacity of Jung, our
role here is simply to carry onward what these giants have produced. The
work is selective, therefore, on grounds of both limitations in competence
(e.g. the treatment of the meaning of the "letters" on the pictures or
lotuses will be minimal), and space. What will be presented is an initial
introduction, in which the basic theory or philosophy of the work is
considered, followed by a description and attempt at understanding of
each of the phases of the practice, in which the yogin advances up his
spinal column (Mt. Meru) both literally and figuratively, develops his
consciousness, and procedes onward towards Liberation and Bliss.

Something needs to be said, in preliminary, about the texts translated
by Avalon and used by him for his theoretical presentation. These are the
Shat-chakra-nirupana ("Description of the Six Centres, or Chakras") and the
Padhuka-panchaka ("Five-fold Footstool"). The second text, of less importance
in our present context, is a fuller description of the highest lotus or chakra,
the Sahasrara.

Shat-chakra-nirupana was written by a Yogin called Purnananda, as part of
a larger work on Tantra, in the year 1577 of the common era. Little is
known of the life of the author, whose descendants still live in the district
of Mymensingh, except that he copied an important manuscript in A.D.
1526, changed his name when he obtained his Diksha (Initiation) from
Brahmananda and went to Kamarupa (Assam), where he is believed to
have obtained his "Siddhi" or state of spiritual perfection. He never
returned home, but compiled several important Tantrik treatises, among
which the work here considered is but a part.

Both Sanskrit texts are accompanied by commentaries written by one
Kalicharana, about which nothing is stated. The latter, however, informs
us, in his commentary, that Purnananda, "wishful to rescue the world
sunk in the mire of misery," took on the task of explaining the principles
underlying the chakras. We shall have ample recourse to quoting from
both Purnananda and his commentator, during the course of our
commentary, which will also give some flavor of the style and attitude of
these religious men.

Before beginning the introduction and enquiry, however, I want to express my deep appreciation to all three men of religion, faith, and scholarship, who have brought forward the fruit of their experience and investigation and have, therefore, made these remarkable pictures and texts available to those of us in the West who are unprepared, in both knowledge of language or the culture, to investigate on our own. Finally, I want to thank my Zurich Jungian Analyst, Prof. Dr. C.A. Meier, who first introduced me to Kundalini in his brilliant and creative introductory lectures to Jungian Psychology in 1957.

Introduction

After I sat for several frustrating hours, impotently trying to formulate the doctrine underlying the Yoga that we are here considering, I had a vision of my inner "guru" (the figure that I mention in the "Personal Statement" section), serenely seated in the classical lotus position, shaped rather triangularly, with a focus on a large eye in the middle of his forehead, the Ajna chakra. Above his head there appeared a larger eye, occupying a circle. That image gave me some calm and enabled me to begin at the beginning.

The seeker (Saddhaka) in Kundalini Yoga aims at the dissolution (Laya) of himself in the great Oneness of Being-Consciousness-Bliss (Sat-Chit-Ananda), while that same Oneness is also creatively manifesting itself in Mind, Life, and Matter. The Oneness of pure consciousness (Chit), the Eye in my vision, also exists in the yogin, who is a miniature version of the universe. There is a "threeness" and "oneness" in himself (just as my "guru" portrayed). It is said in the Vishvasara Tantra, "What is here is elsewhere; what is not here is nowhere." It is with such paradoxes that the One and Many of this doctrine is replete, and so is the difficulty of formulating it adequately.

Let us consider this triangularity in terms of Shiva and Shakti. All that is manifest in the universe -- in terms of mind, life and matter -- is power or energy, which is Shakti, the Great Mother of all. All power or energy, however, must take some shape or form, and that is Shiva, the Great Father of all. Yet the two are one, there is no Shiva without Shakti and no Shakti without Shiva. This Oneness, finally, is the aforementioned trinity of Being, Consciousness, Bliss. There is the ultimate creative reality as it is in itself, untouched and untouchable (the big Eye in my vision), yet this masculine-feminine polarity manifests in all that exists, including the seeker (Saddhaka). Even when there is no universe, the ultimate Power still exists, although at rest, for this static, changeless, background brings Being into existence. In this system, there is no "illusion" -- all is real, both changelessness and change.

The human being is both Shiva or consciousness, and, as mind and body, is a manifestation of power, or Shakti. We mortals are the expression of this power. The aim of the yogin is to worship (Sadhana) and, by these efforts, to bring this power of Shakti to its perfect expression. This is done by raising the energy from the lowest level of existence in gross matter at Muladhara chakra to the highest spiritual level at Sahasrara. In so doing, another paradox emerges: the yogin joins the Shakti with her mate Shiva at the highest, yet the pair are together from the beginning and never separate. If one can grasp this frame of mind, one has begun to form a relationship with this doctrine.

This viewpoint, actually, is not so strange to one who has been involved with Kabbalah or Jungian psychology. The images of God or the Self found there are just as contradictory and paradoxical. As we shall see later on, however, there are significant differences. For example, in Kabbalistic doctrine, the emphasis is upon manifestation, on bringing the divine into fullest material existence, rather than seeking for liberation from this earthly condition. In Jungian psychology, the emphasis is upon the achievement of consciousness and the *realization* of Self (individuation), rather than being absorbed into Oneness.

The "threeness" of the divine and of the latter in connection with the mortal is apparent throughout the system, not only in the well-known tri-partite aspect of divinity of Brahma, Vishnu, Shiva, but also in the very effort of our yogi to unite the Shakti of his being with Shiva. At the base of the spine are the two processes (Nadis) of Ida and Pingala (Moon and Sun), which, when purified and united, join in the central column of Sushumna, like a subtle body, and rise up to permit the next purification and union, until all the chakras are transcended. There is also the "threeness" of states of consciousness: waking (Jagrat), dreaming (Svapna) and dreamless sleep (Avastha). The fundamental consciousness (unchanging in Chit) is here seen as Jiva, enjoying the world of external objects, as seen by the *gross body* (Sthula), internal objects by the *subtle body* (Puryashtaka), and by the *causal body* (Prakriti), which precedes both. The threeness of all these conditions, finally, is resolved in returning to the source, uniting in the unmoved mover, the Sat-Chit-Ananda mentioned earlier, which is both the goal and origin. My vision of the inner "guru" seated in the lotus position, in a triangular fashion, with his "eye" at Ajna, is indeed presented so that the apex of the triangle faces upward, to unite with the "thousand-petalled lotus" at Sahasrara. It is there, finally, that the One (the Atma or Self), is also the Many (the thousand-petalled lotus).

Such imagery is not alien to analytical psychology, which discovered such processes going on in the psyches of western people, as well. Not only does this description of consciousness jibe with Jungian theory (e.g. gross body as material reality, subtle body as psyche or carrier of images, and causal body as the archetypal level), but the imagery of the "fourth" as unifier, as the archetype *an sich*, is also well-known. A significant difference is that analytical psychology, accepting a scientific framework, asserts that psychic reality, the aspect of manifestation, is all that we can know, whereas the Tantrik yogi "knows" that he is both the origin of all, including the gods, yet only an illusory manifestation of particularity, and that the ultimate aim is Liberation (Mukti), to leave this body and all further incarnations. This may be true, but it goes beyond scientific demonstrability.

If we ask what is the function of existence at all, we are again faced with a paradoxical answer. On the one hand, the aim is liberation, the absorption (Laya) of the Saddhaka in God, but the divine periodically manifests itself anew. This seems to be a result of the "ripening of Karma," the residue of unfinished or unevolved (in our sense) consciousness which needs differentiation and, ultimately, refinement. Our yogin, after all, aims at the maximizing of consciousness. Creation takes place, in this system, when there is a stirring of Gunas (the modes of the natural creative principle of Prakriti), in which the ultimate consciousness of Chit is *veiled*, permitting the finitising principle to operate. "Maya," therefore, brings the world into being. Thus there is form arising out of the infinite formlessness. This is effectuated by a Cosmic Sound (Sabdabrahman), and the universe is created. ("In the beginning was the Word . . . "). The paradox here is that there seems to be a simultaneous need for creation, arising out of imperfection, and the need to transcend all worlds. Indeed, the very understanding of evolution and involution are opposite to those of the westerner. Evolution, for our Indian, is to rise out of the materiality of existence and be absorbed in the Infinite. Involution is the process whereby that same Ultimate brings itself into existence. It is just the reverse with us.

Here, I think, we once more find a common imagery, but a total difference in emphasis. Does the Universe exist as the playground of the divine (also a theme in Indian thought), or does the divine somehow need the spark of human consciousness? This latter thought, emphasized in a psychological way by Jung, does not seem to find an echo in our eastern system. Thus, too, is the western consciousness more involved with manifestation and development of matter. So, all too clearly, do we see the introversion of the East contrasted with the extraversion of the West. Is this just one more variation of the Masculine-Feminine, Shiva-Shakti of the divine playing itself out on the cosmic stage? I think so. And it is just this gradual "meeting" of East and West, in my opinion, that is permitting a larger consciousness to emerge. Our ultimate principles can assume a magnitude germane to a world-consciousness, which is symbolized by a globe, after all, a mandala of wholeness, wherein the opposites and the trinities can be resolved.

To return, now, to our lonely yogin, seated there in his meditation, we discover that despite the grandness of the Indian vision, all the effort resides in himself. Completed Yoga, after all, is the Union of Her and Him, Shakti and Shiva, in the body of the Saddhaka (seeker). Some worship predominantly the masculine side of the androgynous figure (Ardhanarishvara), but some concentrate more on the left (feminine) side and call her Mother. She is, indeed, the Great Mother who conceives, bears and nourishes the universe sprung from her womb (Yoni). This is because She is the active aspect of consciousness, imagining the world to be, according to the impressions derived from previous worlds, including the residues of suffering. She it is who is the source of our understanding that *the world itself is an imagination*. This perspective gives us a comparative validation to the western discovery that the *anima* is a projection-making factor, and that the world itself is a product of psyche, of imaginative activity. Does this view arise because the western investigators, like most of their eastern counterpart yogis, have been male? Our *animas* spinning the web for us to worship and fathom? And will this change as more of our sisters become seekers and explainers? I believe this to be true. And it is just such an expansion of the feminine, in my opinion, that accompanies this opening of East and West. For me, who touched the Eastern soul at the seat of the great Goddess Kali in Calcutta, it is moving to learn that the men who worship the feminine realize that She is the awe-inspiring grandeur who is both the creative source of the universe, and takes it back into Herself. Thus, perhaps, is Kali seen as Destroyer, for She destroys both the manifest and illusion, bringing us back to the origin.

This same feminine is also Kundalini Herself, the Serpent Power of energy, coiled and at rest around the base of the spine of our yogi. She is the static center about which every form of existence revolves. The One Consciousness (Chit) is polarized into static (Shiva) and kinetic (Shakti) aspects for the aforementioned purposes of creation. And it is Yoga which resolves this duality. It is for creation that Kundali (the larger, universal form of the individual Kundalini) unfolds in activity, and it is for Liberation (Mukti) and Enjoyment (Bhukti) that our Saddhaka works. He does this by identifying consciously with the Pair. I found that this same method of conscious identification was useful to me, when attempting to rise out of confusion and the inability to move, while writing this work.

My inner "guru" advised me to emulate his Dhyana (meditation), and when I did so, I became calm and centered.

So, whereas the yogin is everything because there is nothing in the universe that is not in the human body, his aim is to bring this power to full expression and dissolve himself. The way this is achieved is by the yogic methods, which we shall next consider.

The forms of yoga are sometimes considered as three-fold or four-fold. The three-fold system includes Karma Yoga, which entails an individual committing himself to *right action* without attachment to the desire for the fruit of this to accrue to him. This is available to anyone in the world, and is rather like what Abraham Maslow called trying to be a "good person." A second form in this system is Bhakti Yoga, which has at its center *devotion* to God, in the form of Upasana (worship) and living from the heart. The third form is Raja Yoga, which involves Jnana, or *intellectual* endeavor in the form of study, scholarship, wisdom, etc. These forms, of course, are not mutually exclusive. Indeed, the individual usually employs all of them, but is centered upon one of them.

The four-fold system of forms of yoga are Mantra Yoga, Laya Yoga, Hatha Yoga and Raja Yoga. All of these entail practice (Sadhana) and control of mind, feelings and body. Mantra Yoga is devoted to rituals, words and practice — things *outside* the body. Since the belief is that mind becomes what it perceives, the practitioner attempts to control it by its own object, basically name and form. The yogin uses images, emblems, pictures, markings, mandalas, yantras (diagrams), mudras (gestures) all in attempting to make modifications (Vriti) of his habitual negative patterns. In short, one uses the mind to break it. The simplest form is to observe the customs and stages of life most honorably — ritual. More specifically, chants and other uses of word and sound are central. We will consider this in more depth below.

Hatha Yoga is concerned primarily with the physical body, using Sadhanas (exercises) to reach the subtle body. The attention is to inner light and breath as well. Most important is Pranayama, or breath control, based on the idea that the breath is related to the life principle itself, and that *Prana* is raised up in the work. Ha (sun) and Tha (moon) are the two forces which are reconciled in the physical discipline, and various Asanas (postures), Mudras (gestures) are used to facilitate this. Even Virya (semen) is made to flow upward to the crown of the head to achieve the ultimate bliss. This is expressed in all of the methods in which Prana (vital energy) enters Sushumna (subtle body of central column) and becomes Laya (absorbed) in Sahasrara (crown chakra).

Raja Yoga and Jnana Yoga, having been mentioned earlier as the intellectual means of attainment, are used in all the higher forms of yoga, particularly in Laya Yoga, an advanced form of Hatha Yoga, which includes the Kundalini Yoga being investigated here. Whereas Hatha Yoga is physical and effects the subtle body through the gross physical body, and Mantra Yoga is concerned with forces outside the body which effect it, Laya Yoga deals with Pithas (supersensible centers) and forces of the *inner world* of the body. These supersensible centers or chakras, and their symbolism, will be of main interest to us in the section which follows.

At this point, it needs to be said that in Laya Yoga there is concern with the *Light*, and with the material forms of *Images* of the Spirit. Of central importance is Dhyana (meditation), which is of three kinds: Sthula (gross), Jyotih (a kind of infusion) and Sukshma (subtle). The first involves the concentration (Dharana) on given images of a very rich kind. One of these is to think of a great Ocean of nectar in the heart, in the middle of which is an Island of Gems; the Island is clothed with a forest of yellow blossoms, and surrounded by a variety of trees; in the midst of these is a Kalpa tree, laden with fruit and blossom; in the leaves, bees hum and birds make love; the four branches are the four Vedas; under the tree there are precious stones and within that a beautiful couch upon which the yogi is to picture himself with the Devata (Goddess). One can see that such richness of imagery clearly is an awakener of psychic life.

The second form of meditation, Jyotih, is to infuse fire and life (Tejas) into any form imagined. The third form, Suskshma, is to meditate upon the Kundalini after it is aroused. All of these meditative methods are precise, differentiated, and given to the yogin at various stages of his development, and are different for each chakra worked with.

How are we to understand these Yogas and the methods included in them? At first, one sees that the Indian has far less of a split between mind and body than we in the West. Our western Yoga, so to speak, in the form of sports, does not aim at spiritual liberation or union with God (although this may occur for some or even be sought after; I am thinking here of the Scottish runner in the film, Chariots of Fire). Our closest kin to this practice in psychological work are the body therapies begun by Wilhelm Reich. The latter, an avowed atheist, was propelled into his own spirituality as a result of his work and evolved a theory which is not so totally different from the Indian, of which he knew nothing (e.g. breathing, orgone, etc.).

The meditative methods are also extraordinarily differentiated and precise. Their aim is magical, in the sense of producing an effect indirectly and of using precise images, rather than "letting the soul speak for itself"

(Tertullian). Modern therapies of image (e.g. Gestalt), might be surprised to learn that their methods have a far older origin and, indeed, far greater differentiation in Indian tradition.

All this seems to be quite right, since a particular goal is aimed at, and there are revealed ancient methods of achieving it. But what are we to make of the fact that relatively few, even in India, embrace these paths of discipline, and of those that do, only a few are accepted by Gurus, and of those accepted, only one in a thousand "attains"? (I get this latter figure from Avalon). This is possibly because most of us merely participate, one way or another, in Karma Yoga, just living our destiny the best we can.

But there is another way that this can be considered. This is that there is so much prescribed direction, that little room for individuality presents itself. Is this why Jung had no interest in visiting the Holy Men when he was in India? Perhaps he expected that only a "type" would be manifest, rather than an individual. I suspect this to be true. Herein, also, lies the difference between spiritual methods as precisely given (see also my essay on this topic in *The Knight*[9]), and the method of active imagination invented by Jung. The latter lets the psyche speak for itself, and aims at a relationship with the powers therein, leading to *individuation*. The Indian methods lead to *Enlightenment* and *Liberation* as well as *Bliss*. No wonder most seekers on the path in the Jungian sense continue to experience suffering, for they are focussed upon individuality. In fairness, the Indian also recognizes suffering as a fact of existence, as long as one is in a gross body; hence the desire to attain total liberation and not be born again in this dimension.

We shall have much to do with the imagery discovered and revealed by these methods in the discussion which follows, but at this point, it is enough to appreciate the richness of this ancient method of disciplining the soul. Before we proceed to that imagery, we must remark that the yogin is not merely engaged in a sort of technical or engineering act -- far from it. There are many principles (Yama) and austerities (Niyama) that are prescribed for the aspirant, without which there is no good result. These are moral principles: avoidance of hurt to the living, honesty, not stealing, sexual continence, patience, fortitude, kindliness, simplicity, moderation, purity. There are also austerities: fasts, contentment with what one has, belief in Veda, charity, worship, study, modesty, sacrifice, and a right attitude. Without these, some say, power may be gained, but to no final avail, since Karma is still built up, and ultimately one must be on the path to liberation. One is here reminded that moral virtues are also required in alchemical work (see Jung, *Psychology and Alchemy*[6], and *Psychology of Transference*[5]), which clearly make these efforts psychological, and not merely a body-training or soul-training or even a spirit-training. Without heart or love, nothing is gained.

A final word, too, on Mantra: Tantrik conceives of a person's two lips as themselves Shiva and Shakti, who between them, utter the sounds (Shabda) which create the universe (the Cosmic Sound mentioned earlier). Letters and sounds are no mere arbitrary datum but are world-creating. Sound, like previously considered aspects, comes in the form of gross, subtle, causal and the "hidden" speech, the ultimate formations of which, the letters of the alphabet are an expression. These fifty letters of Sanskrit (which Kali wears as a garland of human heads!) appear on the petals of each lotus in each chakra, and carry significances, some of which we will have to consider. Here we must only know that thought and its expression in sound is a fundamental power, as real as objects. The Sanskrit root of M as power, in the form of the sound, "Man," means "to think." Mind, as both "revealed" and "revealer," can think of divinity and become it, ultimately. The vehicle is sound and the word.

This conception of the primacy of the word is certainly familiar to us in the Bible (And God *said*, "Let there be light"), just as the "light" is also primary. This special perception of the "subtlety" of the letter and word is also known to us, not only in the view that every word of the Bible is sacred and basic, but in the Kabbalistic conception of the letters as the building blocks of the universe. There is an archetypal sense, then, which sees letter and word-formation as fundamental, even genetic, which is not so far off from the current views in linguistics. The Indian view is that there was once a universal tongue and that same "form" exists in the background to existence. The "gross" letters are produced from the "subtle" letters, and both are the Garland of the Mother revealed in the Mantra.

The causal-subtle-gross distinctions implied here bring up the question, sometimes raised, as to whether the Kundalini energy worked with is "real" in the sense of physical, or "imaginary" in the sense of psychic (See White, John, *Kundalini*[10]). Avalon takes up this issue in his introduction and assures us that both are true. The test for the physical reality of the Kundalini is in heat. When the Kundalini rises, another person can tell this directly by placing his hand over the base of the spine, which will be quite cold. Intense heat, however, will be felt at the crown. Avalon tells us that yoga can be practiced, however, in both physical and non-physical ways. In the former, it is possible to attain the "siddhis," or powers of an unusual nature, and "bliss." This requires concrete effort. But Enlightenment and, particularly, "Liberation" is possible even when body power does not come into consideration. So, it depends upon what one is after. Furthermore, I would add, since physical ability varies a great deal among people, just as mental ability does, not all are able to engage in the strenuous Asanas required. Westerners, in particular, are in no way prepared for such efforts, which can come more easily to Easterners. Even the lotus position, natural to the Indian, can cause lots of pain and strain to us in the West, as every beginner in such meditation knows.

But what does a Jungian say about this? Do we not place emphasis upon "psychic reality" as the basis of both "mind" and "body," even antecedent, the way Tantra also conceives it? We do so, indeed. But my experience, even with the powerful technique of active imagination, is that transformation of the physical is always relative. It is true that we often begin with affects, which themselves are closely related to the autonomic nervous system and, therefore, close to the physical level. Yet the kind of transformation of the instinctive levels -- through image and word -- is always variable, and it is likely that the distinction suggested by Avalon is correct.

Before we proceed on to a discussion of the chakras, I want to correct an impression of limitation I may have given when discussing the "presented" character of the meditations. India, home of religions, is notoriously tolerant of diversity. An ancient saying is "To dispute the religion (Dharana) of another is the mark of a narrow mind. O Lord! O Great Magician! With whatsoever faith or feeling we call on Thee, Thou art pleased."

Chakras: General

The chakras may be defined as "subtle centers of operation in the body of the Shaktis or Powers of the various Tattvas or Principles" (Avalon[1], p. 103). Just as consciousness is not simply a function of the body or its organs, however, just so can we not simply describe the chakras as physiological activity. Consciousness is not an organic conception but is itself primary, or antecedent. It is rather more correct to think of the body and its various centers as "veiled" expressions of consciousness. Indeed, as consciousness goes from the abstract to the subtle to the concrete, we see the increasingly veiled condition of it, so that it can even appear as unconsciousness. Yet all aspects are conditions of consciousness. So, then, when the centers are described, these are seen as in western physiology, even where this is more detailed than in the latter, and transcending it.

Yet it is essential that the physical not be overlooked, since the purification of the body is necessary for the purification of the mind. *Prayanama*, the principle of breathing meditation, is the unifying instance of this, since concrete inhalation-exhalation is prescribed and a transcending spiritual cleansing is intended. If we remember that the Indian mind is less split than ours, we may approach a better understanding. Jung, in Lecture I[3], described the eastern mind as "concretistic," in that an idea also has substance. Here we might even think of it as degrees of substance involving the aforementioned concrete/subtle/causal/primary divisions.

We need also to know that the energy is purified through the Nadis — loosely defined as nerves, the principle ones of which there are fourteen in number, but of which Ida (moon), Pingala (sun) and Sushumna (center column) are the chief. The energy passes through this center as it rises.

The chakras or centers (also called *padma* or lotus), all have different mandalas, numbers of petals, animal symbols, Tattvas or principles and organs, as well as elements and particular Shivas and Shaktis represented. In order for us to better glimpse this complexity, I have adapted a Table of these variations from the work of Avalon, and also included a summary of the psychological aspects as discussed in Jung's work. This might help the reader keep an unconfused orientation in the discussion which follows. (See Table next page.)

How are we to understand the chakras psychologically, one might ask? Jung expressed it by saying that each chakra is a whole world. One might say that this means that a different type of consciousness is being described for each of them. As one looks at the Table, one can see at once that each one carries a world in itself, as Jung says, replete with imagery, elements, mandalas, and types of instinctive expression, as well as functions and conditions of the gods and goddesses. When we go more deeply into the symbolism, we will see that whole world-views can be contained in each of them, indeed whole types of religious attitude. It is little wonder, then, that this ancient tradition has been so long-lasting, and has had its impact on other religions as well.

It would be well to get a flavor of the style of our teacher here, Purnananda, as he begins his Shatchakra Nirupana in the preliminary verse (Avalon, 1, p. 318):

> Now I speak of the first sprouting shoot (of the Yoga plant) of complete realization of the Brahman, which is to be achieved, according to the Tantras, by means of the six Chakras and so forth in their proper order.

Here he is simple and direct, as he is in the concrete descriptions of the lotuses and steps, but he often becomes flowery and adoring, as we shall see. His commentator, however, begins at once with a more elaborate style:

> He alone who has become acquainted with the wealth of the six Lotuses by

CHAKRA	LOCATION (Plexus)	PETALS	MANDALA	ANIMAL	TATTVA (sense-act)	SHIVA	SHAKTI	ELEMENT
Muladhara 'root support'	Perineum; between anus and genitals	4	Square	Elephant	Cohesion; smell; feet	Brahma child	Dakini	Earth
	PSYCHOLOGICAL SIGNIFICANCE: Everyday reality; grown into; family, work, etc. Elephant, domesticated libido.							
Svadhisthana 'proper place'	Hypogastric; bladder, above genital	6	Crescent	Makara crocodile	Contraction; taste; hand	Hari-Vishnu youth	Rakini	Water
	PSYCHOLOGICAL SIGNIFICANCE: Unconscious, devouring, dangerous, negative fish-monster. Moon							
Manipura, 'plenitude of jewels'	Solar plexus; navel diaphragm	10	Triangle	Ram	Expansion; heat; sight & color; anus	Rudra old	Lakini	Fire
	PSYCHOLOGICAL SIGNIFICANCE: Handles of crucible-triangle form of swastika. Emotion, passions; Rudra is destroyer; affects; Belly is action-reaction, no reflection.							
Anahata 'unattackable'	Heart	12	Hexagon	Antelope/ gazelle	Movement; touch; feel; penis	Isha	Kakini	Air
	PSYCHOLOGICAL SIGNIFICANCE: Conscious. Union of opposites, atman (self) appears. Small flame in castle; heart in lungs. Here is reflection, discrimination, judgement. Come to impersonal aspect of oneself.							
Vishuddha 'purification'	Throat pharyngeal plexus	16	Circle	White Elephant	Akasha (space-giving) hearing; mouth	Sada-Shiva	Shakini	Ether
	PSYCHOLOGICAL SIGNIFICANCE: Pure concepts, reality of psyche. World is inner drama, has to do with Hindu idea that word and speech beyond tangible reality (compare John: "Beg. is the word"							
Ajna 'place of command'	Between the eyes	2	—	No animal	Manas (mental faculties)	Shambhu	Hakini	None
	PSYCHOLOGICAL SIGNIFICANCE: Command, no animal means psychic reality does not require animal, bodily reality. Yogin is a psychic content of God.							
Sahasrara	Above crown on head	1000	Lotus	None	None	None	None	None
	PSYCHOLOGICAL SIGNIFICANCE: Shunyata, the void. All being is no longer being. Union of opposites. Advaita (non-two); Nirdvandva (free of opposites), objectless subject. Total union of Shiva-Shakti.							

Maha-yoga is able to explain the principles thereof. Not even the most excellent among the wise, nor the oldest in experience, is able, without the mercy of the Guru (Lord of Mercy), to explain the inner principles relating to the six Lotuses, replete as they are with the greatness of Sha (Final liberation), Sa (Knowledge) and Ha (Supreme Spirit).

Now the very merciful Purnananda Svami, wishful to rescue the world sunk in the mire of misery, takes that task upon himself. He does so to guide Sadhakas; to impart Tattva-jnana (knowledge), which leads to liberation; and also with the desire of speaking of the union of Kundalini with the six Chakras.

So, then, we shall accompany our teachers, Purnananda, his commentator, Kalicharana, Avalon and Jung as they reveal to us this path.

Muladhara Chakra: "Root-support"

Jung's interpretation of the psychological meaning of this center is that the Self is asleep and the ego is conscious. He is thinking, of course, of the statement that the Kundalini Herself, wrapped two and one half times around a central lingam, a phallic energy source, is slumbering and that She is Herself a symbol of the Self, ever-present but needing to be awakened. Our ego, however, is conscious, insofar as we are living our everyday lives. We are "rooted" in the earth, the element of this chakra, and safely seated (like the Bija or seed-mantra of "Lam") on the elephant, Airavata. The elephant in India is a symbol of strength, firmness, solidity. He would be the equivalent of what the horse once was for us in the west, or the ox both east and west: energy for the tasks of everyday life.

Not only are we rooted and supported by the earth, we are under the principle (tattva) of *cohesion*, of hanging together, and connected with that earth reality by our feet, and also by our sense of smell, like the animals. Our mandala is four-square and solid, our connection with life is through the institutions into which we are born. It is Jung's genius to interpret this as the condition of everyday consciousness, in which we are awake only in a collective sense; our true Selves are asleep. This, he says, is also a state of *participation mystique*, and most Europeans are in this condition, as well. But, just as Jung seems to have no high regard for the average consciousness of the European of the early 1930's, he also warns repeatedly that these Indian symbols are "a foreign body in our system" and that they might inhibit our own natural growth in the psyche. Not for the first time, he encourages us to "stand up" to these symbols.

Here we see Jung's continuing ambivalence toward the richness of this Indian tradition and we can see why. All that he said of the qualities of this chakra are certainly true, but there is a seductive promise here in

Kundalini Herself and in the other aspects of this chakra that he fails to mention. Look first at the state of the Goddess, the Dakini who dwells here. This Shakti-Dakini is deeply red, four-armed, holds a sacrificial spear, a sword, a skull-staff, and a drinking cup. She is powerful and bespeaks the need for the suffering and sacrifice of everyday life, one thinks. She is far from asleep herself.

Her consort, furthermore, in his Shiva aspect, is the Child-Brahma, who also has four hands, holds a staff, gourd, and rosary. He makes the gesture of dispelling fear. The spirit form (Shiva) here is a mere child, but he holds the community symbols of containment and prayer and aids us in dispelling the fear of the forces of the Gods and Kundalini when aroused. So it is that the "banality" of everyday life contains the powerful forces of the universe. The gods are not so fully asleep, but reveal themselves to us in their contained condition.

The promise of the as-yet-unawakened Kundalini is shown very powerfully by our teacher Purnananda, who tells us of the sleeping Kundalini, "fine as fibre of the lotus stalk," in Verses 10 and 11 (Avalon[1], p. 347)

> She is the world-bewilderer, ... Like the spiral of the conch-shell, Her shining snake-like form goes three-and-a-half times around Shiva and her lustre is as that of a strong flash of young strong lightning. Her sweet murmur is like the indistinct hum of swarms of love-mad bees. She produces melodious poetry and . . . all other compositions in prose or verse. . . . It is She who maintains all the beings of the world by means of inspiration and expiration, and shines in the cavity of the root (Mula) Lotus like a chain of brilliant lights.

And again, in Verse 13, Purnananda tells us:

> By meditating thus on Her who shines within the Mula Chakra, with the lustre of ten million Suns, a man becomes Lord of speech and King among men, and an Adept in all kinds of learning. He becomes ever free from all diseases, and his inmost Spirit becomes full of great gladness. Pure of disposition by his deep and musical words, he serves the foremost of the Devas.

This is the promise of the as-yet-unawakened Kundalini, but it is significantly to be noted that Creation is the specific suggestion here. Out of the ordinariness and the suffering of everyday life lies the possibility of creation, of the rousing of energy and consciousness which makes one "lord of speech" and "adept in learning." One thinks here of the childhood dream of Jung himself, who beheld in that underground cavern a phallic god not so different from the lingam, and who himself achieved this creativity which both threatened and promised itself to him. Is this not like the presentation here of the Shiva-Shakti, both suggesting the powerful forces and "dispelling fear?"

Jung so much as says this, (Lecture I, p. 14) when he suggests that the Kundalini is that which makes you go on the greatest adventures. It is, itself, a symbol for the divine urge. It is the "lady" for the Knight, and the *anima* for the man. It can be a spark, a fear, a neurosis, anything which indicates that a greater will than our own intervenes in our life. And it effects us just when we are in ordinary life. Jung confirms here that the Indian must fulfill his ordinary existence, usually, before he can legitimately undertake the Yogic path of Kundalini.

All of the foregoing sounds very unique and individual, yet Jung asserts that this is no personal task. No, it is impersonal; the energy itself is transpersonal and if we awaken it, we must be careful not to identify with it lest we suffer inflation. It happens to us as much as we cultivate it. Once more, the paradox becomes manifest: the divine is unconscious, we are unconscious of it; we awaken, it awakens and the sorting out process begins. Yet the system itself symbolizes the "development of the impersonal life," says Jung. "Therefore it is at the same time initiation symbolism, and it is the cosmogonic myth" (Lecture II, p. 23). And it is the creation myth that Jung compares to the Pueblo myth, and the Christian story, too. In both, the step from the ordinary, on earth, is followed by a further step into the water (baptism), just as we now see in the next stage of the Kundalini process.

Svadhisthana Chakra: "Proper place."

Just as the Muladhara is the "root support," the beginning of a process of spiritual growth, rooted in the culture into which we are born, the next phase of development -- after meditation and raising the energy -- is to the "proper place," the region of the water. We have also "risen" from the earthy condition of the perineum, between anus and genitals, to the "root" of the genitals in the hypogastric region, the bladder. After earth comes water, after awakening from ordinary life comes "baptism" or immersion in the spirit.

It is Jung's genius, here, to understand this second step of spiritual growth as an immersion in the sea of the unconscious. What for the East is "up," for us is "down." Furthermore, what for the East is masculine (the moon), for us is feminine. He notes, prophetically as it turns out, that these symbols are made by men and that it is masculine psychology with which we deal. All the same, he notes that in all initiation rites and mystery cults there is a kind of baptism, a descent into water, and so it is here. The way of higher development leads through water, the immersion into our own depths.

What is it that we find there in our depths? Why it is the *makara* fish, a kind of legendary animal, which we might compare to a crocodile, or better, the Leviathan of the Bible[7]. That devouring monster confronts us, I think, with our desire, our lust, our never-ending demands that are never satisfied. It is these *klesas* or desires which are being transformed in the meditative work of the yogi, as he focuses on the Shiva-Shakti, god-goddess who dwells here.

First of all, he finds the Shiva condition as Vishnu, in the form of a youth. The spirit-form has grown from the child-like condition in Muladhara to the youthful one in Svadhisthana. The principle (tattva) under which he operates, however, is one of *contraction*. There is a narrowing of consciousness, from one point of view, and a submersion of that which had shown before as light. Now the *hand* is necessary; one not only stands on the common ground, one is actively engaged and molding one's own psyche as one struggles with the desire and lust which are activated herein. This same youth, who is also a symbol for the time when our own lusts are activated, is called upon as Hari (remember Hari-Krishna?) who is prayed to, as Purnananda tells us in Verse 16 (p. 361):

> May Hari, . . . who is in the pride of early youth, whose body is of a luminous blue, beautiful to behold, who is dressed in yellow raiment, is four-armed and wears the Shri-vatsa (an auspicious curl) and the Kaustubha (a great gem worn by Vishnu), protect us!

And from what should the youthful and beautiful Hari protect us, we might rightly ask? The answer is hinted at in the very next verse, in which we are told that the consort of Hari-Vishnu, the Rakini makes her home here. (Verse 17):

> It is here that Rakini always dwells. She is of the color of a blue lotus. The beauty of Her body is enhanced by Her uplifted arms holding various weapons. She is dressed in celestial raiment and ornaments, and Her mind is exalted with the drinking of ambrosia.

So far, apart from the weapons, we seem to have nothing to fear. Our Goddess is beautiful and exalted, but our commentator has more to tell us about Her.

> Meditate on Rakini, who is blue of colour. In Her hands are a spear, a lotus, a drum, and a sharp battle-axe. She is of furious aspect. Her three eyes are red, and her teeth show fiercely. She, the Shining Devi of Devas, is seated on a double lotus, and from one of her nostrils there flows a streak of blood. She is fond of white rice and grants the wished-for boon.

Kalicharana also tells us, in the commentary to verse 18, that this Rakini cleanses us from the "fault of Ahamkara" which can be seen as egoism, but also includes many of the evil inclinations such as Kama (lust), Krodha (anger) etc. We are clearly dealing with the problems of lust and anger, desire and egoism.

The Goddess, terrible to behold with her three-eyes and fierce projecting fangs, is what we fear and why we need the protection provided by her consort, the youthful Vishnu-Hari. Yet this Goddess, confronted and worshipped, ultimately frees us from the darkness and grants us boons. It is clear that, in our words, the confrontation of the unconscious with genuineness and respect brings about a transformation in the fierceness of our own desire-life and carries us onward on the path of spiritual development.

Jung talks about the destructive aspect of the unconscious itself and it is here, in this struggle, that the truth of this is revealed. Also made manifest is the necessity of the first phase, the orderedness and regularity of a society in which the gods are worshipped and the rituals of existence hold sway. Yet without an encounter with this fierce Goddess, there is no fulfillment of the creativity suggested in the first chakra and the development of the mandala (from four to six petals) would not take place. It is noteworthy that there are six enemies of man, symbolized here by the meditation on the lotus. These are the greed and anger mentioned earlier, along with Moha (delusion), Mada (pride), Matsarya (envy), which all arise from a sense of "mineness," (Ahamkara). When overcome, the darkness of ignorance is replaced by the Sun of knowledge, says our commentator.

Is it only our own darkness which is overcome, or is it the darkness of the gods (nature) which is also being transformed?

Manipura Chakra: "Plentitude of Jewels"

Avalon tells us that Manipura is so named because the fiery Tejas found at this level produces a lustrous gem (Mani). Here we have a ten-petalled lotus, in contrast to the four of Muladhara and the six of Svadhistana. There is more development, differentiation and complexity, we might conclude, as well as more intense movement, symbolized by the fiery element on the one hand, and the mandala of triangles. Muladhara, with its order and clarity, gave us a mandala of the square; the Crescent-moon faced us in Svadhisthana and here we are confronted with the triangles of Manipura. The triangle, like the number three, is a dynamic figure, and the condition herein portrayed is equally dynamic. Within the triangles, furthermore, are to be found three swastikas. These symbols did not, in the day of Kundalini, convey the horror of our modern associations, yet it is not by chance alone that this chakra is connected with destruction, as we shall shortly see.

First, however, we need a view of its various conditions. The animal here is the ram, a symbol of battle and power, as well as Rudra, the Shiva-form here, who is seated upon a bull. Clearly, power is indicated. Furthermore, the tattva condition is Expansion in contrast to the Cohesion of Muladhara and the Contraction of Svadhisthana. Expansion must mean the enhancement of energy and power, as well as consciousness. The qualities of heat, sight, and the "organ" of the anus, confirms this paradox of conditions which add energy and vision (consciousness), yet produce detritus and destruction.

The Bija of Fire is called "Ram." This is a seed mantra, seated on a ram, a carrier of Agni, the Lord of Fire. Here, too, is Red Rudra, smeared with white ashes, and his Shakti Lakini who is "fond of animal food." This, Avalon informs us, is a digestive center, in which the Saddhaka is expected to satisfy the appetites of this devata, Lakini. We are still in the region of desire, and the seeker continues to eat meat, a practice given up at the later chakras.

The verses of Purnananda tell us clearly that power and destruction are the conditions to be dealt with spiritually at this chakra:

Verse 20
Meditate upon Him (Agni, Fire) seated on a ram, four-armed, radiant like the rising Sun. In His lap dwells Rudra, who is of a pure vermillion hue. He (Rudra) is white with the ashes with which He is smeared; of an ancient aspect and three-eyed, His hands are placed in the attitude of granting boons and dispelling fear. He is the destroyer of creation.

This presentation of the "destroyer of creation" is also ambivalent, just as fire is. We are faced with the passions, which Jung tells us is indeed the fullness of jewels, but also Hell. If we cope with these passions, are able to get objectivity, then we rise above the ordinary situation of action and reaction, of a belly-psychology, and can achieve calm perspective (the property of the next chakra); otherwise we roast in the Hell of our own fires.

But here, too, says Jung, is where the sun rises, where consciousness can appear. We can come to a realization of eternity, of an immortal soul, just through these fires. Yet, if we do not transcend, we remain a creature of the abdomen, we think with our intestines. Here, then, is no freedom, only bones and blood (as we will see in a moment in describing the Shakti-Lakini).

When we ask, once more, what it is that we are afraid of, we now find that we no longer deal only with a boy and youth, for the male aspect, as we did in the earlier chakras, but now we face a more ambivalent "ancient" Shiva, who is both a granter of boons and a "destroyer of creation." Now, too, the fearsomeness of the Shakti is becoming somewhat reduced, although Her power (remember, She represents the energy of the universe), is still awesome. Let us hear Purnananda on our Shakti:

Verse 21
Here abides Lakini, the benefactress of all. She is four-armed, of radiant body, is dark (of complexion), clothed in yellow raiment and decked with various ornaments, and exalted with the drinking of ambrosia. By meditating on this Navel Lotus, the power to destroy and create (the world) is acquired. Vani (the power of speech) with all the wealth of knowledge ever abides in the lotus of his face.

In addition to Purnananda's remarks, we have the commentary of Kalicharana who informs us that this goddess Lakini is "fierce of aspect and with Her teeth protruding." He continues:

In her right hand She holds the thunderbolt and the Shakti (the weapon of fire), and in the left She makes the gestures of dispelling fear and granting boons. . . . She is fond of meat and her breast is ruddy with the blood and fat which drop from Her mouth.

Not a pretty picture, but a potent one, and here, too, the opposites (dispelling fear while she also scares us to death!) come into play. All in all, this chakra is a clear representation of the Power principle, when viewed psychologically. One might even think that this orientation is the province of Adlerian psychology, whereas Svadhisthana is that of Freud, and the upcoming Anahata, which brings Self symbolism into play, would be that of Jung. In any case, all of the "lower" chakras confront us with the instinctive conditions and passions, through which we must move in meditation and contemplation, in order to achieve the promised bliss and consciousness of "higher" chakras. Yet we must remember that the flow of the Kundalini energy is, at last, a circular one and that the energy which rises also returns and there is a *circulation* in the ultimate stages, even though this is not emphasized in many texts.

Avalon's interpretation of the "fond of animal food" condition of the Shakti-Lakini is that the appetites of this devata are meant to be satisfied. This seems to bring up the question as to how the various instincts are to be dealt with in the meditation of the Saddhaka. On the one hand, there is the control and sublimation of these desires; on the other hand, there is the tacit indication that these are to be fulfilled. This paradoxical injunction is certainly a condition which is commonly found in analytic work, and the direction in each specific event is a closely watched one, wherein one tries to conform with the total needs of the soul. One wonders how the Saddhakas approached this. Did they, too, fulfill, or only inhibit? If we pay attention to some Tantric texts, there was a sequence: first denial and devotion, followed by service and fulfillment, followed by "indifference."

Anahata Chakra: "Unattackable"

For Jung, the Anahata chakra is where individuation, as a conscious awareness of the Self, truly begins. Until this point, one is immersed in desire, passion, the thousand-and-one things of existence and there is, above all, no detachment. Here, at last, begins reason, a capacity to rise above the emotions. Here, too, one gets the first germ-like glimpses of Purusha, the thumbling of the Self. But one must remember, says Jung, that as long as we are mortal, we can become quite inflated by thinking that we have "arrived" in Anahata; in point of fact, we remain in Muladhara with our egos, but we can and do *behold* Purusha in Anahata as we gaze on it from below. For this, we truly need the mantras, the sacred words, because our capacity for true civilization, for the spiritualization of ourselves, is quite weak. Thus far, Jung.

We can see, in every way, just as Jung suggests, that here is a significant development beyond the previous three chakras. The mandala now is a hexagon (combining the triangles of masculine and feminine nature), the petals of the lotus have increased to twelve, the animal is less demanding and aggressive (antelope or gazelle), the element (air) is more "spiritualized," and the Tattva or principle is significantly changed. In contrast to the previous cohesion, contraction, and expansion — all of which keep one contained in a single place — we now have the aspect of *movement*, which allows one to proceed outside of one's previous condition. Furthermore, there are the further Tattvas of touch, of feeling, and of the organ of the penis, all of which imply relationship, connection. This is quite suitable, of course, to a heart center, which evokes caring, feeling, compassion, and relationship with others in a manner different from exploitation or dominance. We shall now explore this chakra in a more detailed way to see just how this change occurs and what is entailed.

Avalon and Purnananda tell us of the Anahata lotus as "charming," as beguiling in its color (red) as the Bandhuka flower. At last we rise above the fires of Manipura, and now we are in the region of the Vayu, a mandala of six corners, of two triangles entwined, the same as the Star of David or Seal of Solomon. This mandala, in which the male and female triangles are happily united, is smokey in color, presenting a nice contrast to the warm-hearted reds of the chakra. Can one guess that here we find the "smoke" from the Manipura fires below, and here the flame becomes gentle and refined as the flower which charms us?

In many ways, we are told that peace is encountered here, and the wars below are overcome. For example, the Anahata is called "unattackable," because the sound which is heard here (says Kalicharana) is "that which issues without the striking of any two things together." We are reminded of the Buddhist "sound of one hand clapping," and attain a glimpse of that condition in which there is a "steady flame of a lamp in a windless place." (Verse 26).

Furthermore, we are told that the element here is Air, and the animal is that fleet-of-foot antelope or gazelle who is truly gentle in comparison with the previous ones. As we shall see, even the Goddess is less violent here, for her "heart is softened by the drinking of nectar."

Finally, we are informed that a small, secondary lotus is located just below this heart chakra. It is called a "mental lotus," with eight petals, in which there is the Kalpa Tree, a jewelled altar surmounted by an awning and decorated with flags. I have elsewhere (*The Tree*) described this as a "Buddhist Lotus," since serenity is specified at the base of this Tree, and "detachment," is achieved.

The Saddhaka who meditates on this Heart Lotus, as Purnananda tells us, "becomes like the Lord of Speech and like Ishvara, he is able to protect and destroy the worlds." He is no longer subject to the whims of creation and destruction in the universe of his own passions and now, by the grace of the Word, can himself both protect and eliminate. He is thereby, "illumined by the solar region," and full of "charm." Indeed we are told later on (Verse 27) that the yogi so arrived "is dearer than the dearest to women," because he is so skilled in pleasing them, says Kalicharana.

The God and Goddess here are indeed changed as well. Isha is the Shiva aspect here, with three eyes (seeing all), and clad gently in silken raiment. He wears gems around his neck and bells on his toes, as well, and possesses the "soft radiance of ten million moons." Even the Goddess, here called Kakini, becomes "exhilarated and auspicious, benefactress of all." Despite the fact that She still carries a noose and skull, she "makes the sign of blessing and the sign which dispells fear." Her heart (as we have seen) "is softened with the drinking of nectar."

Kalicharana informs us that this softening is caused by the supreme bliss engendered by drinking the nectar which drops from Sahasrara. In any case, her heart "expands with the supreme bliss." One might also add that this Kakini is thought of as wearing the skin of the black antelope. Does this not suggest also that She, too, has been civilized?

Finally, we are told that the yogi who attains here not only has his senses completely under control, but can concentrate intensely, and "is able at will to enter another's body." Kalicharana tells us that this means he can enter the enemy's fort or citadel, even though guarded. We can understand this, psychologically, to mean that such a person is highly sensitive, can intuitively penetrate people's defenses and can also, best of all, protect himself from their darkness ("he may render himself invisible."). Yet we can not discount the statement that Siddhis are here achieved and that, as Kalicharana says, that such a person can "fly across the sky" (Astral travel? Out of the body experience?) and even "enter another's body." Although we can not be certain of the literalness of this capacity, we can surely conclude that, at this point, the transcendence of the yogin is such that he goes beyond the ordinariness of the life and psychology of the lower three chakras.

With Jung, we can conclude that what was begun below in Muladhara is now achieved in Anahata. It is notable that this capacity to come to the impersonal aspect of one's Self is located at the "heart" region, and even has, below it, a "mental" lotus. To think with the heart, as the Pueblo Indians also know, is to truly have consciousness. This is no mere mental activity, as we shall later see.

Vishuddha Chakra: "Purification"

For Jung, the attainment of the Vishuddha Chakra is to reach the level of Psychic Reality. The element of this chakra, *ether*, is a substance which is no substance; it is a conception of substance. It is at a level of abstraction, therefore, which goes beyond the empirical world. The evolution of the yogin's work, then, has him move up from the gross matter and earth of Muladhara, all the way through the *five* elements, now including the final one of ether. This ancient idea of transformation is also found in alchemy, says Jung, and hinges on a kind of cooking process. Manipura, with its "handles," resembles a pot, which is like the cooking process found in the "kitchen" of the stomach, the region where that chakra is located. If Manipura is the center of transformation, via the emotions, then Anahata, which is the *place* of transformation and is invisible, provides the psychic foundation which is fully realized, at last, in Vishuddha, the region of psychological reality.

Jung thinks that civilization as a whole has reached Anahata -- our center is no longer in the diaphragm as it was with the Greeks. Despite this growth, however, we have not yet reached Vishuddha, with its conception of the world as a psychic reality. Only here can one grasp the *Purusha*, dimly felt in Anahata, in which the essence of man is seen as a subjective condition. Jung thinks that when the abstract ideas of modern physics and of analytical psychology are generally comprehended, then civilization will have reached this level of understanding.

There is, then, a great gap between the achievements of Anahata and Vishuddha. To reach the latter, thinks Jung, is to *unlearn* all that was achieved in the progression from Manipura to Anahata. At this point, the world itself and everything in it becomes internal, psychical. To be at Vishuddha is to be with the subjective level of existence: *everything that happens to one's self is one's self*. Or, to see it in another way, the world is a reflection of the psyche.

This progression of the development in psychic reality, says Jung, can be seen by the changes in the animals which belong to each chakra. The elephant, like the horse, is, at Muladhara, both the instinctual urge which supports consciousness, and the cultivation of the *will* to enlarge it. The Makara, or Leviathan at Svadhisthana is the strongest animal in the water, just as the elephant is on the land. These two, in Jung's opinion, are really the same animal[3]: (Lecture III, p. 10-11)

> The power that forces you into consciousness and sustains you in your conscious world, proves to be the worst enemy when you come to the next centre, for there you are really going out of this world, and everything that makes you to cling to it is your worst enemy. The greatest blessing in this world is the greatest curse in the unconscious.

As we continue up the scale, we come to the ram of Manipura, the animal of fire and passion. Here *sacrifice* is central, we give up being mere slaves to our passions and desires. The result is to be found in the animal at Anahata, the gazelle or antelope. This animal is like the ram, but is not domesticated nor is it sacrificed. It is fleet and shy, light as air, and has lost the heaviness of earth. Only here, at last, is a psychic factor realized. It is like the unicorn (Holy Ghost) and bespeaks a psychic factor not even vouchsafed in Freud.

When we come to Vishuddha, at last, we arrive at a level of instinct which transcends all the foregoing, for now we experience a purified condition of instinct (white elephant) in which the power supports human thoughts. Like Plato, there is an appreciation of the subjectivity of the mind, but not just as in intellect. The intellect requires physical evidence for its conceptions, not so the psyche itself, which does not. Consider, for example, the image of God! Finally, as we shall see later on, there is an absence (in Ajna), of the animal itself — there is *only* psychic reality. But here, at Vishuddha, we are in the realm of pure concepts, where the world is itself an inner drama.

This is commensurate with the Hindu idea that word and speech are beyond tangible reality, as we discussed earlier, in speaking about Mantra, and about the letters of the alphabet on the petals of the mandalas. It is noteworthy here that there are the largest number of petals for this mandala, sixteen, and that the center itself is located at the throat, the pharyngeal plexus, without which speech and the word would not be possible. When we also note that this center has as its tattva, Akasha, or a space-giving principle, in which hearing and the mouth are its senses and act-capacities, we are certainly in the region known to us in another tradition: "In the beginning was the word . . ."; "And God *said*, Let there be . . ."

There is more to be said about Akasha: The word refers to a kind of region or condition known in magical and mystical circles as the "place" in which all the psychic "records" of mankind are kept. Here one can find the images and words for all the events, past and present and future, for everyone. To tune in to this region is to be able to read all of one's past incarnations and even to anticipate future ones. Our commentator, Kalicharana, notes that to "see the three periods" of past, present and future is to "see the Self (Atma), and, as all objects of knowledge are therein, they become visible to him."

How are we to understand this conception psychologically? If we were to translate this into archetypal language, we would say that when one is so deeply connected with the unconscious as to be in touch with the Self, then psychic reality transcends our usual, conscious ideas of time and space, and we are then in the web of existence, in which synchronistic events take place. To be so linked, then, is to "know" in a different way. It is, therefore, quite right that the mandala of this chakra is also the seamless symbol of the circle -- no more angles or corners. "God is a circle whose center is everywhere and circumference is nowhere" is a fitting statement of this psychic image.

If we look, now, at the images of the God and Goddess which are given for this chakra, we discover that the male principle has grown significantly in power and presence and that the female principle, already "softened" in Anahata, has become "like light itself" -- white. The male God is Sada-Shiva, and he is seated on a great lion-seat, holding a trident, battle-axe, sword, thunderbolt, great snake, bell, goad, noose, and he makes mudras dispelling fear. In short, he contains all the powers of the previous chakras, but is now in a condition of purification in which all is subjective. Indeed, he is now united with a female principle, is an androgyne, and is known as the "ever-beneficent one." All the implements, meditated upon by the Saddhaka, convey His greatness, but also benevolence.

Something similar can be said for the Goddess here, who is the Shakti

Shakini. She is white, and carries a bow, arrow, noose and a goad. No longer frightening, she still conveys the power, like her consort, to urge the Seeker onward, to continue in his meditation and attain the Akashic level of consciousness. The Saddhaka's senses are now pure and controlled, but this is what Purnananda says about our seeker at this level (Verse 31):

> He who has attained complete knowledge of the Atma (Brahman) becomes by constantly concentrating his mind (Chitta) on this Lotus a great Sage, eloquent and wise, and enjoys uninterrupted peace of mind. He sees the three periods (past, present and future), and becomes the benefactor of all, free from disease and sorrow and long-lived, and like Hamsa, the destroyer of endless dangers.

By this is meant that the Saddhaka has freed himself from the bonds of Maya and will open the gate of Liberation (Moksha), as his next step.

Avalon, in his scholarship, has provided here an additional verse (31A), not noted by either Purnananda nor Kalicharana, but by one Bala-deva in another text. In this verse, the yogi is "in his wrath, able to move all the three worlds. Neither Brahma nor Vishnu, neither Hari-Hara nor Surya nor Ganapa is able to control his power (resist him)." Avalon makes no comment on this strange assertion of the power of the yogi, but we may here relate this to the attainment of psychic reality: when all existence is relativized in the psyche, then the Gods themselves no longer have power, and the meditator can grasp the essence behind the Gods themselves. This, in effect, is the last-but-one step for the yogi to come to the "place of command" in the next chakra and discover that with all power comes no power, and that the yogi himself is nothing more than a psychic content of God.

Ajna Chakra: "Place of Command"

At this level, after a long development and differentiation in which the petals of the lotus increased, we now face a reduction. The petals are reduced to only two, and there is no mandala, no animal, and no element. For Jung, when there is no animal there is no bodily reality; only psychic reality exists. In short, the yogin now realizes himself as a pyschic content of God.

In the beginning, at Muladhara, God or Atman was dormant and the yogin (ego) was aware. Now that God is fully awake, the ego realizes itself as a mere fragment, focussed on the *unio mystica*. This is symbolized in the presentation of the original Lingam once more, but now white. In Vishuddha, furthermore, says Jung, psychic reality was opposed to physical reality. Here in Ajna, there is no longer any physical reality, only psyche obtains.

In his final lecture (IV) of his series on Kundalini Yoga[4], Jung takes up what he considers to be a paradox between the views of India and Hinduism and those of us in the West, particularly as this effects our understanding of Ajna. He does this by interpreting Sthula (which we have translated as the concrete or gross bodily level) as the personal aspect of consciousness, whereas the Suksma (which is generally translated as the subtle-body dimension) as the supra-personal. Jung suggests that each chakra has a sthula or personal aspect and a sukshma or supra-personal aspect. Muladhara, for example, is in the pelvis but represents the world. We, in the west, think of our consciousness as in the head, at Ajna, but we live in Muladhara, in earthly entanglements and causalities. We are also identified with consciousness, and thus speak of "sub-consciousness." All this, however, is strictly from a sthula (personal) aspect. To look at things from a supra-personal aspect is suksma. We begin in the head, it is true, but we do not remain there. India and Kundalini, on the other hand, is entirely the reverse. Indians begin with the suksma aspect, even in Sahasrara, and conceive of man from the top down. We think of ourselves in Ajna, but we live in Muladhara. Here is the paradox:

From the sthula aspect: India is in Muladhara, we are in Ajna.

From the suksma aspect: India is in Ajna, we are in Muladhara.

We shall return to this differentiation, but now, as we discuss Ajna, it is well for us to grasp this strange condition in which we "think" with our heads but do not come to the impersonal aspect of ourselves, and the Indian does not so think, yet he is fully aware of the impersonal aspect of himself.

All of this hinges on the fact that this chakra is the seat of the Tattva of Manas, or the mental faculties. This is stressed in the commentary and also it is noted that there is an additional, minor chakra, said to exist between Ajna and Sahasrara, also devoted to the mental aspects. Our whole understanding of mind, in short, is what is at stake here.

Avalon tells us that Ajna is called "command" because at this point, the Saddhaka receives commands directly from the inner Guru, from above, in both the "manas" minor chakras, and from the Sahasrara itself. All else recedes and loses significance. There are only two petals of the lotus now, and all the letters of the previous petals are exhausted. The mantra, now, is *om*, the ultimate, and fire, sun and moon converge. Here the Atma shines lustrously like a flame, and the yogi gains the final siddhis (powers) which permit him, at his death, to voluntarily put his *prana* at this spot and enter *purusha* directly, needing no longer to re-incarnate.

The Goddess here is described in Verse 32 of Purnananda:

> The Lotus named Ajna is like the moon (beautifully white). On its two petals are the letters Ha and Ksha, which are also white and enhance its beauty. It shines with the glory of Dhyana (the state of mind produced by meditation). Inside it is the Shakti Hakini, whose six faces are like so many moons. She has six arms, in one of which She holds a book; the others are lifted up in the gestures of dispelling fear and granting boons, and with the rest She holds a skull, a small drum, and a rosary. Her mind is pure.

The "holding of a book" is variously interpreted as a gesture which conveys learning or knowledge. The implication is that knowledge is central here, and that the yogin now is connected with the wisdom of Manas, as well as with the purity (white) so received. All the same, the various symbols of death, prayer and limitation are also presented. In verse 33, the Shiva aspect is described:

> Within this Lotus dwells the subtle mind (Manas). It is well known. Inside the Yoni in the pericarp is the Shiva called Itara, in His phallic form. Here he shines like a chain of lightning flashes. The first Bija of the Vedas (Om), which is the abode of the most excellent Shakti and which by its lustre makes visible the Brahma-sutra is also there. The Sadhaka with steady mind should meditate upon these according to the order prescribed.

By subtle, is here meant beyond the senses, and the phallic form of the Shivalinga is here also subtled into whiteness and the chain of lightning flashes.

The Saddhaka who has achieved this level realizes that his "Atma is nothing but a meditation on this Lotus" (Verse 34). He therefore knows, as we have said, that he is only a content of the Self. As such, he becomes the benefactor, and is all-seeing and knowing. "He realizes his unity with the Brahman and acquires excellent and unknown powers." The yogi also "closes the house which hangs without support," meaning that the mind's connection with the outer world has been removed and he is in connection of the infinite.

> . . . By repeated practice (he) becomes dissolved in this place which is the abode of uninterrupted bliss, he then sees within the middle of and in the space above (the triangle) sparks of fire distinctly shining.

Our text here speaks of matters subtle and literal at the same time, thus giving evidence of what we have already seen about the capacity of the Indian mind to be "unsplit." The duality of this chakra, an achievement of meditation, now both tells us of a psychological condition, and describes a state in which the Saddhaka literally sees the sparks of fire which come down to him just above the Ajna center and below Sahasrara. It is here, indeed, that many directions are given in the commentary on how to meditate and produce this effect. For those who think of this material as purely symbolic, the succeeding verses and commentaries should make it clear that concrete experiences are also being described. It is here that fire, moon and sun are joined as different symbols and experiences, but also where the nadis or nerves mentioned at the outset become intertwined. The lotus itself is much like the Mercury symbol and caduceus in our own symbology and it is not by chance that here one experiences full healing. It is here, too, that "The excellent Yogi at the time of death joyfully places his vital breath (Prana) here and enters, (after death) that Supreme, Eternal, Birthless, Primeval Deva, the Purusha, who was before the three worlds, and who is known by the Vedanta" (Verse 38).

When all of this is accomplished, we learn (in Verse 39), that the yogi will then see, above the Ajna Chakra, the form of the Mahananda, and will make manifest pure Intelligence (Buddhi). From this point, there is no other task than to enter into the Sahasrara.

Sahasrara: "Lotus of a Thousand Petals"

When we come to the ultimate aim of the Kundalini Yoga endeavor, the place of fulfillment, Jung is surprisingly laconic. Here is what he says: (Lecture III, p. 17)

> To speak about the lotus of the thousand petals, the *sahasrara* centre, is quite superfluous because that is merely a philosophical concept with no substance whatever for us; it is beyond any possible experience. In *ajna* there is still the experience of the self that is apparently different from the object, the God. But in *sahasrara* it is not different. So the next conclusion would be that there is no object, no God, there is nothing but *brahman*. There is no experience because it is one, it is without a second. It is dormant, it is not, and therefore it is *nirvana*. This is an entirely philosophical concept, a mere logical conclusion from the premises above. It is without practical value for us.

Thus speaks the Jung of 1932, consistent with his long-held theory that without an ego it is pointless and ridiculous to speak of experience. Self without ego is a mere "concept." One wonders how the Jung of twenty or thirty years later (he died in 1961) would have described this. One returns, again, to his dream of discovering himself as a yogin, meditating in a temple, with his ego as an object of the yogin's dream. Would this have changed his view? It is hard to say, but one would guess that he would then emphasize the paradoxical nature of the experience wherein the ego is both totally relativized and "nothing," yet it is the "all" which is flooded with Brahman and, therefore, "everything." But here, in his psychological seminar, he is trying mightily to remain empirical, conceptual, comparative. Purnananda, on the other hand, devotes eight full verses to this chakra which is beyond all chakras, and his commentator, Kalicharana, engages in many paragraphs of distinction of names, concepts, this and that, just as if he were giving us a specific recipe which can be fulfilled only in the prescribed manner. The remainder of the book, furthermore, is given over to the specific directions for doing the work. So much for mere "symbolism" or impractical cogitation.

Before we look into some of these verses, we need to note that, at Sahasrara, not only are there no longer any animals or elements, as was the case in Ajna, but now there is not even a condition of principles (tattvas), nor, strictly speaking, any Shiva or Shakti. At this point, Shiva is the Guru Himself for our Saddhaka and the Shakti, as we shall see, is *Nirvana*. Shunyata, the Void, is achieved, in which all being is no longer being. There is full union of the opposites, beautifully described, as we shall see in a moment, and duality is overcome.

The "lotus of 1,000 petals" is a kind of mandala, but this vastly differentiated totality is both symbol and concreteness, is no longer located "inside" the body but is on top of the head. All the letters are here, supreme bliss, void, supreme light, formlessness. The bliss here achieved is a consequence of *atma* realized. Once fully here, furthermore, the yogin has no further need of rebirth and, if he does not die on the spot, he will not re-incarnate when he does die.

Let us turn, now, to some of the description of the verses of Purnananda:

Verse 40
Above all these . . . is the Lotus of a thousand petals. This Lotus, lustrous and whiter than the full Moon, has its head turned downward. It charms. Its clustered filaments are tinged with the colour of the young Sun. Its body is luminous with the letters beginning with A, and it is the absolute bliss.

The "head turned downward" means that the chakra drops its delicious nectar to the chakras below, thus producing the bliss which is specified. The "filaments" are the multitudinous conditions, names, qualities about which so much is then written and discussed. The luminosity of the body is a consequence of the shining character of all the letters (the building-blocks of existence, as we have noted before) which are contained therein.

Our commentator, Kalicharana, furthermore, proceeds to give details which prescribe meditations which "dissolve all things in their order from the gross to the subtle." These include the five gross elements, all the tattvas (e.g. feet, sense of smell, as well as organs, etc.) Then all the subtle forms are dissolved, and so on, many pages worth.

In Verse 42, the Sahasrara is described as the full moon, "without the mark of the hare," -- that is to say, it does not have what we call "the man in the moon" and is perfect, clear, "resplendent as in a clear sky." This full and perfected light sheds a profusion of rays and is "moist and cool like nectar." Kalicharana explains that this means the moisture which descends to us is cool and produces a "feeling of smiling gladness."

Inside this moon, twice removed, "shines the Great Void which is served in secret by all the Suras." Kalicharana then tells us that the great void (Shunya) is served in secret since:

> Eating (Ahara), evacuation (Nirhara), sexual intercourse (Vihara), and Yoga, should be done in secret by him who knows the Dharma.

We are being told of the increasing separateness and privacy of the Saddhaka as he achieves his final goal and bliss. In Verse 42 we are told of the achievement of Liberation and the end of ignorance and delusion. In Verse 43 the "constant and profuse stream of nectar-like essence" teaches of oneness -- so that this flow of energy also instructs as well as dazzles. Verse 44 takes up the various names of that being encountered and Verse 45, which we will quote, speaks of the fruit of a complete knowledge of Sahasrara, suggesting that the Saddhaka should realize it as a whole and in detail.

Verse 45

That most excellent of men who has controlled his mind and known this place is never again born in the Wandering (Samsara, the world of birth and rebirth to which men are impelled by their Karma), as there is nothing in the three worlds which binds him. His mind being controlled and his aim achieved, he possesses complete power to do all which he wishes, and to prevent that which is contrary to his will. He ever more moves towards the Brahman. His speech, whether in prose or verse, is ever pure and sweet.

Kalicharana tells us that such a man is free from bondage, both virtue and sin. We can understand this to mean that such enlightenment takes one beyond the opposites and the usual moral code as well -- even life itself has no longer any hold on him.

Verse 46 describes the aforementioned "moon" in more detail, calling her "as thin as the hundredth part of a fibre in the stalk of a lotus" and "lustrous and soft like ten million lightning flashes." More such descriptions continue in Verse 47, which also speak of the divine knowledge accruing from this flow. This continues in verses 48 and 49, the last ones which are devoted to a description of the lotuses themselves, while verses 50 to 55 describe the methods used to achieve these experiences.

Finally, we are told, the yogin who has gone through these experiences now "dances at the feet of Ishta-devata" — he is beyond words and deeds, even beyond experiences, and celebrates his joy and fulfillment in ecstatic dance. This is especially poignant, since, at this point in Avalon's book, we are given a series of photographs of a yogin demonstrating the various postures and procedures to be undertaken in this Yoga. The power and frailty of our somewhat wild-eyed Saddhaka makes all this intensely human, in his search for the divine.

What are we to make of this hymn to the sacred along with its recipes and enjoinders? Are we to somewhat haughtily turn up our noses at this primitive, non-scientific presentation? Assert that this is not practical for us, as Jung does? Or, more honestly, assert that this goes beyond our understanding?

I think that the latter is the best response, but we can attempt to draw nearer to understanding by seeing the parallels in alchemy. There, too, we are given vast numbers of words, procedures, enjoinders, along with descriptions of bliss and knowledge. There, too, as Jung showed us many years later, was the attempt to both produce and explain the experience of a Self which is non-producible and unexplainable. In each generation or era, there are those who have such experiences, and they haltingly try to convey these, help others come to similar experiences. Mostly, our experiences are partial and we are both led astray and lead others astray also. We generalize too much, or impose structure where it is not. Yet that same overwhelming content is being approached and, if we are modest enough, we too can glimpse that which is being described and asserted.

The particularity of the Indian, Kundalini experience, it seems to me, is that it combines the concrete and the abstract simultaneously. Very precise exercises, breathing, meditations are given, along with descriptions of *literal* experiences of the rising of the energy. And, unlike in alchemy, the experience is clearly "inner." This Hindu, Indian system, as Jung recognizes, is an Easterner's attempt to grasp the nature of the psyche in its fullness. In our final section, we shall attempt to compare this system with others, East and West.

Epilogue

We come, now, to a general appreciation of this pictorial and verbal material on Kundalini Yoga as revealed in the works mentioned. We have the illumined scholarship of Avalon, one of those outstanding English personalities of the early part of the twentieth century who advanced the flowering of western understanding of the East. We have the classical and impassioned presentations of Purnananda and Kalicharana, devotees and geniuses of the Hindu tradition. Finally, we have the perspective of another twentieth century master, but this time one of the few to be able to truly bridge east and west, Jung.

Another way of comprehending this Yoga is to be found in a comparison of pictures and text of a similar nature but in different traditions. I am referring, now, to the Zen Ox-Herding Pictures and to the Alchemical pictures of the *Rosarium Philosophorum*, used by Jung to understand the transference in psychotherapy. All of these series attempt a portrayal of the process of Enlightenment, whether one conceives of it in western or eastern terms. In *Buddhism and Jungian Psychology,*[8] I drew some comparisons between Zen and the alchemical work. Now we may add some to be found with the Kundalini series.

First and foremost are the several similarities between the Alchemical work and Kundalini. In both cases, there is a gradual development of a "divine" or "royal" pair, representing the fundamental opposites residing within the psyche itself. The pair effect each other and the poor human doing the work. They also ultimately unite at the end. The feminine principle is powerfully at work, so that, in alchemy, the final androgyne is more heavily female than male, and in Kundalini, the final condition itself, Nirvana, is feminine. Not so in Zen. The story is told of a single male, and the feminine is all around him, in symbol and picture and particularly in nature. He achieves by negation, by simplifying, in contrast to the richness of imagery and prescription in the Hindu and Alchemical versions. Buddhism was clearly a revolt against the "excess" -- if one can call it that without disrespect -- of the Hindu tradition. And Alchemy was a compensation, as Jung shows, to the Christian negation of nature.

The Buddhist and Hindu works are similar in that they seek Enlightenment, arise in the context of meditation, and are clearly introverted methods. Alchemy, on the other hand, had a strong admixture of experimentation, of uncertainty whether the "stone" or the "gold" was truly "philosophical," residing within the soul, or also had a material, outer basis.

All three works are replete with fantasy, with the symbols of search, with the prescriptions for self-improvement, and with the need of discipline, study, abandoning pre-conceived ideas, and, finally, openness to the divine itself. It is remarkable that all these works were composed, from so different philosophical and cultural bases, within one hundred years of each other, and at a time when a spirit of renewal was sweeping the world, although unknown to each other. If we add that another set of pictures, the Tarot, related to Kabbalah (as well as magic and alchemy), was in flower, we have a most remarkable synchronistic presentation of spiritual change.

One is tempted to suggest that we are in a similar period now, as the cultures of the world are in open connection, spiritual experimentation is rife, much of the older beliefs in all the religions have died, only to be renewed from within and without, syncretism is rife in cults and sects. It would have been easier to claim this in the late 1960's and early 1970's than now, some fifteen to twenty years later. The cycle of change has returned us, collectively, to a new period of materialism, conservatism, provincialism, yet the Eastern cults and branches which have taken root in the West continue to grow and develop.

It is of interest to note that many of the gurus and teachers who have come from east to west have been corrupted by wine, women, and materialism. Rather, one should say that it was not *our* wine, etc. that corrupted them, but rather their inability to cope with the ready availability of these things outside the cultural prohibitions in which normally one would be "safe." This, in my opinion, in no way vitiates the messages being brought, or even casts a particularly negative light on these masters so "corrupted." It might even be expected. Not because all of us human beings are weak -- which we are -- but that there is much more work to do to integrate the spirit (wine), the feminine (women), and the body (materialism and nature), in an adequate manner. All of our traditions are wonderful and they are all lacking in the present necessity of going beyond the patriarchy, beyond revealed knowledge, beyond, even, individuality. The psyche is in continual travail and movement and *we* are all experiments of the soul, it seems to me, in which it is trying to build up a new image of the Self which is sufficiently inclusive.

In order to do our part toward the gradual emergence of a sufficient world-view, it is useful to integrate that which is already known, as revealed in the image-full presentations here under consideration.

For my own psyche, it has been a fascination to approach these various traditions, and appreciate the particularity of each. I think that I am not alone in sensing that each of them speaks to my psyche, not only as a "part," but even as a totality. It is, rather, that each touches that totality in a particular way, and that no one of them can take the place of another. I mentioned in *Buddhism and Jungian Psychology* that while the world was trying to build up a larger totality of spiritual union, it was at the same time trying to maintain differences, even individuality. That is the creative part of the process; the destructive part seems to be the urge toward the dissolution of everything. Here the Indian mind is of particularly great help. Its perception of the eternity of the Kalpas, of the view of the human condition from the aspect of Sahasrara, of the co-value of creation and destruction, can help one attain some equanimity in the face of these events. Its emphasis upon "dissolution" is positive, in this regard, but far from the value that we in the West, -- as exemplified in Jung's work -- put on both individuality and improving this world.

The process continues, and I am pleased to have been able to contribute my share, individually, in company with respected colleagues, and to the larger psychic events encompassing us all.

References

1.   Avalon, Arthur, *The Serpent Power*, Ganesh & Co., Madras, India, 1953. (Original 1918). 508 pp. plus approx. 100 Sanskrit.

2.   Jung, C.G. *Letters*, Vol. II, edited by G. Adler, Boutledge & Kegan Paul, London, 1976.

3.   Jung, C.G. "Psychological Commentary on Kundalini Yoga: Lectures One and Two" (1932) in *Spring: An Annual of Archetypal Psychology and Jungian Thought*, 1975, pp. 1-33.

4.   Jung, C.G. "Psychological Commentary on Kundalini Yoga: Lectures Three and Four" (1932) in *Spring: An Annual of Archetypal Psychology and Jungian Thought*, 1976, pp. 1-31.

5.   Jung, C.G. *Psychology of the Transference*, 1946, in Collected Works, Vol. 16.

6.   Jung, C.G. *Psychology and Alchemy*, 1944 (English 1953) in Collected Works, Vol. 12.

7.   Jung, C.G. *Memories, Dreams, Reflections*, Pantheon Books, Random House, New York, 1961.

8.   Spiegelman, J. Marvin & Miyuki, Mokusen, *Buddhism and Jungian Psychology*, Falcon Press, Phoenix, Arizona, 1985.

9.   Spiegelman, J. Marvin, *The Knight* (with two essays on active imagination), Falcon Press, Phoenix, Arizona, 1982.

10.   White, John, Ed. *Kundalini: Evolution and Enlightenment*, Anchor, Doubleday, New York, 1979.

11.   *The Zohar*, attributed to Moses de Leon. In Five Volumes, Soncino Press, London, 1933.

Comments on Spiegelman's
KUNDALINI YOGA:
A PSYCHOLOGICAL COMMENTARY

by

Arwind Vasavada

I had occasion to read Tantra and The Serpent Power as a student and as a teacher of philosophy in India. I did not really understand then the symbolism of images in the Chakras. I was therefore astonished at Marvin's grasp of this difficult task, especially the images of the Chakras. Reading the paper, I followed his intuitive understanding and I felt it right. He also sees clearly that Jung could not accept all it said about the process and the stages of experiences beyond Ajna Chakra, and why Jung rejected Sahasrara Chakra and Void and called them philosophical concepts. Marvin correctly wonders what Jung would have said now at this stage when Eastern ideas and experiences have flooded the western mind.

In his writings, Jung did not say anything about that which is beyond the psychic realm. He remained within the realm of psychic subjectivity. Even Self was an archetype for him. Even though he felt the presence of the beyond, he remained confined in the sphere of knowledge. Speculating, he brought in the concept of Psychoid to explain the common origin of Instinct and Spirit.

I often wondered why he remained at that level in his books, when he says in reply to a B.B.C. interviewer that he did not have to believe, "I know." Here he does not mean that he knows God with a rational mind. In his Autobiography he acknowledges the limitation of knowledge and accepts the realm of Eros and surrenders to it. In terms of Indian thought we would say that the path of devotion -- Bhakti -- dawned on him with the realization of the limitation of knowledge.

To my mind, the main difficulty the western mind encounters with Indian thought is the dissolution of the ego and entering the Void. One can understand this difficulty because the words of Indian texts do not and cannot convey what they mean to convey.

Indian thought, like the western, accepts that there is light within each

63

one of us and this has to be followed. The Light is the Guru and guide. Indian wisdom says that this light is veiled over by conditionings — Samkaras. Ego is this light so conditioned. Light is always there. If light were not we would not even be aware of these conditionings. Being aware — reflecting — frees us from identification with conditioning. In this process of Self-knowledge, one learns more and more to be witness to the psychic processes. This witnessing is common to all — it is not particular in the sense of my or your witnessing. It is Self as witness.

Jung's way also helps us disidentify from inner and outer objects. The moments of disidentification are moments of clarity and freedom. These moments are experiences of ease, not dis-ease, togetherness, being at home, in one's own right place. This wholeness is encountered every now and then. It makes us sensitive, to be aware whenever we are caught in polarities. This awareness or sensitivity either helps us to let go of our hang-up or makes us aware, "Oh! I am caught here. I cannot yet give it up." Even this honest acknowledgement and acceptance of where I am is different from being caught and unaware, struggling and conflicted. If one goes through this process, according to Indian thought, understanding dawns that all psychic processes are a play of polarities. One witnesses the rise and fall and temporary balance in the psyche. This is what is continually taking place. Engaging oneself in the process by taking sides is to sustain it. There is no need to engage in the process. Not taking sides is then to flow with what is. One *is* the process, flowing, living spontaneously.

So what this dissolution of ego refers to is the dissolution and death of the conditioned mind—ego, every now and then. The Light always IS.

This is also clear from the understanding of the Chakras, as very correctly pointed by Marvin. From the first chakra, Muladhara to Vishuddha, we have the presence of Shiva and Shakti in different forms. The changing faces of these male and female principles at every stage means gradual transformation from gross to subtle, from heavy earth to Akasa — formless space.

From Ajna onwards there are no elements, there is no subject-object polarity. In totality, all is gathered up in itself. It is wholeness without otherness.

There is nothing lost in this process, but all is transformed. This is clear from the understanding of Sahasrara. All the alphabets are there and more. It is a thousand petalled lotus. It is turned downward from the crown of head and nectar is dripping downward to all the chakras below and nourishing them. There is thus relation maintained with lower ones without otherness.

It seems as if Vishuddha and Ajna symbolise the state of deep sleep of the Divine Mother -- the Unconscious. The creation is in the form of a seed state. It is also called the Causal Body. From Anahata to Swadhisthana is the dreaming state as there is greater differentiation at these levels. With Muladhara, we have the world of objectivity -- external reality. It is comparable to the waking state.

Let us try to understand the implication of Jung's statement that we have no archimedian standpoint outside the psyche. It is true that so long as we are enclosed within the psychic realm, we cannot know the origin of psyche and matter. We cannot know what is beyond. We cannot know the origin of psyche because we are its offspring. Asking to know the source and origin is asking to *know* our mother. One has either to trust the midwife or be the mother.

Let us deepen this question, "I can only know psychic reality." Do I really feel the presence of the Beyond? Do I feel as if I am imprisoned in the realm of psyche? Can I casually say that I know psychic reality and am satisfied with it?

No inquiring mind whether eastern or western can remain satisfied with this situation. A frustrated mind has only two options before it. It can continue exploration of the Unconscious endlessly. This endless inquiry is futile since it cannot open the door to the Beyond -- the source. The creativity of the Divine Mother is not in time, it is timeless. The inquiring mind can get lost in it. We have to understand the level of creativity of the Divine Mother. It is eternity. Her creation is total, all at once, not successive in time as cause and effect. The mind imprisoned in time cannot get there. Only by ending time is it possible to enter Timelessness. Creation at that level is not evolution as we see it. It is manifestation of the Unmanifest, of the Formless into forms. Just as in the dream, dream-reality is created all at once, so is the creation of the universe by the Divine Mother. Just as on waking from the dream, the ego reads time and space into it and weaves a story of it, likewise we see creation of the universe as evolution in time.

If we accept the fact that I do not know and cannot know and stay there, if we have accepted our defeat and really given up the possibility of knowing, breakthrough can happen. The conditioned mind-ego can explode, leaving Light, pure and simple.

Let us try to understand Individuation according to Jung and Liberation according to Indian thought. The root meaning of Individuation is undivided whole. The whole includes all that there is. There is nothing outside of it. It is self-determined, self existing and freedom as such. Jung's description of individuation supports this. In the process of individuation we are freed from the pressures of collective consciousness and influences from the collective Unconscious. Thus we come to Being what we are. This is freedom from becoming this or that. Individual is indefinable. It is Its Self. Can we distinguish wholeness as mine from yours? If it is, it then is fragmentation, separativeness from all. It is isolation and loneliness. Jung did not mean Individuation to be isolation or individualism.

The individual certainly is a unique expression of the whole, hence one with the whole, one with all, one with the lowest of the low and highest of the high. He is all and No-thing.

Thus Individuation or Self-realization and Liberation are not different from each other. The process of Self-realization aims at freedom from past conditioning as much as the process of Individuation. Both aim at the dissolution of the conditioned mind as an obstacle to Seeing. Thus, we can resolve the difference between east and west.

REPLY TO VASAVADA

by

J. Marvin Spiegelman

When I submitted my chapter on Kundalini Yoga to Arwind Vasavada, I had trepidation lest my account be seen as inadequate, in error, or insufficiently appreciative of this great marvel of Indian thought and experience. Hence my delighted reaction when Arwind found it not only accurate and intuitive, but that he also even learned something from what I had to say about the symbolism! I think that I have to thank the "guru" of my dream for grasping and expressing concepts that my conscious mind would have not understood.

Arwind's remarks contribute substantially to the discussion, and I shall respond to certain crucial sentences of his.

"The main difficulty the western mind encounters with Indian thought is the dissolution of the ego and entering the Void." Yes, indeed.

"In this process of Self-knowledge, one learns more and more to be witness to the psychic processes. This witnessing is common to all -- it is not particular in the sense of my or your witnessing. It is Self as witness."

This is crucial. Arwind has put his finger on the central matter. It is the Self who is conscious, witnessing, particularly at those moments -- as he goes on to show -- when one is separated from the conflict of opposites. I think that Jung might agree with this, the later Jung, at least. A way of bridging this disparity of ego and Self is to say that at those moments, ego-identification is transcended and the two are one. I and the Self are one! How do we know this? Only by memory, as we fall back into duality, but a duality which has been "enlightened". Surely that would be acceptable to Jung. Furthermore, we know that the Jung after the visions of 1944 was well aware of this transcendence. He even had that famous Hindu as the gatekeeper to his visions, as well as the later dream in which he is privileged to see his own face on that of a yogi and realize that he is being dreamed by him. When the latter awakes, Jung dies! *That* Jung would have no difficulty at all with what Vasavada says here. He would, I imagine, still hold that *he* experienced that, but could not prove it. As a scientist, he had to maintain doubt (because of lack of proof); as a man he "knew."

The remainder of Arwind's argument is sound, but his imploring us to make the leap beyond the realm of psyche is difficult. For Jung, as a *scientist* this would have been next to impossible. His attitude was probably correct, given the particularly unpleasant Western fanaticism of those who "know," for example, that only Jesus is savior, or that Mohammed is God's only prophet. Such people tend to thrust their own conviction upon those of us who may have had other experiences, and Jung (and science) have added a very valuable corrective in saying, Prove it!

All the same, we can, individually, make the leap of faith or surrender that Vasavada suggests. Jung did not have to do this, since his crucial visions simply came to him! As he often points out, the unconscious also has us, rather than we having it.

Given these differences in emphasis and momentary attitude, we can indeed agree with Arwind Vasavada, and what is more, we can thank him for putting the matter so feelingly as well as intellectually, a gift no doubt, from his own deep and sincere surrender to the Divine Mother!

MAYA, THE YOGINI

I

My name is Maya. I was born in the city of Calcutta, the state of Bengal, and the nation of India forty years ago. I might pridefully add that I come from a long line of gurus and that I am, of course, of the Brahmin caste. In these days of Independence, after the British Raj and when the world itself may be nearing an end, such pride may be rather irrelevant. It is also not entirely true, since my heritage is mixed. My father was an English army officer who had a torrid and romantic love affair with my mother in the 1920's, when the whole world was beginning to shift on its foundations. The man was honorable enough and wanted to marry my mother, but this was not permitted by her parents. She was married, instead, to a decent and equally honorable storekeeper, for whom she was a feather in his merchant caste's cap. Since my father was dark and my own features are quite Indian, my step-father became my only father, as far as the world was concerned. I suppose that this was an advance for the time; in an earlier era they might have stoned or burned my mother and I would not have been born at all, or else been tossed upon a dung heap.

I tell you these details because my peculiar background does have relevance to my story, which will gradually unveil itself. Straightaway, however, you can see that my origins are not entirely conventional, though I was raised in a more or less usual fashion for Hindu girls of my time and of my class and station. I married at 14, had one child each year until I was 19, busied myself at home with my husband and family, enjoyed the social life of the post-war years, was excited by the turbulence of political activity and our new independence. I had several lovers, which is not so out of the ordinary any more, as you might think, but my real unconventionality began just three years ago.

My children had grown and the last of them had married and established her own family. At thirty-seven, I was still attractive, had led a life which was both active and reflective, and I was by no means ready for old age, nor to die on a bier with my husband. I loved him dearly, this man ten years older than myself, but he was not my entire life. Obviously. For some time I realized that I needed to retreat from the world, perhaps follow the path of my ancestors who had been gurus. The men of my family had either pursued a life of meditation or had sought enlightenment in the usual Indian way when reaching middle age. It was still uncustomary, though possible, for a woman to seek a guru but something in me rebelled at that. Here, perhaps, was an independent spirit of my English father, asserting itself against the Indian elders who had deprived him of his love. This thought, however, is more likely to be a romantic cover-up for the fact that women everywhere have changed; we are no longer so willing to be disciples or slaves to men, even if they are gurus. I, as a modern woman, simply did not want to submit my spirit to a man. If I could have met a guru who would be willing to share a spiritual relationship with me, to seek together into the reaches of the unknown world of the gods, I would have been delighted. But I did not know any Indian men who would either desire this or be capable of it. Gurus there were aplenty, but they would want their submission -- especially if they would even deign to grant their time and presence to a mere woman. Besides that, most of the gurus I knew about were rather corrupt and not worth submitting to!

Yet, I needed to retreat, to achieve enlightenment. What was I to do? I had read somewhere that the Masters of old had said that all two-footed creatures of the world could be enlightened, and that the best guru was Shiva himself. One did not need a concrete guru in the flesh; it was the spirit of Shiva, in any case, which came to the good guru. I felt that this piece of wisdom might be right, and, in any case, it suited me. I resolved to go off by myself and meditate. I would live simply and pray that the good lord Shiva would guide me.

My family, of course, thought I was quite mad when I told them of my plan, but they were used to my being independent in other ways and when I assured them that I would return if the procedure were too uncomfortable (I was no ascetic!) and that I would write regularly to them, they assented. The night that I got their blessing, I dreamed that the Lord Shiva came to me and instructed me to take with me, into my wilderness, the pictures of the Kundalini Yoga. I awakened delighted; Lord Shiva was with me! I knew the pictures only casually, but was convinced that I had a guide with me and that my desire to be a Yogini on my own was meeting with divine approval.

Thus it was that I began my meditative experiences as a Yogini three years ago, and that is the substance of my story -- what happened in that meditative retreat.

I went to a mountain cabin, far from the bustle of Calcutta life, but close enough to civilization to buy for myself the few necessities that I would need from time to time. I knew that I was there to be alone, and to come to an inner enlightenment, but I had no need for the disciplines of the flesh that some men seem to require.

After a few days of accustoming myself to a certain quietness and calming of my wandering mind, I sat down with my first picture of the Kundalini series. I prayed to Shiva to be my serpent Kundalini, to guide me and inspire me in the way that he, in his wisdom, would know that I needed. I submerged myself into *dhyana* and allowed myself to be thought, rather than to think. "Oh, Shiva," I prayed, "Let it be you that work in me; you it is who will both coil and uncoil the Kundalini; you it is who will be both enlightener and enlightened, for I am as nought, a mere point on the needle of eternity." I then could look at the first picture, the *Muladhara*.

I sat and stared at this first picture. I studied and looked and reflected for one day, two days, three days. Nothing but stale bread seemed to come from it. I knew that the center the picture connected with was located between anus and genitals. I knew that this mandala was of the earth, that the elephant symbolized everyday reality. I was aware that the four red petals enclosing the center contained the kundalini, "luminous as lightning, shining in the hollow of this lotus like a chain of brilliant lights." That center, basic for smell and speech, contained the material energy of the universe. I knew that coping with this chakra would bring mastery of desire, of envy, of anger, and of passion. All this I knew — from reading. I peered at the picture: elephant, yellow, Child Brahma, Shakti goddess, snake coiled about the lingam. I looked and I studied, but I knew nothing.

Despair was my lot. I had come for nought. I had come to find myself, to meditate and to reach the heights and depths of the yogins, of my ancestors, but I was a foolish, conceited woman who sat only in her ignorance, with stupid books and more stupid pictures. I could not do it.

I sat despaired. I wept upon the page of the picture. I slept. I fasted. Then it happened.

How can I tell you how it began? It is with me yet, and it makes me tremble in fear and wonder. I meditated upon this center near my own anus. I called repeatedly upon Shiva, the great Lord, to aid me. Then I heard a great cackle. It was not the Lord Shiva who came to me! It was not Krishna. No, it was not any male God at all! Out of the depths of my own darkness and ignorance, desire and despair, came a cackle of the great Goddess who was a woman like myself! She was no ordinary woman, this Goddess. Oh, no! She combined the hells of the four thousand aeons. She was Kali Durga, but She gave me no name!

She cackled and spoke:

"So, little woman! So, petulant, demanding little thing! You seek the highest powers! You seek to become as great as the Gods, let alone those yogins who have fasted and torn themselves to pieces to flee from their ignorance. And you expect to find it by yourself, in a moment, with just a book and a few pictures! You are, indeed, beyond yourself.

"I would laugh at you and tear you to pieces if I did not have my own reasons for letting you live in sanity and go on. Indeed, it is a pain to my heart that I am required by my own need to attend to such foolish mortals as yourself. I would be quite contented to let you pass ten thousand more rebirths without achieving enlightenment were it not for my own need."

"What is your need, great Goddess?" said I. I know not wherefrom I had the courage to so address Her, especially after Her initial bitter and explosive and frightening outburst. But I did, all the same, and She answered.

"My need is also the need of my great Lord Shiva, though He does not know it and will not admit it. He has given unto me the secret which He cannot admit even unto Himself."

"What is this secret, great Goddess?" I asked, growing a little annoyed at Her for not coming out with what She had in mind.

"The secret, little one," She continued, "is that the great Lord Shiva needs a change in His consort. He needs Her to be a Sister, an equal, a co-creator of the universe, a manager of the kalpas. Not only does He need Her so, but He needs Her, too, to be a Queen-Sister to His creations, just as He aims to be a King-Brother to His. This is His need for the new aeon. He hardly knows it yet, Himself, but has given it to me to be known. I am His willing and loving consort who will be with Him and bind Him and embrace Him and create with Him. I cannot do this alone, but have need of you, and millions like you. Do not wax rhapsodic at this revelation for I must tell you that this comingling with creatureliness, this becoming sister to my creatures, this elevation on their part and going down on my part is no pure joy to me. I do welcome the elevation of the feminine, however, and of women, for it is a sweet desire that this be true. You, little sister, are chosen just because you come here alone, will not bow down to the gods and to your men. You, just because of your rebellious spirit, your courage, your conceit and your foolish desire, you are chosen to be aided, whereas others, content in their status and achievements, are not. Thus, little one, you secretly partake of my own being."

At this moment, the picture came to life. Now I saw with my eyes; before this I had only heard the words. I saw the child Brahma dispelling fear with his four arms; I saw the goddess Shakti, in Her redness and four-armed dancing wonder. There were the spear, the staff, the sword and the drinking cup. There, too, was the happy elephant, with six tusks.

As suddenly as it had come to life, however, it all vanished. I sat fixedly for a long time. There was no question about the reality of my experience, but I felt cheated, somehow. The Goddess had deemed me worthy, for whatever reason, to talk to me and to show Herself to me. I was part of a Divine plan which was nothing less than a new development, a re-incarnation of the great Gods. I was chosen as a woman, just because of my independence and ... well, it was all true and wonderful, but, somehow, not real enough. Not real enough? I asked myself. Why? ... I felt unchanged. Where was the mastery of anger and desire, of passion and envy? It seemed to be all words, even though I was granted a vision of the image of the Goddess. Was I just the usual stupid female who does not trust words? Then I thought: "No, I am not stupid, but it is true that I have only experienced it in words; I have not yet felt it in my body, in my senses, in my true being as a woman! If the great Lord Shiva wills it and if the Great Shakti wishes it, too, then they must find a way for me to experience them! I refuse, as one who values the flesh, to subject myself to those silly, self-punishing antics of the gurus!"

With that, I obstinately tossed my head. I was silent for a moment, but then laughed. I was quite alone in my eloquent sovereignty, and, in truth, I was only partly convincing myself. I was autonomous all right, but lonely. I had to admit, ruefully, out of my feminine being, that I longed for company. But I stuck to my independence and stayed on in my little cabin.

Days and weeks passed, as I felt the loneliness. I saw not a soul. I ate modestly, walked about the mountain, and waited. There was nothing more for me to do.

One day, when I felt that this whole experience was simply going to trickle away into a kind of "holiday at the mountains," I heard a whisper in my ear. The hiss of the Kundalini serpent came as a woman. "Walk!" she said. I walked, in my imagination, up a hill to a large building. Fantasy it was, but as real as I am. The building was a temple, of beautiful design, upon which were painted and etched, in bas reliefs, all kinds of sexual intimacies between men and women. I went inside this building and wandered about in it. There were beds and couches and tables, but no one was present. Then a woman came toward me. She seemed undistinguished in appearance, but there was something special about her which I could not fathom. She told me, in a matter of fact manner, that she was a priestess of this temple and that this was a place where men were kept to be of service to women. Women could come and go as they pleased and could gratify any and every sexual hunger that they might have, but the men kept here were bound and immobilized -- physically or spiritually or both. These men could do nothing other than what the women wished.

Astonished, I asked how this came to be. I was told that many years ago, in this region, the women did all the work and the men just sat about and talked. Sexually, too, the women were more or less at the convenience of the men. Then, the women discovered gold, and the men took credit for it. They used the gold to establish trade and to grow rich. After a time, they had so much gold that the wives no longer needed to work. Some grew fat and lazy. Others became restless. All the important women of the community began coming up to this mountain, but the men neither noticed nor cared what was going on up there. In truth, on this mountain, the great Goddess had established a temple wherein women could gratify all sexual desire. The men there were generally handsome and of good physical condition, though not always. Old men were there as waiters and retainers, obsequious and silly. The Goddess had arranged matters whereby no man could come to the temple unless summoned, and no man could avoid coming when so ordered. The mystery of the place was that the men, although tyrannized and kept as slaves and playthings, also wanted to stay there, in service of the Goddess. The men so selected, it seems, were the special ones, the better ones, but by no means the socially successful men of the community, though some of them were there, as well.

I was astonished at this story, and wondered why the great Goddess planned and maintained this situation. I was horrified, but also sexually stimulated. I wondered if I, too, could have my desires satisfied. The priestess seemed to know my thoughts at once, for she came out of her blandness and laughed. "Go, my child," she said. "Enjoy yourself, for here women are free and can come and go as they wish. Only the men are bound. They are here because they must be and because they wish it!" Having concluded her story, the priestess walked silently away.

I now began to explore the building to see what kind of activities were taking place. In one room, I saw a woman repeatedly whipping a number of men who could do nothing but cower and wince in pain. In another cubicle, a woman was being licked and sucked upon by several men. In a third room, a woman copulated repeatedly with a long line of men, perhaps fifty in number. All these sights both fascinated and repelled me. I smelled the odor of privies. I began to wonder what sort of sexual hunger I had that might be satisfied, when I spied a man tied to a stone column. As I got closer, I saw that he was European, and very handsome. He vaguely reminded me of pictures of my father, though he seemed, also, to be at least half of our own nation, resembling my husband and one of my lovers. Yet, he was none of these, and a stranger to me.

I went up to him and looked at his sad, deep eyes. I was touched by his suffering. He looked at me with a strange mixture of fear, anger, and desire. When he did so, I was absolutely electrified, for here were mirrored the emotions that I had felt so frequently in my life and in just such a combination. I had experienced a great sexual desire and fear of both the desire and the possibility of its fulfillment. My desires were often of the kind that are frowned upon. Yet I had also felt great anger that my desire was not being fulfilled, or only fulfilled at great cost to myself in pain and guilt. I was instantly drawn to this man, who mirrored my feelings and conflicts. Despite the intensity of his eyes, he seemed half dead, as if he had been whipped and used repeatedly by many women. He said nothing.

I dropped to my knees and began to lick and suck at his exposed genitals. I was fulfilling both my own need, and I think, his as well. For there was love in me, and with love all things are possible, and all dilemmas are resolved -- or so I thought at that point in my life. As I indulged my desire, the man came to life, and I saw that he was like a God. I saw him as Shiva himself, yet a mortal like my father, husband, lover. My lover-God had come to life, but he was trapped in this place. I could come and go as I wished, but the man of my soul was trapped here by the great Goddess. How could I free him, make him the willing consort of my soul, I wondered? Was the Goddess so full of revenge, for all Her rejections and past hurts, that She would not let this be? Or would it be, as I had known and experienced and feared from men, that once free and independent, he would leave me? Men do leave us for others, do they not? For another woman or for some beckoning demon of fame and fortune?

I was confronted with an age-old woman's dilemma. Indeed, I felt the agony of the Goddess, Herself! That is why She had him trapped here, to keep him for Herself! What a despicable woman She was, just like the rest of us! Yet, he wanted to be here, the priestess had said. He must not want to leave Her, as well. He, therefore, must also be undergoing suffering, like me, in order to transform himself. He was chosen by the Goddess, after all, and She is not such a fool as to choose just anyone. She told me, I recalled, that She was serving Her consort, the Great Shiva, who needed Her equality and sisterhood. Then I realized something: this man, this God before me, had reminded me of father, husband, and lover, all of whom had been authorities for me, not really equals like a brother. Was the man of my soul undergoing the trials of the Goddess in order to come down, to become my equal and friend? Was he being transformed from his mightiness and superiority? Yes, Yes, Yes! At once I knew that my own independence, rebelliousness, superiority of spirit were incarnated in this man, and that he too was being groomed to serve the Goddess. Oh, how I loved him, and how I felt the meaningful love of the

Goddess! She was terrible in Her form and in Her spirit, but She was grand and loving, and in the service of love, as well. Yes, here my man was being transformed, as was my spirit at the very same time.

I clutched my man to my bosom. I sucked upon him and upon his spirit and made it my own. I felt his suffering as my own. I felt as one with him in that terrible union of fear and anger and passion. And I knew at that moment and for all eternity that the union of fear and passion and anger is of the great Goddess, that it is Her gift of this conflicted rack to help us find that love. I understood that She undergoes this suffering Herself in the name of Her own great love for Her consort. All this I knew in a moment. Even now, I thrill to this knowledge. I may lose it, in my moments of despair and lostness and meaninglessness and unlovingness, but it comes back as I am there in living memory. I am, once again, locked in embrace with the man of my soul -- He who is my spirit, my consort, and my king -- sharing the sweet-bitter agony of fear, anger, desire, and transformed by love. At the moment that I first experienced this union, Great Shiva was also freed from His imprisonment, and I felt the Kundalini rise up from the region of my anus. The smell of privies was replaced by the sweet smell of flowers.

II

Less than a month passed before I was once again thrown from my perch of joy and self-satisfaction. After two weeks, I had already looked at the second Chakra, the Svadhisthana. I had seen its six vermillion petals, the white water within, and inside that, the terrible Makara fish with the great mouth. I knew that Vishnu, the Protector, lived here, too, but felt Him small in the lap of the Bindu. In this Chakra, above all, dwells the Shakti, Rakini, with Her four hands and three eyes and fierce fangs. Frightening were Her spear and drum and battle-axe. More frightening still were the stream of blood running from Her nostril, and Her wild, mad eyes. That face, together with the terrible Leviathan-like fish Makara, made me shiver.

My book said of this Chakra: "He who meditates upon this stainless Lotus is freed immediately from all his enemies (the six passions of lust, anger, greed, delusion, pride and envy)." These words gave me little solace. I did not gladly meditate upon this lotus. I would gladly have rested content with the freeing from ignorance that I had achieved with the first Chakra, Muladhara. But I was not to be so lucky as to escape. After three weeks, I began to feel the repeated need to empty my bladder. It was quite unusual for me, but I needed to urinate many times a day. I then realized that the Svadisthana Chakra is located above the genitals, and that the kidneys are related to it. What was in that dark water, I wondered? With a shiver of fear, I said a silent prayer to Vishnu, the Protector, and proceeded to meditate upon this Chakra.

I did not have long to wait. The Shakti-Rakini made Herself manifest and I cried out in terror and horror. She gobbled white rice ravenously, despite the continual pouring of blood from Her nostril. It reddened the rice, but she heeded it not. The Makara fish appeared and changed into a hundred wild animals which raced by me as I stood perfectly motionless. It stopped and transformed into a demon which approached me. I became so frightened that I could hardly breathe. I was as if in a terrible nightmare from which I tried to awaken. There was nothing for it but to look deeply at the face of this demon, but I could not. My breath faded and I fainted.

When I recovered, I looked about me, and saw that everything was the same. Even the page of the picture was unchanged. Perhaps it was only an overwrought imagination, I thought. But the pain in my belly, my feeling of weakness and a shivering fright made me think otherwise. An awareness was dawning upon me. With the Muladhara, I was privileged to unite with the God, Brahma, and to free Him from the imprisoning grasp of the Great Goddess. Now, I had to meet Her again, to face the Mistress of the temple, with whose priestess I had talked. I had to confront the Goddess, and free *myself* from Her terrible grasp.

At that moment, I felt the sharp talons of Her vulture-like claws. I chose to look into Her horrible face, to peer unflinchingly at the blood and into those mad eyes. I fainted once again. Who can look into the eyes of the Goddess and see therein the lust and greed and anger and delusion and pride and envy and still remain conscious? Who can do that? Surely not I.

I wept and wept. I was abased. I was frightened. I was horrified. I was rent asunder and felt split into a million pieces. There flashed before my eyes the vision of every greedy act of my life. I tasted the bitterness of my own failures and hatreds. I tasted my own briny tears. The water ran out of me. Worst of all was the wordless rending asunder that I felt. No words had I. No answers. Only pain and delusion and fear and ignorance.

"Oh, Goddess," I prayed, "Why do you torment men so? Why do you turn them into demons for Your sake? Why?" My belly ached. I felt repeated pressure to relieve myself. No answer came, only pressure of water — tears and urine, urine and tears.

After a time, the water stopped, and there was stillness. Just stillness. No answers, no change, no redeeming thoughts. But stillness was preferable to the horror. I resolved to stay with this stillness, and did so for a long time. There was something peaceful in the silence. Was this an answer to greed and lust and pride and envy and delusion? No. This was an answer only to the mad lovelessness of the Goddess. It was surely no use to confront Her with any of these things. It was like blaming Nature, with its evolutionary processes, for its lovelessness. There is love: I had learned that with the Muladhara. I knew now that there also existed an opposite to Love. What was that? Raw power? Yes. Selfish "mineness"? Yes. Power and greed and lust and envy and pride and anger, all blamed on another. Blamed on us by the Goddess and by us on the Goddess. Enough. Enough of my words. I will be silent. Once I have spoken in complaint. Twice have I spoken in prayer. Now I will cover my mouth. I will be still.

I sat in stillness for many days. I began to understand how it was that my ancestors the yogins could sit for hours and days, utterly alone and silent. It was not a stuporous condition, but a state of total wordlessness and movinglessness. After a very long time of the agony of the stillness, I began to weep. The tears came gently from my eyes, but it brought release from the pain, the tension, the stillness. There were no sobs, nothing to change the soundlessness, yet the movement of the water seemed to break the quiet as well. As if one can hear the flow of tears.

I smiled. Imagine, "to hear the flow of tears." That made me smile. I noticed that I previously had not paid attention to the sounds in the mandalas, which seemed rather meaningless to me. Now I guessed that the sounds had an abstruse meaning, like "to hear the flow of tears." I left that paradox, not wanting to break myself into pieces again, and allowed myself to breathe freely and happily. I soon fell into a deeper reverie.

I found myself transported into space -- or so it seemed. There was water above, through which I went, as well as the water of the oceans below. You in the West, do you not have such a statement in your Bible of "waters of the firmament" above and below? I am not sure if that is what is meant, but this is what I experienced. I knew that I was about to take an astral voyage.

I soon found myself on a planet which I could not fathom. It was dark and the earth was black. The ground was rocky and there seemed to be little or no vegetation. I wandered about in the very dim light, which came from a source I could not divine. I knew I was on a planet, but I did not know which one it was. Was it Chandra (or the Moon, as you call it), or was it Mangala (Mars)? The barren nature and the rocky ground suggested both of these. Then I came across a tree. It was a seemingly ordinary tree in shape and size, like one of your elms, perhaps. But the leaves, the leaves! They were shimmering yellow. It may not be unusual for there to be yellow leaves, but here was a black tree with shimmering yellow leaves which appeared to shed light from a source within the leaves themselves!

I stood looking at this strange tree, when suddenly, a most lovely young girl came close to me and smiled warmly! I looked at her rather astonished, as you can imagine, but she smiled once again and placed her arm on mine. "Fear not, Maya" she said, and I wondered how she knew my name. "Fear not," she repeated. She said not another word but communicated to me silently, as if by telepathy. She informed me that this planet was, as I had guessed, Mangala (Mars) and that she was from Shukra (Venus). Mangala was, indeed, barren, though it had once had a very great civilization. This civilization was destroyed by the ever-recurring wars that it had suffered. These wars, in turn, were caused by both the people and the atmosphere of the planet, which was heavy and crass. The people were healthy, aggressive, and positively physical in nature, but this vital essence was overly enhanced by the electric thickness of the atmosphere. The two fed off each other and caused destruction. The beautiful tree that I was now looking at was one of the black trees of Shukra, of which there were many. It was planted here, as the first of its kind after the catastrophe. The atmosphere of Venus-Shukra was very different from Mangala-Mars, though not opposite to it. These trees were being introduced to Mangala-Mars to help change the atmosphere, and then a new civilization would develop, even greater than those which existed before.

I took in this strange idea that people and atmosphere were dependent upon each other. I knew, of course, that the atmosphere could affect people, but the other way about? That was strange. And yet, it seemed possible and reasonable to me. We do affect our atmosphere physically, do we not? Why not psychically?

I closed my eyes and was led by my new friend to the planet Venus-Shukra. We went through a very hot and gaseous atmosphere in which I thought I would die. At the last moment -- if one can speak of time in the ordinary sense in such astral voyaging -- the poisonous and destructive vapors gave way to a hard earth which opened up to receive us. We continued to fall for a long time, as if magnetically attracted toward the center of this planet. Finally, we landed but it was not on solid ground at all. The earth -- if one may call the strange substance on which we stood "the earth" -- swayed as if it were an ocean. My thoughts quickly went to the western myths, of sea-born, foam-born, wave-born Aphrodite, the Venus of the Greeks. I had read of the wave-floating earth of Venus, as written by an Englishman. The Greeks and Englishman were right about Venus, but why was Venus-Shukra bringing to mind these western associations? Then I remembered. My natural father, after all, was an Englishman, and a soldier (Mars) who risked all for love (Venus). I smiled, for I was his daughter, was I not?

Be that as it may, here I was deep within the planet of Venus itself, finding it hollow like a cave, with no sun nor moon. Instead there was a glow of mellow light, now red, now yellow, now blue, now green, a changing rainbow of colors, but so subtle and diffuse that the eye was not aware of the changes, unless it focused upon them. Yes, this was very different from Mars-Mangala! I remembered a scrap of knowledge from Hindu astrology: Shukra's color was that of the rainbow! Now I understood what that meant: the light of the atmosphere changed like a rainbow. This surely would be something that would be worthwhile to transfer to Mangala. My friend easily divined my thoughts and nodded to me. I realized that the black tree with the yellow leaves, giving a light from within, was the first of many trees to be transferred from Shukra to Mangala. Eventually there would be many, many such trees. I realized, too, as I looked about Shukra, that there were so many varieties of tree that the eye could not comprehend them, but what they had in common were leaves of all shades of the rainbow. Most remarkably, all these leaves -- red, green, yellow, blue -- all had a luminous glow which came from within the leaves themselves. I realized that one day Mangala would have such trees and that the atmosphere would change to these various colors. How then, I thought, would this go with Sun and moons, which Mars had? Here was a mystery which seemed deep and problematic, though I knew not why.

I looked again at my friend for an answer. She said nothing, but I had an inkling of the meaning nonetheless. Something about the union of the diffuse, rainbow-light of Shukra and the solar light of Mangala, piercing and direct -- the union of these two would be a marriage of Gods. Indeed, I had the distinct impression that this had already occurred in the pleromatic world of the Gods, and that the realization would gradually take place on the planets. I was vouchsafed a glimpse of coming events, but I did not know what form it would take, nor why I was given that glimpse.

I looked again at my friend, and I saw something very strange: one eye seemed alternately gay and happy, and then sad and tearful. While these changes were going on, the other eye changed from being wild and fearsome, to being still, deep and fathomless! Two eyes: four conditions. The opposites were not happy-sad, on the one hand, nor still-fierce on the other; no. Happy-sad made one union, while still-fierce made another, and the pairs were opposite. More than that: I was in the presence of the Goddess Venus-Shukra-Shakti Herself! Here, my guide, this ordinary girl, who had seemed sweet and benevolent and in deep communication with me, She was the Goddess and was showing me Her vision: Her two eyes and four conditions. I laughed now, for I understood. My Goddess was showing me and choosing me, just as She had said and promised in the Muladhara. It takes two eyes for the perception of depth, after all, and now She was showing me that happy-sad as one eye, and still-fierce as the other eye, made a pair and a foursome which gave her perception of depth! All my pains and changes and feelings, and angers, and fiercenesses were attributable to the Goddess! I fell at Her feet, embracing Her ankles and Her knees. She lifted me up and kissed me. I knew that I was free of the Goddess, as I wished, but free because I accepted Her, loved Her, submitted to Her. Most deeply of all, I understood her! I danced with joy. Suddenly, I found myself once again on earth, beside my cabin in the mountains of Bengal.

During the following days, I pondered and turned over in my mind the opposites: happy-still; sad-fierce. The words and the states gave some sense to my feelings, but I was not satisfied. How, I wondered, did all those feeling states in the atmospheric rainbow of the Venus-Shukra unite with the Sun and moons of Mars-Mangala-Kuga? And how was that warrior planet, so masculine and vital, going to change? This I needed to know, or else I would not be able to free myself from the Chakra. At once I realized that I needed to be freed not from the Goddess, but from Svadhisthana Chakra! To be freed, I had to further overcome my darkness and ignorance.

The Goddess had explained much to me, about the atmosphere and the planets and the feelings and the unions. But I had to know more before I could proceed to the next Chakra. Who would tell me? The Goddess had unceremoniously deposited me back upon my meditative doorstep. To whom could I turn? I thought for a time, and then it came to me: Vishnu, the Protector, of course! Did he not live in this same mandala of Svadhisthana? Would not this great Lord, who had appeared so often when the world was threatened by evil powers, would He not incarnate Himself again?

"Oh, Vishnu," I prayed, "Oh, savior of humanity. You have become an avatar for humanity's sake so many times; You, who have been both Krishna playing the flute over the mountains and our hero Rama; You, Vishnu, incarnate yourself for me. Perhaps I ask too much for myself. I know that my need is to free myself from this place of ignorance. I know that what I need to know, of the marriage of Shukra and Mangala, of rainbow and sun-darkness, and what emerges therefrom is as nothing to You. I should pray, I know, for a greater boon from You: to be savior of mankind. That we all pray for. But you do not answer us yet. So then, Vishnu, perhaps You will vouchsafe your maidservant a vision, an answer to her question?"

I received no answer to my prayer. Unlike the time when I began my meditations, when I sought the guidance of Shiva, the great Guru who is beyond all gurus, I had no answer to my prayer. That is, I had no answer that I expected! I waited a few moments, and then I heard a laugh. This time it was no female cackle, such as the great Goddess gave me. No, it was a very male laugh. It is hard for me to explain, for the laugh had humor and benevolence in it, along with sneering and harshness. I heard the laugh, but I saw no person. I knew, however, just as I had known with the Goddess, that I was in the presence of the God. He was Vishnu, the Protector, and Mangala-Kuja at the same time.

I was not transported from the spot, nor was I moved at all. No, I sat absolutely still, in my lotus position, and felt the world around me change: the heavens opened up and became as if swallowed by the great fish Makara, and there was only darkness and a very dim light. Through the dimness I saw the planet Mars-Mangala-Kuja come hurtling toward me as if it were some great spacecraft. It hurtled so close and was going so fast that I instinctively held up my hands over my face as if to ward off the blow. How foolish our inadequate little defensive instincts are; as if my little arms could protect my vulnerable body from the great planet.

The hurtling stopped and now I was audience to a spectacle of the planet itself. How can I describe this to you? It was as if I were observing a history of the planet in time, and as if all of it were going on simultaneously. Time was being visually portrayed, serially, in terms of events, and simultaneously, taking place in different parts of the planet. And I was aware of it all at once. I had only to cast my eye on this place or that, and I would see it all. The word "all" is the right one, for it is a totality which is a totality all the time. The part, at the same time, is the whole. Is that confusing? I imagine so, for it confuses me as well, and I still do not rightly grasp it all.

What I saw might be termed "A Natural History of Aggression." The first part showed the battling and devouring of animals who were instinctive enemies: cat and mouse; fox and goose; lion and deer, and so on. In each case, the battle was for good, or for territorial defense, or for sexual partners, or for leadership. It was horrible and natural. Then there were scenes of men, and it was the same. Civilization after civilization, the heights of achievement were increased and the destruction augmented. I saw civilizations rise to great peaks and, like Atlantis and Lemuria, go down under waters of Malekaric destructiveness. I watched all this with a cold eye, as if I, myself, were the Sun of Mars-Mangala-Kuja, looking down upon it. But, as our sun is not cold, perhaps the analogy is better with the moons, those two moons of the planet. They, indeed are cold.

But no, it was a combination of both: I looked with the coolness of the two moons as two eyes, and with the clarity of the sun, but without its warmth. I saw coldly, without fire nor feeling nor horror, nor agony, nor even pleasure. As I looked with these two cold eyes of two cold moons and with this one bright eye which saw all without warmth, I saw the continuing development of the "natural history of aggression," as I have said. The light grew dimmer as I looked, until I saw the planet devastated by its aggression. I watched as the people grew more and more aware of what was happening. I saw them withdraw from the cold moons and clear sun and retreat into the depths of the planet, to build their cities and their civilizations away from these cold eyes. All became barren outside, and the life that went on inside the planet was not available for me to see. Now events were occurring in the time-scale I had experienced when brought there by the Goddess: I saw a great black tree being planted, and on this tree were beautiful yellow leaves. As I watched, I saw more trees being planted, just as the Goddess had informed me. Before long -- it could not have been more than fifteen or twenty million years -- many, many trees were planted, and the cold dim atmosphere began changing. There seemed to be a strange union going on. During what seemed to be the middle of the day, the bright sun had full command and cast its clear light on all sides. In morning and evening, the rainbow light had its sway and gorgeous colors filled the sky. At night, all was dark, except that one moon shown, and the other broke up into thousands and millions of particles that became stars.

With this union of the atmosphere, of Venus and Mars, of Shukra and Mangala, the people came out from under the earth of the planets and began to communicate with one another. One knew that things were happening: the cold-eyed aggression of the one was transformed with the feelings of the rainbowed other. And the simple continuity of trees which shine with an inner light was joined with the greater light of the one Sun. Whereas before this Sun was simply a cold orb, seeing all, now it was filled with heat and light and warmth and fire and passion.

Numbers appeared in the sky: the two plus two, of the two eyes of the Goddess, mingled with the one plus two of the sun and moons of the God. It was a strange sight: two and four of the Goddess; one and two of the God. They united in equally strange ways. The two of the Goddess merged with the two of the God, making four. There was the One of the God, the Two of the God and Goddess, the Three of the God (with his own one sun plus two moons) and the Four of the Goddess (with Her two plus two). Together they were as One and Ten, for they sum to ten and are as One, are they not? In the Heavens and in the Waters and on the

Earth, they were united in embrace, Shiva and Shakti, Vishnu and Lakshmi, God and Goddess. And I was freed from the bonds of Svadhisthana.

III

Many days went by, but I did not feel the joy and freedom of enlightenment which I had felt after I had escaped the bonds of the Muladhara. Had I really freed myself from Svadhisthana? Was my vision, my astral voyaging, only a dream, only a self-deception, only an illusion? I smiled ruefully, for my name meant "illusion" and, it was true, I could hardly tell if I, myself, existed. How could I know? I had seen, I had heard, but -- and now I knew that a part of me was not freed from Svadhisthana -- I had not tasted. And taste was the very center, the very purpose and point of that Chakra! The Tattva of taste was not dissolved.

So, I was not free. I noticed that again, as had been happening every day for some time -- one eye began tearing. It was strange. I was not really sad, and only one eye wept. I reached up and with my finger took a tear and tasted it. It was salty. I reached down and took some of my urine. It was bitter. I laughed. Yes, now I tasted: the salt of wisdom and the bitterness of my lack of enlightenment! I was freed from Svadhisthana, all right, but I was still only half, and cool, and not . . .

Enough. Whatever I was lacking had to be redeemed as I proceeded. I had been through the earth of Muladhara, the water of Svadhisthana, and now I needed to face the fire of Manipura. It was just this fire, this heat of tapas which would transform my meditation into the freedom that I desired. It was good; now I would continue my *dhyana*.

I fixed my attention on the Manipura, the "plentitude of jewels" which was at the navel. I looked carefully at the picture. Facing me was a central crucible of red fire, triangular in shape. I looked at its three handles, the swastikas. Inside the fire was the Ram sacred to Agni. There, I knew, was a central place. I also looked outside the triangle, and saw the God Rudra, the Destroyer, seated upon the bull. I saw, too, the Shakti Lakini, blue and three-faced with three eyes in each. She had four arms, fierce teeth, and chewed rice mixed with meat and blood. Rudra was white, smeared with ashes. They both made the signs dispelling fear and granting boons, but their visage said otherwise. Only the outside of the Mandala, with its ten blue petals, seemed to suggest peace.

These were the Gods ruling the Chakra: the Destroyers! Dare I descend into the heat and fire? I had read somewhere that the fire-walkers were those who had mastered this Chakra. But who could go into the fires of hell and emerge unscathed? Not I. I said this with full knowledge of my limitations even in terms of self-mastery -- I did not even think about the desirability or meaningfulness of walking on coals concretely.

It was many days before I could directly view the task of this Chakra. It seemed that I had already been through so much, why should I expose myself to the fire and pain of the Destroyers? At last, however, I could set myself apart from these Gods, and look, even so, into the burning crucible and fires. I waited, and the vision began to form for me. I felt the heat rise and fill my eyes with the colors that are meant for the Gods.

Now I saw them there: Rudra, pure vermillion, white with ashes, gross and barbaric, on his unattractive bull; the Shakti Lakini, blue and vicious, with bloody mouth. It was then that words began to form within me. I am moved to call them a prayer, since they are addressed to the Gods, but I had never so spoken to the Gods in this way, and you might even find me rather blasphemous in my statements. In hopes that you will understand, and -- dare I say it -- even share the sentiments with me, I will relate what words formed in me:

"Rudra, Great Destroyer! I do not count you Great. As I contemplate my navel, I sense a sickness and nausea within my belly which leads me to want to throw up the pain and rancor and resentment which lies within me! And it is You whom I hate. You and Your rotten Consort. Look at You. I see in You every tiny little tyrant, every fat Rajah and vicious potentate who has burdened and drained and deprived my people of their joy, of their material blessings, of their livelihood, while You sit in Your fat splendor, unmindful of their suffering. What care you? You care only for the sacrifices which are given to You. You care only for the sweet scent of the smoky spirit of the animal as it rises up to Your wicked nostrils. Yes, Ram sacrifice you wish, as well as Goat, or Lamb. It is as nothing to You. You care not that the animal eats when it is hungry, makes love when it wishes, fights only for its security or food -- all these natural and good things are as nothing to You. For You care not about Ram or Lamb, unless it is of use to You. You care not about Man, unless he is of use to You. You care only for gifts and sacrifices, and that Man sing Your praises! Yes, now I will tell You, and make no more cowed response to Your threats. For what can You do to me? Kill me? That is no great threat. For I tell You that I despise You! You, God, I despise You, and curse You! I am no atheist who foolishly believes that he can dismiss You. No, it is much worse; I know that You exist, just as these petty tyrants, and hypocritical leaders exist. They exist, just as You exist, and they serve You. And they make us all serve You, do they not? Well, I will not serve You willingly, though bow to You I must. I know that I am impotent to overthrow You. I know that I can only rant and rave and groan and weep, though You can and will have Your way.

"And You, Great Shakti Lakini! Neither do I count You Great, though You, too, are the Destroyer. What are You, with Your three eyes and three heads and bloody mouth, only out for itself! Your Consort and Lord is after Power, at least, though He gets it in his devious, bitter, mean and skulking ways. You do not seek even that! You want only to devour poor souls. You want only to torment us, feed upon us, drive us into all sorts of temptations and experiences and emotions, and then it is You that feed, unmindful of the feelings of others, unmindful of their pain. You simply keep the whole bloody mess of life going, get Your bounty of flesh and rice and blood — and mankind weeps and groans. What is worse, You incarnate Yourself in us, and get off freely! Oh, how I despise You!

"These are my prayers to You, You Gods, You Destroyers! I heave up my pain and my wrath and my bitterness. Eat, therefore, of this pile of vomitted words which are my prayers to You!"

My words reduced my nausea and I felt a brief respite of the pain in my belly and pressing on my navel. But the Gods neither moved, nor made any sign at all that they had heard me. Not even a sneer from Rudra, nor a cackle from Lakini! Rudra merely sat, pompous and self-satisfied, on his gross bull; Lakini devoured her meat and rice like a vulture or hyena.

I sat and looked at them and sighed. What was this? Why did my efforts have no effect? Was this only egotism and self-centeredness? Did I just see there, in these Destroyer Gods, my own power and hunger and selfishness, which were not apparent to me within myself? No, I would not fall into that trap for myself, for I had often been there; it is easy for me to simply say, "Oh, yes, that is my own darkness and evil." The Gods love us to do that, do they not? They love to indulge every whim and get their sacrifices from man and then have man feel the guilt and pain and agony and suffering. Lastly, if man takes the burden on himself, he is the sacrifice for their grievous behavior! Yes, they want their Ram-Lamb sacrifice, do they not?

Now I remembered a ritual at the temple of Kali in my fair city of Calcutta. I recalled the sacrifice of the Goat, and his one eye staring wildly and painfully up at me. A sacrifice to that Kali who needed to be cut up in many pieces and spread over the entire land! But we can cut Her up no more, for She can re-unite Herself easily. It is illusion to think that we can destroy the Terrible Mother! Why then, I thought, do they want sacrifices and prayers and praise? They seem to need that from us. And this poor goat? This poor Ram or Lamb, with his eye staring up? Then I thought in satisfaction: Yes, that is it! That is it! It came to me in a flash of lightning, like the energy of the Kundalini itself! I spoke in words of declaration, not prayer:

"There, Great Goddess Lakini! Look at that Ram, with his One Eye showing. Look at that animal creature! He, in his littleness, in his naturalness, in his goodness, knows more than You, with Your Three Faces and Three Eyes in each. For your Threeness is as nothing! You see all, have all power, but You are incomplete! And I, as a woman, know what it is to suffer from incompleteness. You are only moving and dynamic and changing and devouring, no rest. Your three faces need a fourth face, and your three times three eyes need a fourth and tenth. It is the Ram's face, and the Lamb's eye, and the Goat's being that You want. Without that, You are incomplete! You need that natural animal to satisfy You all the time. Praise us, Mankind, for you need us to offer these sacrifices to You! Without us, You simply do not have Your totality!

"And You, Great God Rudra! In your impotent and little fury! You get all Your power from the Bull, and You do not know it. You have everything, but You do not know it! The One-Eyed Ram-Lamb-Goat sees more clearly than You, with Your Two. Look, tyrant, look! You are a lesser animal than the Ram! For he, at least, is pure animal and can be nothing other than pious in following his nature. You, great Monster of a God, act worse than any animal, yet claim and show a human face as well!

"Well, you Gods! I reject You and despise You, and now let me hold up a mirror to You and show You how You look!"

With that, I took the Eye of the Ram and held it up to the Gods so that they could see therein the vision of themselves. Until this point, both Gods seemed quite oblivious of me and rather uninterested in anything that I had to say. I did not even know if they heard what I said. Nonetheless, I offered the Ram-Lamb-Goat eye up as a mirror, as an angry and vengeful and superior kind of sacrifice. I then became aware that They — these great and powerful and awful Gods — were interested and moving towards me. Now it was I who sneered, and I who laughed and cackled at them! For I had the mirror eye, the one thing that these vicious, uncaring, monstrous Gods needed — the capacity to look at themselves! I had it from the spontaneous nature of the Ram-Lamb-Goat himself, and from my own nature. So, now, I held up this Eye, and they looked.

The Shakti-Lakini looked and saw the horror of Her three faces and three eyes in each. She retched at Her blue color, and grew ill at the sight of the blood and meat in Her mouth and, I presume, at Her greed. She fell back in horror, it seemed, and gave the Eye to Her Consort.

Rudra looked and saw His ugliness! He saw the grossness of His being, His pomposity, His self-centeredness, His power-seeking, all of which really showed His impotence! He then looked at me, His little nothing of a female being, and at his Consort. He awakened to the fact that She had more power than He and that I had more insight. He shrieked in agony! The Two Gods clawed at themselves. I showed them the great burning vat of fire, with the swastika handles. They shied back in fear, but I reached out and pushed them in! What joy and vengeance, that those who had kept men in the heat of ovens of pain and desire and having to sacrifice for the Gods, that these Gods should now suffer as men have suffered! I shouted aloud, for I understood a deep truth: It was not man alone who needed to be transformed, but the Gods needed this! The Gods, in their lack of insight and consciousness of what it is to be a Human Being, needed to be burned and transformed in that self-same fire!

I sat before that crucible of fire and looked at the red, boiling, bubbling mass of thick liquid. It was like fire and blood at the same time. I was still, without pain and without passion. I was even without thought. I said only, "Let them stay in their broth, for they so willed it and wanted it."

With that, I took the Eye of the Ram-Lamb-Goat and swallowed it. I felt as if the eye went quickly and easily down my throat and into my belly, to lodge beneath my navel. I then imagined that it looked up at me from the opening in my navel, and I looked down at it. And then I laughed! I laughed and laughed and laughed! It was no sneering laugh, as that of Rudra; it was no cackling laugh of horrible glee at another's suffering, as that of the Shakti; it was no giggle of a girl. At that moment, despite my years and despite my having had husband, lovers, children, much experience in my life -- at that moment, I became a woman! I became a woman in spirit! I laughed with joy and with self-insight and I laughed also at myself and my own pretentiousness. As I laughed and felt myself to be a woman in the spirit, by one of those meaningful moments in which Nature and Spirit, Man and the Gods, are one, I began to menstruate. The blood flowed freely and warmly, and I felt its rich, fiery quality pulse through me. I put my finger in it and tasted it, and I found the blood tasty and good! I felt at One with my Sister, the Shakti, for I, too, could look at myself, my animal nature and laugh!

Then I thought of Rudra, puffed up and pompous, like the silly tyrant He was, and I laughed once more. I laughed, for this is what I, too, saw in the mirror of the Eye of the Ram-Lamb-Goat. This natural creature, without conceit, without selfishness, without even consciousness of itself, this creature's eye showed me my terrible vanity and pride. I saw myself full of ego and pomposity, searching after praise. I laughed and laughed and laughed. I did not sneer at myself for these things. For this is what it meant, I knew, to be both an animal and a God! We, poor human creatures, were in-between! I knew, once again, all that I had known from the Gods in the Muladhara and Svadhisthana, but now I knew it in a different way. How can I say it, better than I have already? I cannot. Know only that the Gods need to be praised, the animals need to be praised, and Mankind needs to be praised, for we are all One!

With those words of laughter and joy, I saw the Great Rudra and I saw the Great Shakti Lakini rise out of the boiling red fire and blood of the crucible. They rose up as if transformed into jewelled, golden statues which emanated a glow from within. They were still and lifeless like statues, yet they had a numinous luminescence. I had an inkling of what it meant, but I cannot put it into words, lest I, too, become only a destroyer with words.

But now I could see that which I could not see before. These same great Destroyer Gods, were also moving, changing, Creator Gods. "Oh, my Gods!" I said, and I fell to the ground in utter awe and wonder: The Creator Gods and the Destroyer Gods are One! I saw then the motioning of the one hand in each God, which said, "Fear not." For with one hand they destroyed, but they also, as it is written, "dispelled fear and granted boons."

This great vision was too much for me and I held my hands over my face. I felt the warmth of my own blood, and I felt tears rising and blood rising, from the lower regions of genitals and navel upward. The Kundalini was rising. I was freed from Manipura, and the plenitude of jewels therein.

IV

Anahata, the "charming" lotus. "Charming" perhaps, because of its gorgeous reds and oranges and vermillions, of the "shining colour of the Bandhuka flower." No other Chakra, for example, says a commentator, has the "rays of the Sun on its filaments." They are like twelve soft leaves which give off a lovely light. Charming, yes. But what does it mean? Does it mean that he who achieves liberation with this Chakra shall be warm and friendly and give off a sweet light? And be charming? Yes, perhaps so. For at the very end of the verses, it is said that the Yogi will be "dearer than the dearest to women." As a woman, I understand that he will be gentle and loving. Yes, that would be nice. I would like to be that way, too.

What I really want is Anahata, the "Unattackable." Ah, that would be the redemption and liberation which I would seek. Imagine, no longer being at the mercy of the violent winds which sweep one. No longer at the mercy of the others who can split one in pieces with their *avidya* and desire and unconsciousness! Imagine! Would that be possible? That is what the verses claim. The commentator says: "He is able at will to enter the enemy's fort or citadel (Durga), even though guarded and rendered difficult of access. And he gains power by which he may render himself invisible, and fly across the sky." Yes, I understand that poetic language. To me, it means that the Enlightened One can enter the Self of another, can connect and understand him, even if the other is guarded and defensive. He must do so by intuitive means. The Enlightened One can also "render himself invisible" — that is, he can hide in his own "citadel," inside his own Self — and can "fly across the sky." I suppose that means that he can vanish into his own or the general spiritual atmosphere and thus be safe. Yes, I do believe that I understand this. I am even rather flattered that I can translate the poetry of the old Guru Masters of hundreds of years ago and understand it with my modern, post-independence mind!

But to achieve it; ah, that is another matter. How I have learned that to know only with the mind is to be possessed only by Shiva! How I have learned that to know only with the body is to be possessed by Shakti! The Form and the Power; both are always present. How can they be united? Here is where I must find out.

Let me look at the Lotus. All around are the beautiful orange and red and vermillion leaves, each with a letter. I had not attended to the letters of the lotuses before. Just like a woman, I suppose. But now the letters are not just letters; within this lotus is heard the sound of the Shabda Brahman, "the sound which issues without the striking of any two things together." That is the sound, the "Om," the Mantra which even caused a new religion to develop. The sound that issues without the striking of any two things is, indeed, the primordial sound of the universe, the tone of all creation. It is said by another commentator that many varieties of this sound can be heard: the sound of a swarm of bees; a waterfall; high humming of a holy man; roaring of the sea; ringing of a bell; rustling of tiny silver chains; flute notes; shrill, high whistling; the sound of a drum; distant thunder. All magnificent sounds, and I think that I know what is meant. Is it not like the Buddhist's "Sound of one hand clapping?" Yes, yes, and this may be a "Buddhist Chakra" for other reasons, for there is another little lotus beneath this large Anahata lotus. That little lotus has eight red petals, and inside it there is not only the great Kalpa-tree, the wishing tree, but the Ishta-deva with an awning, and trees laden with flowers, fruits and sweet-voiced birds. That little "mental-chakra" is, no doubt, the place of the Buddha. I sense that he sat under his Bo Tree, which was, on earth, the same as the Heavenly Kalpa Tree, and that he faced all the devas and demons as they swirled at him. It is certain that he proved his "Anahata" — his unattackableness — and was enlightened. For all his fruits and all the fruits of those that followed surely came from his

Bo and, in sooth, from the great Kalpa Tree in Heaven. This is, indeed, a Buddhist Chakra!

But look inside the Lotus of Anahata. There is the Vayu-Mandala, a smoky-colored, six-cornered one. Grey as a mass of smoke is it, and in the shape of interlocking triangles, male (apex upwards) and female (apex downwards). In the West one calls this the Star of David, or, perhaps, the Seal of Solomon, the union of Macrocosm and Microcosm. So, a Jewish symbol, too! Well, could it be that there meet Hindu, Buddhist, and Jew? Yes, it could be. For here, it is said, the great Jivatma, the Atman, the Self, first makes its appearance. The union of the opposites, the end of division and enemies. A fitting place for the union of the highest and where at least three religions can meet.

What does it mean that the smoky region, with its six-pointed star, is here? Let me read further. Inside the smoky region is a Shakti-Trikona, a female triangle which is like "ten million flashes of lightning" and is a Shiva Linga of shining gold. Here, too, is the half-moon, the crescent which might join the Muslims to us.

What does all of this mean? It means nothing less than that the core of one's being, the spark of the divine, which flows "like the steady tapering flame of a lamp" is inside the smokey-grey citadel of protection. It is a fire which is safely lit and never goes out, for it is in the region of protection. Oh, to have this flame which can be blown by the winds of heavenly desire and joy and not have it go out! Oh, to have it protected by the union of the Male and Female. Could one but have that citadel in which it is safe! And oh, to have the lovely outer perimeter of reds, to show to the world! Oh, Shiva, Oh, Shakti, let this be so for me!

There is more. There, in the Lotus dwells also a lovely black antelope or gazelle. It is light and graceful, fleet and fugitive. Perhaps it is the instinct that one needs to know danger, to run when there is trouble. Yes, to flee within oneself to the smokey union of the citadel and its ever-burning flame within, to the great sound of Om, and stillness. I can almost taste it! But this is the region of touch, and the tattva is of touch and motion -- I must feel it and touch it.

Still more. For this is the region of the Heart, is it not? And the heart is in the region of lungs, of the Air. In this Chakra, after Earth, Water, and Fire, is the region of Air. The Heart has feeling, and Air has the spirit. Here I shall no longer be perpetually hurt or misunderstood! Nay, not so. I shall surely still be misunderstood, but I can protect myself in my citadel. I shall know my heart, and feel my flame and be able to go out to another, but to stay within my own chest, my own treasure, as well. For here, too, it is said, that the one who meditates herein will be smiled upon by

Lakshmi, that benefactress who gives wealth and prosperity. What greater wealth and prosperity than to have safe and sacred one's inner treasure of one's Self? Yes, I hunger after it.

Finally, let me look at the Shiva and the Shakti who dwell in this Lotus. There they are, in their little mandalas. The verses say that here is Shiva-Hamsa, of the Sun, and He is also Shiva-Isha, with three eyes. He is "lustrous like the Sun, and his two hands make the gestures which grant boons and dispel the fears of the three worlds." He lives in the "Abode of Mercy" and is described as "wearing a jeweled necklet and chain of gems around his neck, and bells on his toes, and also clad in silken raiment." A commentator says of him: "The beautiful One possessed of the soft radiance of ten million moons, and shining with the radiance of his matted hair." Ah, how he has changed from the previous Chakra! What a great Sun-Shiva is He, benevolent and granting boons and dispelling fears!

I look to the Shakti. What say the verses of Her?

"Here dwells Kakini, who in colour is golden like unto new lightning, exhilarated and auspicious; three-eyed and the benefactress of all. She wears all kinds of ornaments, and in Her four hands She carries the noose and the skull, and makes the sign of blessing and the sign which dispels fear. Her heart is softened with the drinking of nectar."

"Her heart is softened with the drinking of nectar." Oh, would that were true! One commentator said that "Her heart is made joyous by the drinking of rice-wine." That may be. It is hard for those of us who have suffered from Her to see and experience Her "heart softened." Yet, here it is so. For it is in the heart region, is it not? The Shakti must surely have transformed in between, has She not? Yes. But here, too, it is said that She is dressed in the skin of the black antelope. So surely She is now covered with the sensitivity of the animal and its darkness. Perhaps she has gained from my encounter with Her and my showing Her the eye of the Goat, in the Manipura.

So, there it all is. All that is necessary is for me to feel, to touch, to bring it into my own being. I left out only one tattva; the penis is the organ of action, the tattva to be dissolved herein. All is there: Heart, air, mind, spark, flame, penis, Self, mandala, citadel, leaves, sounds, Om, sweetness, protection. Wholeness. I see all, but do not have it. Let me pray again to the God and Goddess. Let me pray to their union, to the One who will protect it like a flame amidst all attack.

I pray to thee, oh Shiva-Shakti. I pray to the One who combines flame and citadel, and You, who dwell in Heaven and in my Heart, You who already have the Kalpa-Tree which goes beyond what one wishes, You know what it is that I want and need. I pray in silence.

I stayed with my prayer for many days. I knew clearly what I needed to achieve. I knew clearly -- with my head. But what good was it, to know with the head, when above all, one needed to experience it, to possess it, in the heart. The heart, this unattackable citadel. To have it in the head was to be only with Shiva.

Now I knew: Shakti was of the world. Here was I, upon my quiet mountain, retreating from the world in which Shakti had her sway. Surely She could reach me here with Her passion and desires, but here, with the Eternal, with the Formless Forms, here I was safe from Shakti as She could present Herself in the Form of other human beings and animals. No sooner did I become aware of this, than I knew that the test of my citadel (if in truth I had it) would come from meeting other souls and not being destroyed by them, or undermined by them. I could not do it alone, here upon my mountain. I needed the encounter of my fellow creatures.

The same morning when I recognized this fact, there came to me, for the first time, a visitor. It was not that my cabin in the mountains was so isolated. No. I needed to walk only an hour to come to a village where I could purchase food and other necessities. My nearest neighbors, farmers, were no more than minutes away. My isolation was self-chosen and enjoyed, but, as I had assured my family, I was no recluse nor hermit, and certainly not a self-torturer. Yet no one had yet been curious enough or interested enough to come and see the strange lady who was living alone in the cabin. My neighbors had left me pretty much alone. So, as I say, it is peculiar, but by no means strange to the ways of the Gods, that the day that I recognized my need to find and test the citadel in myself in relation to my fellow creatures -- that same day should be the first that a visitor should seek me out.

It is more astonishing yet that this same visitor should be a foreigner. For the lady who came to me was Greek. She had been visiting my family in Calcutta, having been a friend of my sister many years ago when they were in school in England. She had a dream. She dreamed that a kind and benevolent woman had visited her and told her to come to me. She was told by this woman that I, Maya, was a special sort of woman, singled out by the Goddess Shakti. She said that I was especially courageous to go off alone, to face the Gods alone, and to attempt what all the Gurus had attempted. I was foolhardy to do this alone -- as a woman and without a guide -- but was also to be congratulated for this. The Greek lady was to convey this message to me. Why was the Greek lady singled out to do this, she asked? Because she, too, had been courageous and insightful, and was also a seeker and a modern woman, but she was a medium and, in particular, she was a medium of the Goddess' love.

When the Greek lady told me this, I was astonished. I was suspicious, but I was moved. Tears began to fall from one eye. At last, I was receiving the love of the Goddess, and this lady was Her mediatrix. I listened and took it in. I thanked her. I did not know if this were a Deva or not. Then I knew: The demons can come with love or destruction. They can come with insight or with darkness. They can come from men or from the Gods. I did not know for certain, but I had to listen to that within me which told me. This "something," this inner flame told me in a quiet manner that what the Greek lady said was true. For the Greek lady also added that I should just be about my business and be modest. The modesty meant "being about my business" and not a false humility. I laughed, for only a Greek, after all, can speak with authority about Pride. That is their greatest problem, is it not? Modesty: to be about one's business, and only one's own business. A lovely definition. It was true. The Goddess acknowledged that the flame existed. The flame was burning inside me, and the Goddess acknowledged it. I laughed again.

After that, the people came. First came a friend who said that I should be back at home taking care of my family. Then came a man who thought I should be serving his particular cause. Then came a seducer. They came in variety. What I felt forming in me, in reality, was a deep inner flame. This great warm and tender Sun, giving off a glow of crescent Moon. Around it was the smokey Star of David. I knew that this smoky mandala was my citadel and my fort. Here was the three-sided union of God and Goddess: they were united in the smoke of my emotion. Whenever my emotion was aroused, there was the union of God and Goddess. The smoke was that airy spirit and that effect of the inner flame: that dark and volatile "something" that was the product of flame and matter and air. The airy region of my lungs enclosing the fiery center of my heart. The emotion was my citadel: when aroused, the smoke appeared. I could either express my emotion — a way of saying "Who goes there?" — and wait to see if it were friend or foe, or listen to my antelope and flee back inside, without a word. The antelope, with its horns, could defend itself, or flee. But the smoke, beloved smoke! There was a dark grey, murky and potent citadel! There, oh union of Goddess and God, in emotion You are to be my fort and protection!

But I must not forget those reddish little leaves, those outer edges of my lotus, which delicately and feelingly exist, as well. For how can I reach into the fort of another without these delicate vermillion leaves? Yes, I need them very much. Yet I must not cry when I do not have them. I must not punish myself when I feel no warmth nor delicacy moving outwards. At such moments, my own citadel needs attention. My emotion tells me that, does it not? Yes, I no longer need to be a sacrifice for the Gods. I was such a one many times, but no longer. The Manipura has taught me that!

When I realized that I no longer needed to be a sacrifice for the Gods, that I was no longer a Lamb, nor Ram, nor Goat, I felt that I, myself, must go back into the world. I realized that many times in my life I had offered myself as a sacrifice for the greed or lust or power of another -- just because of my own need to be of service to the Gods, and to be a sacrifice. Now I needed to find out if I could be in relation to my fellows without being this unconscious martyr.

I went into the world and watched carefully for my reaction to others and them to me. Many were glad to see me, since I had been away so long, but I realized that most people were busy taking care of their own needs and their own little worlds which were just as rich and busy and difficult for them as mine was to me. Now I listened to the antelope within me. I was like a careful animal observing and listening, and bounding away to my inner citadel or even physically away when there was too much danger of being assaulted. To my surprise, it worked well! My citadel was strong.

I went back and forth between my cabin in the mountains and my life in the world, for I knew that I had to have my Anahata, my citadel and my union and my strength and totality, in both worlds. Otherwise I would just be a fraud! I knew that I was a person who served the Goddess, not just the God, for I needed love and my relationships with people every bit as much as I needed to transform and be transformed by the Gods in my solitude. The Gods, after all, are to be found among us, are they not, and not just within us?

But, in the world I experienced much pain and fear, for my sensitivity had been increased by my meditations. Alone I experienced pain and fear as well, in addition to loneliness, uncertainty, despair, guilt, and so many of the other dark emotions which tended to make my light, my inner sun, go out.

Finally, I sat alone in my mountain cabin. I knew that I had my mandala, my Anahata continued, but still I did not see the face of the Goddess soften. I did not experience "Her heart softened with the drinking of nectar."

I sat in silence, in my lotus position. I sat in silence, determined, like the Buddha, not to be moved until the Gods really granted me the boons that their gestures had promised.

I now sat in the open, exposed to the elements. It was not that I was like the ancient gurus, proving my invulnerability to elements of heat, air, water, earth, or fire. No, it was merely that I felt the need to be exposed -- not as a test. It is hard for me to explain. I felt stronger, was healthy and needed to be out in the elements. Know, only, that it was not a test, nor a challenge, but an openness.

Thus I sat for three days and nights. I think it was three days; I lost track after the first day. I was not troubled by the cold nor by the wind, nor by the rain, or heat. This, I think, was because I was so deeply immersed in my inner search and waiting. It was a passive search and an active waiting. It was just so. I had said my prayers -- the Gods knew what I needed.

The third day, just when the sun was at its highest, the God appeared to move. The great Shiva-Isha smiled, or so it seemed to me. He pronounced the syllable Om and moved out of the great Throne in the firmament which He occupied. He came toward me and embraced me. As He embraced me, I felt an intense thrill which made me tingle as I never had before. My fingers trembled rapidly and my skin crawled. I moved and began a strange dance which I did not understand. Every pore of my body was undulating and vibrating at an enormously quick pace, yet my larger movements seemed to be slow and deliberate. I was like a great dancer, I am sure, although no one but the Gods were there to observe it. I had never danced in this way before nor since! It was a dance of and by the Gods that was miraculous. I danced, as I have said, with very fast movements of fingers and toes, of sensitive pores and skin, but slow and deliberate motions of hands and arms and head, at the same time. My feet made a mandala. They formed the pattern of the whole Anahata, the gentle leaves, the smokey Star. For the last, was left the central flame, the inner sun, the inner Shiva-Hamsa. At that point, my dance stopped and the syllables of word-music which accompanied me stopped as well.

Shiva-Isha smiled again. He lifted me, as if I had the weight of a small stone, and put me beside the pattern that my feet had traced. He then took a great stone lingam and placed it in the center, where the central flame was to be. At the same moment, he touched my chest and I felt as if a phallus were growing out of it. I looked down. It was no phallus, but the flaming power of the lingam was pulsating inside my heart.

At the same moment that I felt the flame in my heart, the stone lingam on the mandala spontaneously burst into flame. It was a miraculous sight! I felt the flame within and viewed the flame without. The winds blew, but the flame did not go out. My passion blew, but the flame did not go out.

Then Shiva-Isha became as one with Shiva-Hamsa, and I knew that the God without was the same as the God within, the Suns were the same. To my surprise, a gentle wind came, the sun went behind the clouds, the flaming lingam went out, and I felt my heart-flame stop. All was silent for several moments. It was as if death had filled the air. And then, just as it had gently gone out, behind the clouds and stilled, the flaming fire of the lingam, the sun, the candle in my heart, re-ignited. All was warm and light again. The God said nothing, but He smiled again. When He smiled, I was reminded of a dream I had when a great Guru, the outstanding one of my time, had died. In the dream there was a birthday cake, with many candles -- about as many as had filled the years of the Guru. The candles were lit, and a gentle wind blew them out. In the next instant, the candles lit themselves again. I saw the Guru smile and I knew that there was immortality. The words of my dream came back to me now: "The flame goes out; but it comes on again!"

The warmth and wonder filled me all that day and into the night. It had rained a little, but the wetness merely added pleasure to the sensations playing upon my skin. At night, a crescent moon appeared. At what I would guess to be the midnight point, the witching hour, I saw the face of Shakti-Kakini in the moon. Her hands held the noose and the skull, and Her face was hard. I looked on in sorrow. Words formed in me: "Oh, Goddess. I fear neither death nor silence. I long for peace, for softening. Would that nectar would soften Your heart as well. But I submit to You, and bow my head." As I bowed, the Goddess came down from the moon. She was like a little child in my arms and suckled at my breast. I do not know if there was, indeed, milk in me, but it felt so. The fluid which came out seemed like milk and semen and wine, all at once. I laughed, for I thought of myself as a strange sort of creature: a manufacturer of good things for the Gods. My gifts flowed freely from me to the Goddess, as it had flowed freely from the God to me. The Goddess was then back on her throne in heaven, gorgeous in Her golden beauty, with the many ornaments. I was stunned at Her glory, but She laughed and did the dance of the mandala which I had performed before. She danced with a grace and charm which was exhilarating and calming at the same time. I knew that the Goddess had been within me when I danced. The Goddess smiled again, and seemed to leap into the Anahata mandala.

She jumped to the "mental chakra" beneath, and clothed herself in the tree, the great Kalpa-Tree. I knew that She was showing me that She and the Tree were One. Then She hopped, as if it were a child's game, playfully, into the spot on the larger Mandala where Her image would appear. She made a crescent sign over the flame, and playfully did the same in my heart. The crescent moon over the fire -- play and exhilaration and joy -- is that what She meant? She nodded. These words came to me: "Play and Flow, Flow and Play." They conveyed the thought that Life was a woman's game, with play and flow of mother milk, and semen, and wine. We live it and suffer it and both give and take of it; it is all of and by the Goddess. The Fire is of the God, but the glow is of the Goddess.

I joined in the Dance of the Goddess. She and I were One. My eyes flowed and Her eyes flowed and the liquids flowed from everywhere. We danced, she and I, the Dance of Life, with great intensity and speed, and with great calm and deliberateness. We danced as the flame moved us, for now I knew what it meant to be "Unattackable." Anahata and I were One, and our Hearts were softened.

V

The joy and exhilaration which came from being freed from the bonds of Anahata, the liberation I felt in my achievement of my "citadel," did not last long. I went back into my life in Calcutta, to test my new-found condition and, within a very short time, the flame of the candle went out.

This is how it happened. One day, I chanced to meet a cousin that I had not seen for very many years. She was the daughter of my step-father's brother and we had never gotten on well together. As we greeted each other, she said, "You look just like your mother!" This annoyed me, though I thought — and said — "You look just like your mother." In truth I despised her mother. There had been something of a family feud throughout my childhood years, my own mother taking a bad beating emotionally from my father's relatives. Well, in short order, we were in painful talk. I am not sure what happened, but in retrospect I saw that I had fallen back into my childhood and had lost myself. I was reacting as a child to the aunt that I had despised, and also reacting from my mother's troubles with that family, not my own. The same was true when my cousin spoke badly about my father. It was true, what she said, but I grew angry and threw it back at her. I was again carrying the unexpressed animosity between the brothers, which was never shown openly. This exchange overwrought me very much. I sheepishly felt that I had lost Anahata, and the heart of the Goddess was not softened. All the same, I returned to my cousin the next day and repaired the damage that had taken place. I told her what I thought had happened, and was able to listen to her views. It was better between us, more human, and I immediately felt the flame inside my citadel rekindle.

I returned to my mountain retreat in a chastened frame of mind. What was this strange wound which was so easily opened? Why was I so vulnerable to this dark act of the Goddess? How was it that I could cope at the vast cosmic level of the Goddess and failed rather miserably in my own childhood family? These rueful questions were with me, as I returned to my meditations. I felt that the "softening" had occurred, but there was something more that I needed to know from the Goddess something that was not clear to me. It was with this attitude that I approached the next chakra, *Vishuddha.*

I reflected upon the meaning of Vishuddha, "Purification." Curious that purity should be beyond "unattackable." But this was surely true. There was still something impure in my mandala, was there not? My reaction to my cousin had proven it. Here, perhaps, my further liberation would include a purification.

I looked at the Lotus: A smokey purple with sixteen petals, each one carrying a vowel in crimson, of the Sanskrit language. Quite right, I thought, purple, the royal, religious color, blend of blue and red, perhaps it is beyond the smokey Anahata with its reds! All the vowels are here in crimson, this is the center of sound, speech, and hearing. These tattvas will be resolved herein it is said. The word, the word, the pure reality of the word, which is beyond the reality of the senses!

I looked further. Within the lotus is a circular mandala, "white like the full moon." Within that is the white elephant. A great and rare purification of the animal -- the elephant has become white. I recalled a saying of a sage: at Vishuddha, one comes to the reality of the soul. Here what was started at Muladhara -- with its "root support" of the elephant and square -- comes the final transformation from the reality of everyday life (which is, in truth, illusory), to the reality of the soul. In Vishuddha we find "purification," the white elephant and the circle, more perfect forms. Grey changing to white, square to circle. Now, then, I could expect to find the reality of the soul.

Here, too, within the circular mandala of the moon was the Bija of Ambara. This reminded me that Ambara, the Ethereal region, made this Chakra a place of Akasha, of Ether, and the element herein was Ether. What was Ether, after all? I did not know. I knew only that its center was in the throat, and my throat was sore. I smiled. For my meditations always kept me close to my bodily centers, even though I did not follow the Masters exactly. I felt that the mightiest Guru, Shiva, was still with me.

I must still describe the Shiva and Shakti of the lotus. Herein, the Shiva is Sada-Shiva, the Beneficent One. He is snow white, three-eyed, five-faced, with ten beautiful arms and clothed in a tiger's skin. Here He is also "She" for He is Androgyne. In addition to His great male half on a lion seat, there is, too, "The Eternal Gauri," His other half, "the Mother of the Universe." I pondered. The unity has occurred, for here the Great God is united with His Goddess: He is white and silver, She is golden.

In addition to the Androgyne form, there is also another Shakti in the "lap" of the mandala. She is the Shakti Shakini, clad in yellow and carrying the noose, the goad, the "sign of the book" and she makes the Jnanamudra, by touching a thumb and first finger and placing them over the heart.

Such is the simple lotus. Simpler than before with only four verses describing it. Let it only be added that the Sadhaka, the meditator who attains the purification of this lotus, achieves, among other things, a vision of "the three periods" (past, present, and future), subjection of the inner senses, and becomes free from disease and sorrow. Above all, peace. Yes, that would be nice, thought I.

So, I meditated upon this Chakra. I felt the pain in my throat and fixed my eyes upon the image itself. My eyes fixed themselves upon the Shakti Shakini. I felt strangely sad, but was warmed by the goodly yellow color of Her garment. I looked ruefully at Her four arms, and ruefully understood that the noose and the goad were still very much there. I was continually goaded by my need for Nirvana, for Enlightenment, and my neck was much in the "noose." I was still very much tied to the process of the work, the yoke of the yoga. No wonder my throat was sore.

I nodded my head and saw the Goddess smile, ever so faintly. She took one of Her arms and made the Jnanamudra on my own heart, as if she already recognized that I had achieved the Anahata, and she was verifying it.

She nodded at my understanding, and showed me her other hand. There was a fluttering, for this was a beginning of the "sign of the book." Now the Shakti Shakini became very white, like light itself, and Her hand beckoned me to follow Her. My eyes did so and saw Her face go into the region which was not a place but a state. I saw clearly a lovely building, situated in a natural forest of great beauty. My eyes followed Her inside this building and I saw therein many, many books. She took down one book and nodded at me once again. At that moment, the petals of the mandala, with all its vowels, began fluttering, and I knew, too, that the whiteness and the region were of Akasha, the Ether. The petals leaped about and formed the vowels of Akasha. It was given to me to understand that the books were the records of Akasha, the library of the placeless state of Ether where all the deeds of one's past lives were kept. I realized that the Shakti Shakini kept the record of my previous lives. Each book contained the story of each of the lives. Some books were thick, some were thin. Some were gorgeous and had lush, golden bindings. Others were spare and drab. Still others were not of paper at all, but were picture books of animals or plants. There were numberless books. Not exactly numberless, for they were finite, but very many. I realized that I had lived many, many lives in many aeons, and that here were kept the records of all of those lives. The record was kept for me to see, if I wished, or for another, if he was so inclined. But there was no record keeper. We all have our own libraries, or records of Akasha, in that Ethereal place which is no place, and we have merely to go there, when we are ready, through that

Vishuddic center which lives in our own throats. For it tells us of the transmigrations of the soul.

I looked at some of the books of my previous lives. In my last one, I was a recluse philosopher in a Scandinavian land. I had pondered long and deeply upon anxiety and despair and upon the meaning of God, but I had been afraid of women and had despised them. This was partly because I was abandoned in childhood by my mother, but this was also a consequence of unredeemed karma from previous lives.

In the lifetime before that, I had been a poet in England -- a wild and romantic figure who had loved the ladies gaily and had hurt many a heart. My natural father of my present incarnation had been my son in that life, and I had left him to pursue an idealistic cause in Greece. There I died in violence. I realized that I had not done right by my son in that incarnation, nor by my natural father -- the same person -- in this incarnation, and that I must go and seek him out in England and make peace with him before I saw, too, that the Greek lady who had been a friend of my sister had also been Greek at that time, and that we had a passionate love relation. It was a true love, hence her help for me at this time.

In the previous three lives, I had been a woman, an ordinary woman living in various parts of Asia. In China, I had suffered very much, losing several children in famines and wars. Two incarnations before that, in India, were not especially notable. These lives, as shown by the thinness and drabness of the books, were ones of karmic "ordinariness" -- apparently teaching me to be prepared for the "specialness" of my past two lives.

Before those lives, I had been a temple courtesan in India, a prostitute in Greece and North Africa, a Catholic priest (austere and removed) in Germany, and variously a tradesman, farmer, wife of tradesmen and farmers in both Europe and Asia. The main tenor of my lives as they presented themselves, was a struggle between male and female, spirit and flesh, idealism and materialism, love and self-sacrifice -- all destined to lead me to my task in the present. But before I come to what my task in the present was, I must say that I saw into further books, where there were pictures -- no words. I had been, at various times, (and these had been my lives in Africa, Oceania, and America) animals, birds, insects, and plants.

These books were sad and beautiful, all at once. There was a great book of a hyena. I knew, from within, that the hyena was unjustly maligned as a scavenger, and that he is really a great figure, seeking his own game, and running only before the lion. In short, it is the lion who scavenges the game of the hyena, and not the reverse! Perhaps a scientist will note this one day.

I saw, too, my life of great anxiety as an insect. I knew that what a great Sage had said was not quite right. He had said that insects were, in reality, bits of plants and trees that had broken off and lived lives at a level between plant and animal. Well, he was not altogether wrong -- in a sense he was correct, because they do meet midway. But in another sense, he was wrong. He implied that the insects do not feel or think. That is wrong. I saw the book of my lives as an insect, and I knew that I felt and thought --not with words but at a deeper place. One life, in particular, was very painful. I had been an insect with several legs, some of which I had lost in battle, and I lay, upside down, in great pain, waiting to die. I was terrified of death and longed for it at the same time! It was a deep hell, the karma of which had come from previous lives as an insect, and the effect of which lasted down even into the present. I had a deep knowledge of death and suffering, and needed to understand it ever more deeply, no matter what form of life I embraced.

I had also been a tree, and flowers, and therein, life was good. But life took on its problematic quality only as I advanced in evolution, up the scale of life toward the higher animals and being human. I understood that being human was in no way "better" than being a cat or a flower or a spider, only "different." All was part of God. All was part of the vast evolution of God and His creation. What mattered only was to live the best life as a flower or spider or hyena or man -- which was to fulfill one's Karma. This I had done, aeon after aeon, for I was quite an old soul. But old souls are not better than young ones -- we are all part of the great Brahman, the mind of God, which is, itself, undergoing evolution. I saw that in my present life I was ordained to repair much of the damage which had emerged during previous lives. I was destined to make a big advance in my development. I saw, furthermore, that I had been full of the agony of the life of woman, full of the agony of the pain of death, full of agony at the injustice of life. Now, in this life, I was destined to achieve the union toward which my heart and mind and soul had longed for many a long kalpa -- that attainment of Nirvana, the enlightenment, which united the Gods with men.

Now I saw that the great image behind it all was the Androgyne Shiva -- the union of the Great God with the Great Goddess, Mother of the Universe, and all in one Golden-Silver form. To this great union the Universe sings.

I looked ahead to the future. The books of the future were there, too, but the pages were blank. It was as if many books were destined to be here written on this planet Earth but, as I advanced on my path, I would help write them more and more. I would more and more be responsible for what was written therein. For that is what it means to be human: we have greater share in our karma, its making and unmaking, than do the plants and insects who have less will. But I saw, too, that evolution was not just in life on this planet. There were books that hinted at other forms of being and evolution, on other planets and in other systems. These, too, stretched into the future. Time and space were annihilated for me as I glimpsed the records of Akasha spreading ever more deeply into the Ethereal regions.

My true Enlightenment was more than this glimpse of past, present and future. My true Enlightenment was that I did not really need to "know" all about my incarnations. It was enough that I was part of the divine plan, that there was growth, decay and new growth, and that we are all Gods. That is the message which I bring from my Enlightenment, that is my Vishuddha, my purification. We are all Gods, and ye are all Gods: man, animal, insect, flower, yea even stone, we are all Gods. With that realization, came Peace, which was promised by this Chakra. The Moon doth shine, the elephant glows in his whiteness, the syllables do mutter, and I know the Reality which is beyond this reality and all the realities — Shiva and Shakti are One.

VI

Ajna, the "Place of Command;" the last Chakra, since Sahasrara, the Lotus beyond it, the Sages have said, is not in the body at all. I felt Ajna, that "third eye" between the eyebrows, but I felt it as a cold in my head, and as a headache. So, when I sat down to meditate upon this highest of Chakras, I was cool as the moon, and quiet, but expectant, as well. For here, the Sages had promised, one met Vishnu, Himself.

I looked at the Lotus. Simple. White. A great round moon, with only two petals, white. No animals, not even the white elephant. A Sage had said that no animals meant that experience no longer required the animal reality. Something beyond the reality of the soul? One must wait and see.

Within the Lotus, what? First the Shakti, Hakini, white, with six faces and six arms, seated on a white lotus. She holds a rosary, a skull, a drum, a book, and makes the sign of the mudras, granting boons and dispelling fear. Above Her, in a triangle, the Shiva-Itara in His phallic form; above Him the Pranava, Om, as a flame of radiance. Above them, Manas, the mind, and above them all, in the region of the Moon, Shiva and Shakti, united.

The commentator says that one should meditate upon them all in that order. Now, for the first time, I have the deep desire to do just as the old Sages demanded, and I even wish to do the Yoni-mudra, to free the Manas, the mind, from the world outside. Does this mean that I am, at last, fully ready to submit to Shiva, to Vishnu, my Lord, as man, and as tradition says? I do not know, I go only step by step, as the Supreme Guru has instructed me. And so, I do as instructed: I put my left heel against the anus, and the right heel on the left foot. I sit erect with body and neck and head in a straight line. I take in air and hold it. I close my earholes with thumbs, close eyes with index fingers, close nostrils with middle fingers, and close mouth with the rest. I keep the air within, and meditate upon the Mantra, the Pranava, Om, and thus, realize the unity of Prana, the vitality of life force, and Manas, the mind.

Yes, I feel it. I can say, with the Yogis of old, "This is Yoga, the favorite of Yogis!" The warmth of Kundali rises within me, from the centers below to Ajna, the place of command. My Guru commands, and I obey. I meditate, as prescribed, in the right order. Let me then look upon the Shakti-Hakini.

There She is, with Her many heads and many arms. I look at the rosary, and know that they symbolize Her prayerful, orderly attitude, and I know that I, too, now have it, and I have it from Her. I look at the skull, and know that I have embraced death, my humanity and my changing, just as She has embraced Hers. I look at the drum, and know that the sound of the drum is the sound of Om, and that my step beats to It, and to no other anthem of nation, caste or class. I look at the book, and know that wisdom is contained therein, the wisdom of Manas which I must come to know. I look at the mudras, and trust that I both give and receive boons, I both feel and dispel fear.

Now I look into the eyes of my six-headed Goddess. The heads move; they rock back and forth just like the dancers of my youth. I am enchanted and charmed by the movement. But, look! The six heads, like six Chakras, blend as they move, and I see that each is just a phase of the ONE, just as the six Chakras are just a phase of the One. Now the six become one head, and I look deeply into Her eyes. What I see there is both a shock and the most natural thing in the world. For what I see is my own face and my own head and my own body. I look into the face of the Goddess and I see my own. I know that I am the Shakti, and that She is I. I look into her face and I wonder, who has the reality? Is it I who dream of the Shakti and She a figment of my mind? Ah, now I know what the Sage meant when he said that here one goes beyond the animal reality, and beyond the reality of the soul: I am a content of a dream of a Goddess, and the Goddess is a content of a dream of mine. Both are the same. No more pain and sorrow, says the commentator, and such it is. For this knowledge places me beyond myself; pain is there, suffering is there, but it never shall be the same again. Oh, Shakti, I adore you!

Now I look beyond, to the triangle above, wherein dwells the Shiva-Itara, in His phallic form. Yes, I see Him, and I see the lightning sparks which emanate from His head, like the semen from below which rises to nostrils and unites in one strange whole. It is, as they say, the Mount of Meru; it is mountain and wings, with Snake wrapped around; it is the western Caduceus of Mercury. Now, I see it, and my headache goes and my cold vanishes. But what is this lightning-like union? Is it healing alone? What is this phallic staff with snake wrapped around and flaring nostrils above? The wings above and snake below. Phallus and nares; semen and air. I cannot tell until I look above, to the great flaming candle and fire which is just above it. Now, out of the brilliant light, I see my Lord. I finally see, in naked flesh, my Supreme Guru who has guided me throughout my yoga, my meditation and my trials. Oh, Lord Shiva, I see you and I know! I know that Your light is blinding but true: for you are eagle and snake, wings and body, semen and air, spirit and flesh. And I know, too, what it means that You are Vishnu, the Preserver, and Shiva, the Destroyer, for behind it is Brahman, the Creator. The Two are One, and the Three are One. Oh, my Lord Vishnu, I am ravished by you as Krishna, mighty singer. Come to me, for I am your Shakti! I am enflamed, enveloped and enraptured, for I know, above and below, and am Queen of the three worlds!

But I will not dwell in this ecstasy, oh, my Lord. For my embrace with You and Your radiance enables me to ascend to that Great eye of Ishvara, the Supreme God who is beyond all creation and dissolution and who is one and the same with Your Trinity of Vishnu, Shiva, and Brahman. I know from your embrace that Your three-fold form is the same as the One, and exists only as You descend into Being. Shine, now, your light of Manas upon me, and enlighten my mind. Show me the pure light of Buddhi.

With my prayer and self-abnegation, I waited a long time, perhaps several hours. And then, in the dim light, I saw a wizened old man. He was a combination of Gandhi, a Sage I once met, and an old monkey. He held up first a magnifying glass, then a telescope. "One eye has each, to make the small big and the distant near. But the one eye of wisdom has to see the 'smaller than small, bigger than big' and that, of course, is Purusha, the Atman, the Self."

This is what the little old man said to me, and then he went on: "Wisdom is not great bundles of facts, nor big words which hide their meaning. Wisdom is Consciousness: to see with the inner eye, the eye of the mind. And that is Ishvara, a creative consciousness. Do you know why it is creative? Because it is to be found only in Ajna. The Shakti here loves to eat of the marrow of the bones. Creative consciousness is the power of the mind along with the marrow of the bones; wings and snake, semen and air. Do you remember your incarnation as a hyena? Yes. Well, then, you know that hyenas have the strongest jaws of all animals, stronger even than the lion. For they can chew the marrow and digest the deepest inner contents. And that is what wisdom is: to know and sense in the bones; to chew one's experience down to the depths of the marrow. If one, then, also sees with the inner eye, then that is all, that is what it is: creative consciousness of Ishvara.

"One must get to Ajna to see it. Kundalini Yoga is not the only way. Many do it in other ways. Look in the bazaars. Look at men. Many have achieved it. Many have gone from Muladhara through Anahata. But in Ajna, you must know, one must rise and see, as well as live and experience." The old man went on speaking:

"Brahma, Vishnu and Shiva are the names for functions of the one Universal consciousness operating in ourselves. Yoga is our means of transforming the lower into the higher forms of this same consciousness. In this, Shiva and Shakti serve you, and you serve Shiva-Shakti.

"But what are Shiva and Shakti? All that is manifest is Power, and that is Shakti. Shakti, the Power, is Mind, Life, and Matter. But there is no Power without a Power-holder. And what is that Power-holder? It is none other than Shiva. Power is Shakti, the Great Mother of the Universe; the Form is Shiva. Together they are Consciousness (Mind), Being (Life), and Bliss (Matter). 'Isness' is the ultimate reality, beyond all form and power, which is what these three connote. They become particular, and thus limited, in the many. The One is the Isness, the Many is the Isness become manifest. Do you understand?"

I thought I understood and I nodded. The old man continued. "I am not so sure. Maya. Your name. Your namesake. Maya is not illusion, any more than you are illusion. In the words of the Shakta Sadhaka Kamalakanta, Maya is the Form of the Formless. You, Maya, are the living reailty of the Formless taking Form. And you, and all human beings, are the Power-holders. All is real: Changeless and Changeful, Activity and Rest, Being and Becoming. Man, in his Mind and Body, is the manifestation of Shiva and Shakti, Power and Power-holder. The object of his worship and his Yoga is to raise this Power to its perfect expression, to raise his own particular and limited experience to the unlimited and whole, and thus to Perfect Bliss. But his yoga is also to bring the Whole and unlimited into the particular, so that the One can become the Many, and evolve.

"Any why must it evolve? Because that is the nature of its opposites. Creation and dissolution, activity and rest. World after World, and Kalpa after Kalpa. All is energy, the Shiva of static energy, the Shakti of kinetic energy. All is potential that must come into being.

"The particular power whereby the dualistic world is brought into being is Maya-Shakti, which is both a veiling and projecting. Consciousness veils itself to itself and projects from the store of its previous experiences. This projection is Samskara, the world in which it suffers and enjoys. The universe is thus the creative imagination of the Supreme World-Thinker, Ishvara. That is why you are both dream and dreamer, Maya. Thus the Self knows and loves the Self."

At that point, I needed to pause and understand what this old man was telling me. If I understood rightly it was none other than that Karma was the effect of previous experiences. My Karma was the result of previous experiences which projected my life further into the world. That is the witch of Shakti. She veils and projects, and that is my life. It is Maya, and illusion, but the true reality as well. Little by little I would eat up my Karma by absorbing the marrow in my bones. I would integrate all my experiences and projections, and be projected no more. But I was in no hurry. There were many lives for that. And eternity as well, for more lives and beings and more consciousness.

I suddenly grew weary with the lives and beings and consciousness. I felt I wanted to flee from the Samskara of suffering. I wanted Nirvandva, freedom from life and the opposites. My Guru spoke again:

"Maya, you can flee whenever you wish. There is the bliss of sleep, dreamless and total. That is a Nirvandva. There is the fleeing to the dream, in which the subtle body lives. And then there is your gross body, with all its states and degrees of differentiation. But the best fleeing is Yoga, the magic when you are with the inner eye of manas. It is the yoke which brings freedom.

"There is no need to throw one's eyes into the heavens to find God. He is within. Whatever of Mind or Matter exists in the universe exists in some form or manner in the human body. As stated in the Vishvasara Tantra: 'What is here is there. What is not here is nowhere.'"

I thought about what the Guru said. Yes, man is the microcosm of the great macrocosm. The body is matter and mind is the consciousness of that same matter. Together they live in life. I understood the magic. But I missed the bliss.

Then I felt myself rising, even beyond the great Eye of the Guru. I was gently rising above the wisdom of consciousness. I rose to the place where Shiva and Shakti were in union. I watched them in Maithuna. They were in sexual union and I felt a thrill go through me. I knew that there was, indeed, something higher than Consciousness, higher even than what the Guru had told me. Because higher than consciousness was the Bliss of

Love and of Union. Then I saw my vision. I saw that Shiva and Shakti were two seeds in a gram. The sheath of this gram, this chick pea, was Maya, the world as appearance. And the whole, made One. I was that chick pea contained in the Great Maya. But I, little Maya, contained the seeds of Shiva and Shakti. I felt them embraced within me, and I felt the thrill of their perpetual union. I knew that when they were united there was the bliss of Nirvandva, and when they parted there was the bliss of creation. With Creation, came Form . . . with Brahma, comes Vishnu and Shiva. Shakti takes form in Shiva. I cannot say more. I feel it in the marrow of my bones, and I thrill.

At that moment, my own personal, particular Kundalini rose and merged with the great Kundali. The power of the Shakti rose beyond Ajna, and I felt it at the top of my head, and round my scalp like a thousand vibrating petals, each with a thrill of wonder. It went above the head, like a halo. I knew that the Chakras were all pierced and now there was *Sahasrara.*

There was the glimpse of the Void, the Shunya which is secret and subtle like the ten millionth part of the end of the hair. All opposites were united, and there was no division. But I could not stay there. The Kundalini did not stay in the Sahasrara, but immediately began to descend, down into Ajna, back into Vishuddha, and all the way down through wonderful Anahata, Manipura, Svadhisthana, to the root support of Muladhara. I could not keep Kundalini there, in Sahasrara, and I knew that I would need many, many transformations before Kundalini would permanently stay there. Only then would I achieve final Liberation, true Mukti. Only then will the union of Sada-Shiva and Chit be complete. But I did not mourn. And I do not mourn. I celebrate Shiva-Shakti. I know that all centers are needed. I know Shiva-Shakti are present in every human act. I celebrate every act as a ritual and a worship. I glory in the Muladhara as much as the great Anahata or Ajna. For the body is Shakti. Its needs are Shakti's needs. When I take pleasure, Shakti enjoys through me. The Spirit is Shiva, and it creates form. Shiva and Shakti are one. I embrace my humanity and my limitation, for the process is the goal.

With that, I came down from my cabin in the mountains. I celebrated my family, for I had been gone for most of three years. I went to visit my natural father in England and to give and receive blessings. I lived, for I knew that I had achieved Enlightenment. I knew that each Enlightenment would be more than the last, and that each act of the Yoga of Kundalini, whether alone in the mountains or in the Karma of Life would be greater than the last, but also the same as before, for all was one.

But before I could fully take up my life again, I slept and awakened here.

So, my friends, I find myself here among you. I see the Great Tree of which you speak. I see thereon the many symbols of my own voyage and dhyana. The Tree itself is Mount Meru and the Snake doth wrap around it. I can see all your wanderings therein. My friends, we are here together, why, I know not, but I embrace you!

PART THREE

ASPECTS OF
HINDUISM AND JUNGIAN PSYCHOLOGY
by Arwind U. Vasavada

With Comments by J. Marvin Spiegelman

Yogic Basis of Psychoanalysis — 1941

The Process of Individuation and Self-Realisation—
    A Comparison — 1957

Alchemy and Catatonic Depression — 1960

A Reflection on Jung's Autobiography — 1964

Philosophical Roots of the Psychotherapies of the West — 1965

The Unconscious and the Myth of the Divine Mother — 1971

Dr. Jung, a Psychologist or a Guru? — 1971

Fee-Less Practice and "Soul Work" — 1980

Meeting Jung — 1986

YOGIC BASIS OF PSYCHO-ANALYSIS (1941)*

by

Shri Arwind U. Vasavada, M.A.

This paper attempts to find justification of the Psycho-analytic method of cure in the Yoga philosophy.

The two knowledges, though differing in aim -- one out for attaining liberation and the other for the harmonization of human personality -- have certain identities. On the basis of these identifications alone, there is the justification of bringing the two systems together.

On deeper insight, it might seem that Psycho-analysis is a special application of Yoga in a special case. Or, in other words, we might express that Psycho-analysis becoming self-consciousness is Yoga.

Psycho-analysis, as we have said, aims at harmonizing the personality of the abnormal so that his life in society may run smoothly. An abnormality may be understood as undue violence of some of our instincts, which bring a sort of dissociation within the personality. The ego is unable to bring about a synthesis between the world of desire and reality. Different types of abnormalities are nothing but different mechanisms through which our instinctual desires manifest in our personality. The distance of the gap between the two worlds depends upon the intensity of violence of instincts. Disguised manifestations of instincts stand as the other or not-self, as an opponent before the ego.

Psycho-analysis by its method brings the realization to the patient that the other was his own voluntary creation. This knowledge abates the undue violence of the instinct as the opposing force. This knowledge with the re-education of the personality cures the patient.

Yoga considers the whole life of man as an abnormality -- a false identification of self with not-self. The process of world manifestation is due to this confusion between the *Purusha* (Self) and the *Prakriti* (Nature). From another angle, it is a sort of dissociation of self from the pure liberated self. The ego which arises out of the false identification with the *karmas*, stands as an other to the Pure, Ideal, Liberated self. The ideal of personality in Yoga is God Who is *Ishvara* (God), *Sadaiva Mukta* (Ever

113

Liberated), *Sadaiva Ishvara* (Ever, the Lord),[1] which one has to achieve by means of Yoga practices. In Psycho-analysis, the ideal is the full-fledged, socially harmonized personality.

In both, the ideal is achieved by way of detaching oneself from the false identifications. The concept of *Vairagya* (Detachment) is the very basis of the cure even in Psycho-analysis, which is overlooked by some expounders.

Every psycho-analyst believes that the cure consists in the re-education of the personality. Knowledge of the incidents connected with the repression of instinct is only a means to abate the violence of the instinct. It cannot remove the attachment: this can only be brought by the education of the mind, which consists in *Vairagya* (Detachment). Even a normal man feels the evils of some of his bad tendencies; he knows them fully, yet they are not removed thereby. It is knowledge through *Vairagya* (Detachment) that will eradicate them.

Thus, the basic tenet of psycho-analysis has its justification in the concept of *Vairagya* (Detachment).

False identification of *Purusha* (Self) with *Prakriti* (Nature) is, according to Yoga, the cause of this world and the individual's identification with the not-self. Identification produces an outward-going activity in the *Prakriti* (Nature). *Samsara* is thus the outward manifestation of the Unmanifest, *Avyakta* (Unmanifest). The check of this activity, therefore, is the means of liberation in Yoga. In the individual the outward-going *citta* is to be checked and detained by *Nirodha* or inwardization. In other words, a habit of continued detachment and dissociation is enjoined there. If I remain a spectator of my mental ocean, I do not plunge in it and identify with it. Such a continued habit brings absolute separation of *Purusha* (Self) and *Prakriti* (Nature), which is liberation.

It is not very easy to be the spectator of one's own self. It is a process towards abstraction, which is against our common nature. There is a definite meethod laid down by the Yoga philosophy which progressively takes one to this stage. One is required to practise the *Astangas*. They are: *Yama, Niyama, Asana, Pranayama, Pratyahara, Dharana, Dhyana,* and *Samadhi.*[2] We shall discuss the nature of only four Angas, viz. *Asana, Pranayama, Dharana,* and *Dhyana,* these alone being relevant to our purpose.

The main purpose of *Asana* is to make us the least conscious of our bodily processes.[3] Our object is to arrive at the stage of a spectator of our *vrttis,* which is possible only if we can rise above our body and its attachments. Any easy posture, if practised regularly, is sufficient to do this. Even after this, we are conscious of our subtle breathing process. *Pranayama,* therefore, helps us further by its gradual control over our breathing process.[4] The progress is now to be made towards concentration. Any object may be chosen for concentration; one may begin with a gross external object and may progressively develop to concentrate upon one subtle idea or image. The process of *Dharana*, thus, consists in the selection of the object of concentration.[5] While *Dhyana* means concentration or absorption of mind in that chosen object.[6] Such a continued practice leads to objectless concentration or abstraction. At this stage, mind becomes so detached and master of itself that it can look at its own inner working with ease as a dispassionate spectator.

Let us now see, how psycho-analysis employs this procedure unconsciously. It will be in the fitness of things to describe causes of abnormalities.

Psycho-analytical findings reveal that *do's* and *dont's* of ignorant parents and their careless nurture cause the child-mind to fix itself on one of the partial manifestations of the sex instinct. As for example, fixation may occur in oral or anal zone or in some other partial manifestations. This inhibits the normal growth of the sex-instinct. Therefore, at the climatic periods, there is a conflict between mind and body, as they have not developed together. The mind has fixated at the lower manifestations of sex instinct, while the body has advanced further. This conflict weakens the ego, causing regression and neurosis.

The psycho-analytic method aims at curing the neurotic by excavating his memory through word-association, and leading him to recall the originating causal incidents. At each step, the excavated material is interpreted, which, if correct, leads to further recall until the last knot is solved by proper interpretations.

The practical aspect of the cure consists in asking the patient to recline easily on a sofa or an arm-chair, so as to make him least bodily conscious. He is then asked to concentrate upon a part of his dream or the incident of the outbreak of neurosis; after that he is to relate all the ideas arising in his mind in associations with the object of concentration. He thus gradually becomes the impartial spectator of his inner working. A practised analyst knows how many sittings it takes for a patient to come to this stage. In this manner, the patient, under the guidance of the doctor, unconsciously practises some of the *angas* of Yoga. *Pranayama* is altogether overlooked by these expounders of science.

It will not be too much to say that if *pranayama* is included in it, it will expedite the process of cure.

It is evident that one who gives others insight into the subtle workings of their minds, should have thorough knowledge of his own self. Psycho-analysis has, therefore, rightly emphasised the need of the analyst being analysed first. The analyst must be free from every conflict of passions in his mind. He must be a fully synthesised personality. In comparison with Yoga, a Guru -- a Yogi -- holds the same position in relation to his disciple. This need is much more realised in the final stages of cure of a patient than in the beginning. Analysis begins with implicit confidence of a patient in the doctor. Confidence comes out of reverence for the doctor. In the final stages of cure, the patient develops a peculiar kind of relation with the doctor, which varies with the type of abnormality from which he suffers. It is here that the mettle of the doctor is tested. The patient in freeing himself from the complexes, deeply attaches himself to the doctor. The doctor has to handle him very carefully at this stage. It is from here that the process of *re-education* of mind begins. This process of re-education will be fruitful or otherwise, in so far as the doctor is a fully synthesised personality or not. A slight mistake in this stage may worsen the whole situation; it might disorganise the whole personality of the patient. In Yoga practice, a *sad-guru* is the proper person to guide a disciple in the higher path of liberation. He, having removed his *samskaras*, knows full well the working of the various instincts and has the power to see into the inner working of others; therefore he will smoothen the course of liberation of the disciple.

Some broad suggestions regarding developing a theory of
Indian psycho-analysis.

The exact nature of the Unconscious is still a matter of controversy among the scientists. Freud emphasises wholly on the violence and repression of sex-instinct, while Adler and Jung do so on Egoism and Love for life or *Elan vital* respectively. In this connection the *Yoga Sutras* have a better suggestion to give. We are asked to believe that the false identification of self with not-self is due to five *klesas* viz. *Avidya, Asmita, Raga, Dvesa,* and *Abhini Vesa*.[7] Each one of these may be taken as layers of Unconscious, the lowest being *Abhini Vesa* or love for life and the deepest *Avidya*. Moreover, it is repository of our *samskaras* or the tendencies of so many lives we have lived.

This and other reasons to be shown below should warn the psycho-analyst against using the Western method of cure and interpretation of the complexes especially in treating Indian patients.

If the phylogenetic origin of the Unconscious is granted, we should believe that our Unconscious will be different from that of the Westerners, and consequently our dream symbolizations and mannerisms of abnormal diseases will greatly differ. New interpretation through new symbols is an absolute necessity with Indian patients. It is possible to discover the symbols by the study of our mythology embodied in the *Puranas*.

It may be objected that human nature being the same everywhere, mental mechanisms of two nationalities need not differ. We do not question this proposition but maintain that a different conclusion is derived from the same premise. Nature of thinking -- Logic -- is alike in human nature, yet there are different languages. Human nature is identical, but its manifestations need not be the same in the different parts of the world. Manifestations depend a great deal upon a nation's social and religious traditions.

It may be more concretely expressed thus. Our philosophic and religious tradition is marked by the concept of *Vairagya* (Detachment) and *Tyaga* (Renunciation). From times immemorial, our Unconscious has imbibed these ideas. The present era being that of transition due to the confluence of two cultures -- Eastern and Western -- it is possible that most of our complexes may be due to *Asmita, Raga* and *Abhini Vesa*. An interpretation of our complexes from the Western point of view would harm and hinder rather than improve the condition of a patient.

Secondly, it is necessary to clear the misunderstanding about the idea of free expression of instincts. No free expression of any instinct can remove its violence. It is not meant thereby that the instinctual needs are to be repressed. Repression consists in ignoring the existence of the desire and reveal the weakness of the personality. It is truly a flight from the reality. But not to repress is not identical with free expression: Identity will be clearly to misunderstand the whole thing. There is a mediate way possible, shown by *Yoga*, and which is the very basis of it. It says, "Be the spectator of your passions, and do not give vent to them, but look upon them dispassionately." To remain a spectator is not to express them. This is possible since it has some higher and sublime ideal before us to hold on.

We can glean some mental mechanisms and methods of detachment from desires in the writing of Shri Meher Baba.

He compares gathering of *samskaras* into the Unconscious with the winding of a string around a stick.[8]

Firstly, cessation of *samskaras* is made possible by gradually freeing ourselves from the bodily needs through fasting and solitude.

Secondly, the *samskaras* can be allowed to be worn out by withholding their expression into action. It is like a wound string which wears out on the stick due to lack of use.

Third process is called unwinding of *samskaras* as we might unwind the string from the stick. It consists in "annulling the past *samskaras* by mentally reversing the process which leads to their formation." This process is exactly like one used in psycho-analytic method. Penance and self-humiliation can bring out the same process of unwinding.

Fourthly, the energy of the *samskaras* can be diverted and sublimated, thus the *samskaras* "get dispersed and leave and have a tendency to disappear."

Lastly, the final wiping out of *samskaras* can be brought by the grace of a perfect Master, by implicit self-surrender to Him.

While discussing these processes, Shri Meher Baba rightly says, "they represent the different principles characterising the psychic processes which take place while *samskaras* are being removed."[9]

We see that there is more than one method of freeing ourself from the thraldom of our passions.

The above suggestions may prove fruitful in developing an Indian theory of psycho-analysis. The Indian psycho-analyst should experiment upon the patient from such an angle; with the study of *Yoga* and mythology, he should find out a new theory of psycho-analysis.

* Read in the Psychology Section of the Indian Science Congress Session, Benares, 1941.

1. *Yoga Sutra*, I. 24.

2. *Yoga Sutra*, II. 29.

3. *Yoga Sutra*, II. 46.

4. *Yoga Sutra*, II. 52. and I. 34.

5. *Yoga Sutra*, III. 1.

6. *Yoga Sutra*, III. 2.

7. *Yoga Sutra*, II. 3.

8. *Meher Baba Journal*, April 1939: "Shri Meher Baba on the Removal of Samskaras" (Part I.)

9. *Ibid.*, p. 3.

COMMENTS

by

J. Marvin Spiegelman

This is the first psychological paper of Dr. Vasavada, written half-way between the receipt of his Master's degree and his Doctorate. It is both naive and original, as he himself commented recently, when he wrote that the paper "contains a confused state of thought seeds which become differentiated later." What is particularly original is the comparison of the "detachment" sought from the turbulence of the psyche in both psychoanalysis and yoga. What is naive is the perception of the role of the guru and the psychoanalyst. Whereas the former makes use, so to speak, of the transference, the latter aims at its ultimate resolution. But Dr. Vasavada was some time away from undergoing his own future analysis at this point. The article, all the same, is a refreshing comparison. One could only wish that the two fields really did share a common spiritual aim!

THE PROCESS OF INDIVIDUATION AND SELF-REALISATION
A COMPARISON

by

Arwind Vasavada, D. Litt.

An attempt is made in this talk to compare the process of individuation according to the Analytical psychology of C.G. Jung with the Indian way of self-realisation.

It might be considered presumptuous to compare the age-old eastern tradition with a new scientific approach from the West. But in the matters of Spirit there is nothing new nor old. Spirit reveals itself to a sincere and devoted heart as much as to keen scientific inquiry.

The scientific approach of Dr. Jung and the traditional way of India agree on the essential and fundamental point that the knowledge of the Self and its realisation is the highest value and supreme satisfaction to the seeker.

> ... So always the inner experience of individuation has been appreciated as the most valuable and important thing in life. It is the only thing that brings any lasting satisfaction to a man. Power, glory, wealth, mean nothing in comparison. These things are external and futile. The really important things are within. It is more important to me that I am happy, than that I have the external reason for happiness. Rich people should be happy but often they are not, they are bored to death; therefore, it is ever so much better for man to work to produce an inner condition that gives him an inner happiness. Experience shows that there are certain psychological conditions in which man gets eternal results. They have something of the quality of eternity, of timelessness, they have the quality of reaching beyond man. They have a divine quality and yield all that satisfaction which man-made things do not. (*Dream seminar.* Vol. I, p. 210., Unpublished works of C. G. Jung.)

The Indian way is religious and dogmatic in the sense that it takes for granted on authority that experience of the Self is the reality; its realisation is the *summum bonum* of one's life. Moreover, the path of realisation is almost marked out for everyone with freedom for individual variation. In this matter a *Sadhaka* is a recipient from the *guru*.

120

It is different with Analytical Psychology. Dr. Jung started with no tradition, since such a tradition is almost lost to the West. His way is a search into the unknown claiming no finality. We, in India, face similar situations with our young men.

> These revelations happened to those people; they grew out of them just as the apple grows from the tree. For us, they give great satisfaction to the intellect, but for uniting the pairs of opposites they serve nothing. Suppose a patient comes to us with a great conflict and I say to him, "Read the Tao Te King," or "throw your burden on Christ." It is splendid advice, but what does it mean to the patient in helping his conflict? Nothing. To be sure, the thing for which Christ stands does for Catholics and partly for Protestants, but it does not work for everybody, and nearly all my patients are people for whom the traditional symbols do not work. So our way has to be one where the creative character is present, where there is a process of growth which has the quality of revelation. Analysis should release an experience that grips us, or falls upon us from above, an experience that has substance and body such as those things occurred to the ancients. If I were going to symbolise it, I would choose the *annunciation*.
>
> *Seminar 1925. p. 110 (Unpublished works of C.G. Jung)*

This brings about a basic difference in the understanding of self-realisation. With us, self-realisation comes to be accepted as a metaphysical concept and sought as the goal of life, an ideal to be striven for. It is understood and accepted as the ideal of a perfect personality which one has to emulate. Individuation is not the goal in this sense. It is a natural process, a sort of fate which leads some to live up to what they can become.

> It is in first place a purely natural process, which may in some cases pursue its course without the knowledge or assistance of the individual, and can sometimes forcibly accomplish itself in the face of opposition.
>
> **C.G. Jung,** *Two Essays on Analytical Psychology. p. 108*

It can be expressed only negatively. It does not mean conforming to any imagined ideal or a goal, nor is it living up to one's natural instinctual propensities. An individuated person is not against collective morality, but is, rather, a unique expression of it. In some way, however, he is a revolutionary.

> Individuation, on the other hand, aims at a living co-operation of all factors. But since the universal factors always appear only in individual form, a full consideration of them will also produce an individual effect, and one which cannot be surpassed by anything else, least of all by individualism. *Ibid. 172*

> Individuation means becoming a single, homogeneous being, and, in so far

as "individuality" embraces our innermost, last, and incomparable uniqueness, it also implies becoming one's own self. We could therefore translate individuation as "coming to selfhood" or "Self-realisation." *Ibid. p. 171*

It is an amoral concept; nothing concrete and definite can be said about it, since what satisfies one, need not satisfy the other. To put it in Indian terms, an individuated personality is self-distinguished (*Svalaksana*). As against perfection, Dr. Jung finds completeness a more correct description of the process of individuation.

The process of individuation is founded on the instinctive urge of every living creature to reach its own totality and fulfillment -- the trend of nature in this respect is more towards completion than perfection.
E.T.H. Lectures. 1940-41. p. 4. (Unpublished works of C.G. Jung.)

Each stage of development brings about the completion of what is wanted in the situation. Thus, individuation is an unending process during the lifetime. Clinical observation has shown that each conflict solved or transcended brings wider and heightened consciousness but never the end of the play of opposites.

It appears from the above as if the ideal of the self-realised person is a moral concept when equated with a perfect personality. It must be pointed out that it is not a moral concept although moral considerations are important in the attainment of self-realisation. This requirement is considered equally important by Jung, too. If one reads the description of such a personality according to Indian tradition it will be evident that both the Jungian and Indian standpoints agree. A perfect personality or a realised person is a balanced person. He is inwardly ever in touch with the self and outwardly, in behavior, he remains undisturbed, calm and tranquil amidst the play of opposites. He does not get entangled in the play of opposites. This description of a perfect personality, to my mind, does not conflict with what Jung has in mind. Jung, however, has never stated very clearly about this stage of realisation. He has more often concerned himself with the process itself and has left for each one to experience the result of the journey.

The Indian tradition calls it perfection; it is the *Achyuta pada*, from where a fall is inconceivable. It believes that such a stage can be reached in this lifetime. A *Jivan Mukta* transcends once and for all time the dualities of life. A scientifically-minded Jungian argues on the ground of his own experience and his analysands that the contents of the unconscious do not seem possible to be exhausted and in the present state of their knowledge it seems absurd to believe that they can be exhausted. Such a state would mean the end of life since life is based on the tensions of opposites.

The Indian approach to self-realisation is through the study and understanding of conscious problems, while the Jungian way developed through the study of conscious and unconscious, in which the techniques to deal with unconscious material has come to be of immense importance.

The situation between analyst and analysand is human, it is some neurotic trouble which brings the analysand to the doctor. Only at a later stage, through transference, may an archetypal relation develop between them. The deeper problems of spirit may never be discussed if the analysis does not demand it. It is true, however, that Jungian analysis aims to make the analysand realise the inner symbolic meaning of all conflicts confronting him. It attempts to take the problem to a higher level through the transcendent function.

A guru does not claim to deal with other than the spiritual problems of the seeker. Right from the start, it is an archetypal situation between guru and disciple, in so far as the guru is meant to be accepted as a super-person who is fit to bestow grace and to lead the disciple out of the dualities and tensions of life. The seeker definitely seeks the highest with a guru. Thus, there is a conscious acceptance of a mana-personality or the wise old man in the person of the guru; this, however, is a matter of unconscious projection on the analyst in an analytical situation.

The guru is aware of this projection. He neither rejects it nor accepts it. He knows full well, as it may be said in a Jungian way, that they are both encompassed by the archetype of the Guru. Becoming aware of it, he transfers this projection on to the impersonal *Adi Guru* -- the original Guru.

The guru, on the basis of his own experience and that of scriptures, makes the seeker conscious of his false attachments to not-self and makes him think through these problems with an aim to give him the foretaste of the indefinable God-Experience. The Guru is an embodiment of peace, bliss and the abounding joy of *Brahman*, pure consciousness. He tries to lift the seeker out of his attachments by means of his selfless love and wisdom. He will actively interfere in case a disciple is passing through a critical stage. He exorts, warns and does not wait for the indication of the unconscious of the analysand to help the disciple cross a stage or overcome an obstacle. There is definiteness and surety with which a guru deals with the seeker. The seeker, however, may be halting and hesitating and not able to follow the guru. The seeker has lost his identity, he is caught up in the "Ten thousand things of the world" because he understands and believes that he is his body. He is caught up by his ideals and imaginations, his thoughts and emotions, because he believes he is his mind. Man, in waking up from the deep sleep of childhood existence and in developing his ego, has fallen into identification with mind functions. He is identified with things and persons of the world through his body. It becomes the task of a guru to help him awaken from his slumber to the awakened state, the state of enlightenment. He is taught to separate the awareness or consciousness from things and psychological functions. The seeker has to realise whether he is his body or he is aware of his body as he is aware of any other object in the outer world. He has to realise whether he is aware of thoughts, emotions and other functions or he is the thoughts and emotions. This realisation is to go hand in hand by living up to the realisation. This is cutting the bondage of false attachments. This is the process of getting into a deconditioned state, as contrasted with a conditioned one.

The seeker, becoming aware of his body and through it his relation to things and persons is different from his previous simple awareness or consciousness. This is comparable to the analysand becoming more aware of his persona and disidentifying with it in Jungian terms.

In the second stage, he becomes aware of his psychological functions and their processes. This is also different from his previous consciousness, for now the seeker learns to notice the subtle unconscious working of the mind behind all his conscious activities and the play of opposites. This can be compared to dealing with the problems of the personal and collective unconscious, that of *anima* and *animus* in Jungian terms.

The fullest realisation by the seeker, that he is neither his body nor his mind but a witness of whatever is happening to him, is a fiery ordeal in so far as it cuts at the root of all attachments to his outer and inner world as he had known it earlier and had learnt to relate to it so far. He experiences a state of complete disorientation. This may be compared to the "Night Sea Journey" in the Jungian way.

On the basis of an understanding of the four stages of consciousness, from the personal experience of having gone through them, the guru stands by the seeker with all his abounding love and care in this period of darkness. His own solidity and his constant reminder to the disciple of the vision he gave him before, sustains the seeker in this dark period. The guru also makes full use of the rich tradition of mystical experience among sages, etc., to help the seeker go through this fire of agony. It is because of the care of the disciple that the guru is called "mother" in our tradition.

The analytic situation is different in this respect. It is a human situation, the analyst does not claim any perfection nor does he aim to lead the analysand to any preconceived goal. The analyst, through his experience, and with the cooperation of the analysand, tries to help him to understand his problem and find a solution. In all this process, understanding of the conscious and the unconscious reactions are the guide for the solution of the problem. The analysis, therefore, goes step by step, and both analyst and analysand cooperate with each other and keenly watch the indications from the unconscious for the possible solution of the conflict of the moment. Only if the analysand is prepared and the unconscious indicates, the analysis can proceed further into deeper levels. The analysis may come to an end at any stage if the analysand is not prepared. There is no active interference from the side of the analyst. Even in the case of interpretation of the unconscious material, the analyst hints at possible interpretations, but leaves it to the analysand to make his own decisions. The aim, therefore, is that of developing greater consciousness on the part of the analysand.

Archetypal situations can now set in, if the analysis proceeds further. The unconscious begins to present archetypal figures, especially that of the wise old man and its opposite in the person of the analyst. The Jungian analyst, on the basis of his experience, seeks to resolve this kind of transference as soon as possible by not accepting such projections on him. He considers such a type of situation as very critical and frought with dangers for both the analyst and the analysand if not properly handled.

In understanding the dangers of this situation, eastern and western traditions agree. Personalities of both guru and disciple can be wrecked at this stage, a stalemate in the progress of both may come about or the disciple may break into schizophrenia. The difference is, however, that in the Indian way the archetypal situation is consciously accepted by the guru and he is not hasty to overthrow the projection of the disciple.

As in the Indian way, Jungian analysis automatically leads to the experience of the void or what is called the *Night sea journey* if the situation naturally grows into it. Leading the analysand to his experience is identical, in principle, with our tradition. All interpretation of the unconscious material during the course of analysis tends to exemplify the rule that whosoever tries to live by accepting one pole of the opposite is ever thrown to the other. The analysand comes to realise this after a bitter struggle of being kicked from one pole to the other. This brings about, from the unconscious, what is known as the "transcendent function." This appears in the form of symbols of union of opposites which make for a solution of the problem. Going through this period of darkness, or the *Night sea journey*, is a characteristic experience of Jungian analysis. It is a terrible situation for both the analyst and the analysand, since both are affected by the situation. They have to keep their eyes open to the meaning of the symbols that emerge from the unconscious and read out the solution. Correct interpretation and patience alone is the guide in this difficult period. Since a Jungian analyst does not accept any preconceived goal to be sought, but tries to understand whatever the unconscious hints at in the symbolic material, it can be a very trying situation for the analysand, at least for an Indian who believes in a goal and in the evanescence of all mental phenomena ultimately. He would miss all that support which he gets in a similar situation from a guru. He will also feel the interpretation of dreams, etc. to be hesitant and halting since they are all broad hypotheses.

At this stage the greatest difference comes to be seen in the two approaches. Jungian analysis, being a scientific approach, starting without any preconceptions, wishes to know in each case what the unconscious wants to hint at for the solution of the problem. It has reason to believe, on the ground of analytical experience, that different solutions are possible in different cases. It wishes to know and study the unique manifestation of the unconscious in each case in its concreteness and detail. The Indian way, on the basis of its long tradition and because of the personality of the guru, goes more definitely and with surety but it is not interested in the concrete details of the solution. It is left to the disciple to find it. The guru is not concerned with giving any concrete help but with giving broad hints and the invaluable strength of his personal realisation.

Another point that might strike him is the occupation of the Jungian analyst with the images and symbols of the unconscious. The guru is trained to see and go beyond all images and symbols. It should, however, be remarked that though the Jungian analyst occupies himself with images and symbols, it is always done as a means of incorporating the inner meanings of these images at all levels.

It should be said, in fairness, that both methods can be dangerous if not properly conducted. The halting and hypothetical procedure of the Jungian analyst can be as devastating as the sure and resolute way of the guru. The former can do so by missing the correct interpretation or by over-assimilation in the transference situation. The latter may miss the present need of development because his eyes are fixed on the ultimate; he fails to recognise that the spirit creates itself through each one of us at every moment. Dangers are thus possible in both ways, one may overemphasize the expression and the other may underestimate it.

The above comparison brings out one important question for discussion, the ideal of perfection vs. completion.

Our tradition believes that complete freedom from the bondage of Maya is achievable in one's life time, i.e. *Nirvandva* is an achievable goal. Metaphysically, it is argued that Brahman is pure consciousness, simple and partless; ego-consciousness presupposes the reality of such pure, partless consciousness. Differenceless consciousness is considered to be the highest achievement; ego-consciousness is a state of bondage. Since it is a mystical experience, one who has reached this stage can alone verify whether it is a state of complete freedom from the dualities of life. For us, it is a matter of faith and we are prepared to accept this on the authority of our scriptures and the strength of a guru.

A scientist -- or a man uprooted in his tradition -- is a skeptic and will only accept that which stands the test of his experience. The analytical experience very clearly shows how, through the transcendent function, one gets over his conflicts and reaches a wider horizon.

> In the meantime I had learned to see that the greatest and most fundamental problems of life are fundamentally insoluble. They must be so, because they express the necessary polarity inherent in every self-regulating system. They can never be solved, but only outgrown.
> **C.G. Jung and R. Wilhelm,** *The Secret of the Golden Flower.* **p. 89**

> This "outgrowing" as I called it previously, revealed itself on further experience to be raising of the level of consciousness. *Ibid. p. 88*

So far, however, complete freedom from life's tensions has not been seen, nor experienced.

> Personality as a complete realisation of the fullness of our being is an unattainable ideal. But unattainability is no counter-argument against an ideal, for ideals are only sign posts, never goals.
> **C.G. Jung,** *The Integration of Personality.* **p. 287**

The mystical experience is short-lived. Man, is, afterwards, left alone to bear the burden of his suffering in life and to hold onto it with his best effort.

On the ground of experience, a Jungian argues that life is possible only through the tensions of opposites. Complete assimilation of the unconscious does not seem possible nor does it stand to the logic of life.

This controversy cannot be solved on the level of arguments, it seems to me. It is a matter of personal experience and one who has it can alone give the final verdict. However, this much appears very clearly: the Indian way keeps its stand in the realm of the Timeless; it believes that endless time-orders are possible within the womb of the Eternal and the Creative. (Such an understanding may develop in the Jungian school as the problem of synchronicity is developed and its implications understood. *See Psyche and Nature,* Jung and Pauli.) It, therefore, has grounds to believe that such a state is attainable. This evidently leads them to accept that ego-consciousness is something which is linked up with the consciousness of time, and thus not so real as pure consciousness. However forceful this argument may appear to the Indian mind, it lacks empirical data for the scientist. It would be considered to be a metaphysical statement rather than empirical. A scientific mind (including the Jungian) takes his stand on self-consciousness as the starting point, that is his reality. It is the pain, agony, and the conflict of this split that makes for his progress onward. He has reason to believe that throughout the first half of life, there is a need to develop a strong ego, and the analytical procedures should aim at building such a strong center. Experience has shown that those with a weak ego have easily succumbed to the contents of the unconscious, leading to schizophrenia, as they succumb to the world. Only a person with a strong ego can stand the confrontation with the fateful process of individuation.

This emphasis on the building of a strong ego does not go counter to any spiritual tradition, since discrimination (Viveka) is considered necessary for the sifting of the real from the apparent. But the mystic tradition of the East affirms that even this discrimination is to be given up in the end. This is the last and the final dissolution (Pralaya).

Yet, if one does not get involved in the above metaphysical arguments, one should be able to perceive significant agreements with the findings of Dr. Jung, especially in what he has to say about Completeness.

Even in our tradition, perfection is not understood in the moral sense. It is an amoral concept. Whatever way it may have been understood by the common man, any writing of a saintly person, and life itself, will testify that the ideal sage is not bound to anything, he is beyond moral considerations, he has transcended far beyond the moral outlook. Perfection is more an attitude of mind rather than concrete actions performed.

Completeness or wholeness, according to Dr. Jung, comes to be exactly the same as above. In accepting one's uniqueness at each stage, man finds himself realised and fulfilled and he is led to accept all that, not on the grounds of something external, but on his own inner necessity. Only a man of courage can accept the totality, which is constituted of as much dark shadows as the illuminated bright points.

The modern age is the one of self-consciousness. We all wish to grow into knowledge through personal experience. Authority does not have the same hold on us as it used to have. Moreover, self-realisation is a personal question. The scientific approach by Dr. Jung to self-realisation becomes very interesting to the Indian mind when he finds the age-old truths brought to personal experience in a man who started from scratch. It is very fascinating to see how the self-regulating psyche unfolds its drama of integration in dreams, visions and phantasies. To one who has been trained to read meaning into this drama -- which is not very easy --

the unconscious almost becomes his guide. It would not be too much to say that Dr. Jung has found a way for the western mind and those uprooted from their spiritual tradition to be initiated into the deeper realm of spirit and to accept true religion.

COMMENTS

by

J. Marvin Spiegelman

This paper comes after Dr. Vasavada has completed an analysis and a deeper study at the C.G. Jung Institute, Zurich. The naivete of the 1941 paper is over and one can see that he, too, has undergone a "night sea journey," and not at the hands of a beloved "mother" guru. Knowing his analyst there (who happened to be the same one I worked with), I smile sympathetically, for Dr. Meier was one to "hang-in-there" with the process, but was rather sternly detached and grandfatherly in that process. I could assure Dr. Vasavada that other analysts are different, since I experienced six of them, altogether, and some, indeed, are more directive or supportive. Each analyst's approach and attitude has its value -- once more, individuality wins the day. Vasavada is quite right, however, in pointing out that the western way has no preconceived goal. The Self emerges -- if it does -- out of the psyche of the analysand, and is neither known nor "perfect." We sympathize with Dr. Vasavada's struggle, now, to do justice to both of his experiences, that of the guru and of analysis. The "union" is not yet achieved here, nor should it be. The reader may get the idea that the process that Dr. Vasavada describes here is typical for all Jungian analysis. It is not. Like the stages described in Jung's *Two Essays*, these are merely descriptive and each analysis is different. Relatively few, as a matter of fact, "go the whole way" implied here, and the ultimate union is rare. Yet all of these aspects are present in some way.

ALCHEMY AND CATATONIC DEPRESSION (1960)

by

Arwind Vasavada

The patient was directed to me for analytical treatment on 31-8-60. He came with difficulty, sat with drooping head on the stool before me. He was a picture of acute agony. It was difficult for him to answer even the preliminary questions. One could see the struggle of an acute nature coming on in him; all he could do was to raise his head, putting his hand on his heart, turn his chin in a peculiar way and utter an indistinguishable cry, a cry of despair and agony. He dropped down to a rigid posture for the whole hour of the session.

After a couple of days in which he needed help desperately, he uttered that he was dying of grief and repentance. The therapy consisted, during this period, mainly of feeling with the patient and urging him to unburden himself. It helped. He came out with some bits of information about himself and a few incidents of his life.

The early life of the patient seemed to be lonely, without much care and love from elders. Mother died when the patient was eight years of age. He is the eldest in the family. Later, father married another woman within a year of the death of his first wife. Step-brother and sisters came in later. The patient had to live in hostels run by the religious sect to which he belonged (Jain). He came in contact with different kinds of holy men. One of them gave him a Mantra to repeat which he carried on till he broke up. Somehow this contact also attracted him to search for the Wish-giving gem (Cintamani).

He married at 14, after studying up to the IV grade. Professionally he was not successful. He started learning to make caps and was fairly well off in it for some time, but he had to take up the post of a constable in the Railway police when it did not continue. He could not go on as a constable since it went against his moral grain. As a result, he had to become a day labourer to earn his living. It was a hard and strenuous life. Later he took up some trade and slowly got involved in speculations which brought him heavy losses. At one time he had to sell off his wife's ornaments but that too did not relieve him from debts. This seems to be one of the causes of his first attack in 1958. He was admitted to Jodhpur Mental Hospital where he was treated with E.C.T. and insulin for two months and discharged as improved. A few months later he had a relapse and was admitted at Jaipur where Insulin treatment was given to him. He was discharged as cured after six months. But he was admitted in Jodhpur shortly, for the third time.

Symptoms of the first attack.
He would move in circles and become violent, often going out into the forest for days. He complained of someone strangling him and pressing upon his chest. He also used to write Mantras of his own making, and sat under the sun for hours in summer heat.

Symptoms of the second attack.
He beat his wife one night and went away into the jungle in a dazed condition. He explained that a figure of a departed soul directed him to a holy place and left him there. Then another soul came and brought him to the city. He found himself later in the hospital.

Relating the incident of the beating of his wife, he broke into a piteous cry and repented it.

After a week he became mute, probably due to increased doses of Insulin which had already started. He began to communicate slowly after a week. This time combined treatment had started (E.C.T. and Insulin). In sessions with me, he showed much fear of E.C.T. and often asked me to intervene in it. I could not do so.

The period after this, he slowly came out of the depression and with proper emotional support he was able to unburden what he called a few secrets of his life. His memory was as if overcrowded with details and he used to break into them without concern for chronological order. The facts recorded here are those which could clearly be understood by me.

As he grew up, along with repeating the Mantra, his search for Cintamani continued, which brought him in contact with different holy men. This often led him into internal conflicts. At the instance of such a person, he began feeding the dogs in a jungle near a shrine. Later he contacted another holy man who gave him another Mantra and he did not know which to follow, the earlier one or the later. One of his outbreaks, probably the first, was due to his feeling that this saintly person got annoyed with him and he went into panic.

Shortly after his return from Jaipur, which was his second admission, he accidentally lay hands on an ancient manuscript giving details of making gold. He fell for it and during this period he began experiencing auditory hallucinations and great apprehension at a voice which called him into dark cavern. Later he began having visual hallucinations of his ancestors, one of which led him into a shrine at midnight and another back to the city after the episode of beating his wife.

All throughout this we should not forget his financial situation which was extremely bad.

It was difficult to systematise the whole of the overcrowding material that came out from him. I could pick out the main trends, the search and research in Alchemy. Often I would drop hints as to what the Alchemical gold actually meant. Could ordinary gold relieve him of his troubles? Could a really saintly person initiate a disciple into worldly things? Has not he misunderstood the import of the text? His financial condition may have misguided him.

I used to make him halt and inwardise over these questions whenever the reference came to such things. When he would pause and slow down, I gave him a symbolic meaning of gold and the Philosopher's stone. I referred to utterances of saints in this connection. He began to take in what was being told. I could feel that he was beginning to realise where he was mistaken.

Secondly, I often put questions regarding his tendency to accept every guru he came across. When he asked me if he should start repeating the formula and which one, I left it up to him, though he was not totally convinced till the time when the therapy broke up, suddenly, due to my accident. I often asked him to see behind his credulousness. I also pointed out how different kinds of Yoga, not suited for everyone, led to the same goal. It seemed he was not clear whether he approached a holy man for spiritual or worldly gains. He, however, maintained that he cared for the spirit. He was shown the contradiction in his belief and practise of making gold. He accepted it.

The naive attitude towards holy men came out prominantly for discussion in the course of time. He said that he followed holy persons because they all were holy. I often had to put the question if he was intelligent and dispassionate enough to judge persons. I think he did not have sufficient intelligence for it, because he believed in them blindly.

This communication lasted for about a month, during which he felt much better. He began to take note of his problems in reality. He felt the desire to work sincerely by honest means without side-tracking which he had done so far. Twice he was released on parole which showed good results and reports. He, however, still complained of a humming noise in his ears sometime. The sessions broke off on 14th Nov. 60 due to my accident. It is reported that he is carrying on well in his profession.

The whole history of the patient shows the over-powering influence of the archetype of Self in the form of Cintamani and Alchemical gold. The patient was as if caught in its thrall. He became an original Alchemist himself in so far as he wrote several formulae and Mantras of his own fancy sometime. He, however, did not know the meaning of them.

During the period of sessions lasting for about 2½ months he had two dreams; one of night pollution which he did not state clearly out of shyness and another one as follows:

Dream. 1/11/60.
He saw a merchant of his acquaintance who has a packet of silver leaves. He shows them both and says, 'Paper burn and leaf dissolve.' He felt that the merchant meant some trick and showed enmity. Then he saw a holy man whom he asked, 'Have you any means to prevent this?' He replied in negative.

The condition of the patient took a turn for better after this. The dream seems to mean his disconnection with wrong alchemical enterprises.

COMMENTS

by

J. Marvin Spiegelman

This case-presentation is a treat for those of us in the west who have heard hundreds of them in clinics of various kinds. It is, on the one hand, the attempt of a psychotherapist to be clear and fair about his work and to report to others about it. In this way, the report is much like those done in western clinics. Even the depression, the catatonia, the confusion over personal and impersonal, over material and spiritual aims, can readily be found in our western cases. The background, however, of holy men and mantras, of jungles and marrying at fourteen, of strange religions (Jain) and struggle with integrity, have a ring different from our own. For us, it is notable that alchemical symbolism plays as much a part in the Indian psyche as it does in our own. The result seems favorable, although we know the difficulty in bringing consciousness of this nature to one who has been so disturbed. One notes, also, that shock treatment and insulin were just as common in the India of 1960 as in the United States. Have the later drugs, one wonders, been in use there also? I imagine so. I imagine also that there are many spiritual seekers there who utterly fail to come into the province of the psychotherapist, since they are quite happy and contented with their gurus -- a condition of far less frequency, one imagines, in the west, although the United States, now, has surely vast numbers of gurus and disciples. Dr. Vasavada's description leaves nothing to be desired, and is a caring presentation of a difficult work with a not-easy patient in a troublesome setting. (e.g. He could do nothing to "intervene" in the use of electro-convulsive therapy.) We appreciate this description.

A REFLECTION (1964)

by

Arwind Vasavada

A book review of *Memories, Dreams, Reflections.* **by C.J. Jung.**
Edited by A. Jaffe. Pantheon Books, New York, 1961.

Soon after Jung's 80th birthday, I was hearing whispers from quarters nearest to Jung that he was engaged in a work never undertaken by him so far -- a sort of confession, an outpouring of a soul. *Memories, Dreams, Reflections*, recorded and edited by Mrs. A. Jaffe, is the product of this labour. She has fulfilled the trust and we are much thankful to her for this service.

It is difficult to write a review of this book because it is difficult to assess the worth of a guru. *Memories, Dreams, Reflections* is Jung's inner and outer side of his being in its unity; his whole life and his development are revealed in honesty and sincerity. Jung answers questions which he never did before, not even to his intimate friends and associates. Reading the book, one gets a glimpse into the development of Jung's personality, as a representative western man becomes self-conscious. In Jung's deepest stirrings and end results, as shown in this book, one can plainly see western culture itself become self-conscious and self-aware. Highest knowledge, the gnosis, is not a statement about anything objective but is a condition of becoming self-conscious or the process of making statements of all kinds. It is non-judgmental, it is pure awareness of oneself, the age and the culture one represents.

Sensitive since childhood, Jung became aware early of his inner voice, his Daimon, "personality No. 2." Inner tension, conflict and dialogue between the two -- himself and personality No. 2 -- paved the way for increasing self-awareness and also for the founding of Analytical Psychology. Jung's *Memories*, from this angle, is indispensable for anyone who wishes to understand his psychology. For here one finds how Jung's life, his thoughts, deeds, and psychology, are closely linked together. He wrote about nothing which he did not experience himself first and then gathered sufficient material and evidence to demonstrate it. In all this, he showed perseverence, strength of conviction, infinite capacity for suffering and an obstinate fighting spirit.

In the early years before he chose his profession, Jung was holding a sort of balance between his two personalities, though No. 2 at times had the upper hand. Later he gave expression to No. 1, at the instigation of his dreams, but he maintained an inner relation with No. 2, who became his guide and Daimon. Jung never became a blind follower to the promptings of his guide. Throughout his life, he remained obstinate in his questionings, in order to be fully convinced of anything. He followed closely to the Gita: "Learn that, by humble reverence, by inquiry and by service." Thus Jung emerges from this book as a man of destiny, who carried out his inner dictates to the full, and to its last limit, without regard for its consequences, good or bad, in the spirit of real detachment and love for truth. Jung, and some of his associates in relation to him, had to face unsuspected turns, heartbreakings, unpleasant episodes. Truth was first and foremost to him, other things and relations secondary. "I have offended many people, for as soon as I saw that they did not understand me, that was the end of the matter as far as I was concerned. I had to move on. I had no patience with people -- apart from my patients. I had to obey an inner law which was imposed on me and left me no freedom of choice. Of course, I did not always obey it. How can anyone live without inconsistency?" (p. 356). It made Jung lonely and brought him much suffering. Those who have been near him (or near a guru also?) have felt the blast of it. Few were able to bear it and still remain with him.

Jung's main mission in life was to make available all that he experienced and to demonstrate this to people who cared to listen to him. Guided by his Daimon, he made descents into his inner world and also worked upon old, forgotten materials, such as alchemical, gnostic, and Christian texts. He forged a link in the history of religious spiritual thought of the West and established its corroboration with Indian and Chinese traditional spirituality. Because of this he could talk most meaningfully and intelligibly to people who had lost the tradition. We would expect Jung to talk like a mystic but he did not want to; rather, he avoided it. The spirit of the age demanded empirical demonstration and the language of science. And with these instruments one can only hint at and lead; experience remains the concern of each individual. There was another reason why he consciously maintained the persona of a psychiatrist. If he did not, what he talked and taught would have been thrown out as another mystic utterance to be avoided by the intelligentsia.

For these reasons, Jung's writings and interviews have been an enigma for an Easterner. Jung presented his deep and profound silence on ultimate questions like the Buddha or humbly said that he was only a healer and not a priest. Deeply charged by his own religious mystic experience, he left each one free to experience his own God for himself (p. 300, 349). Even when he used a term only after careful selection, e.g. Self, he was careful to amplify it by symbols and pointed at the experience, because a word as such meant nothing; it is everything if illumined by experience.

As compared to the training of a Sadhaka in the East, Jung started with handicaps and lack of equipment. Mystic tradition is almost obsolete in the West. Science and rationalism long ago obliterated this and with it the running thread of connection between the isolated islands of the old traditions in mysteries, gnosticism, alchemy, and Christianity. When Jung felt inspired by the dictates of the Daimon, it was a tremendous task for him to unearth these threads, to make them meaningful to people and to transmit them through experiences. He was a lone worker in this field. His task consisted, first of all, in understanding his inner world -- the Self. His inner experiences with dreams, visions, and fantasies were the models. *Sadhana* stands upon three supports: the scriptures, the guru, and one's own experience. For Jung, alchemical and other texts were the scriptures or Vedas, his inner guide was his guru, and lastly he was confirmed by his own experiences.

With maturity, Jung grew into the stature of a guru, from our point-of-view. Jung worked and taught as an individual and never as an institution. The Institute in Zurich grew up independently of him; that is why the *Memories* do not mention it. In spite of being the nearest and the closest, the most understanding and sympathetic, he was bitingly critical, volcanic in anger and bitterly cruel in slashing and disrobing his pupils of their falsities and self-deceptions. One felt himself in the presence of a scorching fire and ran away, or swarmed to the sweetness of a beehive at other times. This was Jung as guru.

Jung was never sparing towards anybody, including himself, or his own culture when it came to exposing untruth. The rationalistic onesidedness of scientific cuture came to be exposed by him as much as the hollowness of the Christian faith in modern times. Jung rises above his time in this and remains true to his experiences in which East and West meet. He analyses the malady of the West as due to its being caught in the irreconcilable opposition between good and evil. In a characteristically saintly way, he points out how negating evil or attachment to good, will not solve the problem. "In any case, we stand in need of a reorientation, a *metanoia*. Touching evil brings with it the grave peril of succumbing to it. We must, therefore, no longer succumb to anything at all, not even to good . . . Every form of addiction is bad, no matter whether the narcotic be alcohol or morphine or idealism." (p. 329) The solution lay in each individual moral decision, the exercising of moral creativity.

"On the contrary, the myth of necessary incarnation of God -- the essence of the Christian Message -- can then be understood as man's creative confrontation with the opposites and their synthesis in the self, the wholeness of his personality. The unavoidable internal contradictions in the image of a Creator-god can be reconciled in the unity and wholeness of the self as *coniunctio oppositorum* of the alchemists or as a *unio mystica*. (p. 338)

Jung's encounter with the Unconscious compelled him to experience it more deeply by contact with the primitive mind everywhere. He, therefore, undertook journeys to Africa, America, and India, all of which were symbolic. Through these, he allowed himself the opportunity to experience the deeper layers of his own unconscious. He opened himself up to them with a view to assimilate them, all of which is portrayed in his dreams at the end of such journeys.

The account of his journey to India is not quite complete: one should add to this account, Jung's foreword to Zimmer's Biography of Sri Raman Maharsi. We Indians are apt to miss something in his journey to India, and with our spiritual arrogance will hastily brush it aside -- the whole book -- as uninteresting and uneventful because he did not meet any saint, even the Maharsi so exalted by his close friend Zimmer. Was Jung afraid of such a contact and encounter? If one recalls what Jung wrote about the so-called perfect person in his *Two Essays* (p. 192), one might get an idea that Jung did not permit himself to come closer to such a person.

However, Jung has made clear in this book that he did not wish to see a saint in India because he wished to experience the truth himself. "I did this because I had to make do with my own truth, not accept from others what I could not attain on my own" (p. 275). He visited many places and was deeply affected by the upright, religious life of an ordinary house-holder.

Despite all this, if one keeps an open mind and understands the mission to which Jung was compelled by his inner demands and the demands of his time, one can easily see that he was in tune with the deepest Self, a deeply religious soul who never arrogated to himself the claim that he reached the end of knowledge.

"When people say I am wise, or a sage, I cannot accept it. A man once dipped a hatful of water from a stream. What did that amount to? I am not that stream. I am at the stream, but I do nothing. Other people are at the same stream, but most of them find they have to do something with it. I do nothing. I never think that I am the one who must see to it that cherries grow on stalks. I stand and behold, admiring what nature can do" (p. 327).

Jung had to speak to his people in their own language. He remained unknowable and unpredictable to many, in spite of being in the midst of a close circle. Even after having revealed all that he had to, it seemed, there was still something held back. This is because Jung never spoke of things that were inopportune.

Of all thinkers, Jung is nearest to the spiritual tradition of the East, but it is sad and unfortunate that he is not much understood and read in India, as it appears from the review in the newspapers.

Jungian Psychology opens the way for experiencing the Self to a man of any culture and religious belief just as any *Guru Marg* does. The study of Jungian Psychology is necessary for us at this juncture as it enables us to discover our tradition.

Memories, Dreams, Reflections, written with such deep, vibrating emotion will surely help us understand Jung, invite us to study him deeply and later to experience his path, which is so essential at the moment.

One cannot help being affected and inspired by the vibrant, dynamic and towering personality of Jung as one reads through the pages of his book, especially the last part when Knowledge surrenders to Love (p. 353-6). The book will surely be received well and be an inspiration to many.

COMMENTS

by

J. Marvin Spiegelman

It is nice to read this appreciative account of Jung's remarkable memoirs. Most of us who have read that autobiographical work shared Dr. Vasavada's admiration of this "towering personality." It is also fun for us to tune in on a sharing of Easterners in the approach of a western "guru," where he is an "enigma" (scientific, empirical) or not submissive (did not seek out Indian saints). What we in the west treasure, they find strange. But Vasavada shows a full picture and we, too, can share his loneliness as the sole representative of Jungian psychology on the vast sub-continent of India. A stranger in both east and west, no wonder that he, like us, finds in Jung a kindred soul. And does he not say that there are enough spiritually uprooted people in India who might be pleased to follow a Jungian path?

PHILOSOPHICAL ROOTS OF THE PSYCHOTHERAPIES
OF THE WEST* (1965)

by

Arwind Vasavada

I have chosen for my subject the philosophical roots of the psychotherapies of the west. I will endeavor to show how the recent trends in the different schools of psychotherapy are moving in the direction of Eastern wisdom and opening a way for better and closer understanding between the East and West. It will be clear from the brief account I shall give you that a sincere scientific attitude, honestly pursued, leads to fundamental truths of life. And it should open the eyes of many of us in whose life this synthesis between science and traditional spiritual lore has not yet occurred.

The progress of different schools of psychotherapy in modern times in the West is bringing into greater clarity the fact that the causes of psychiatric illness are to be found in the alienation of man from himself. Beginning with Freud, going characteristically the scientific objective way, the West has gradually laid, step by step, the foundation for a system and a method which has brought it unconsciously nearer to the spiritual roots of Eastern wisdom, the knowledge of self. We can confidently say that the psychotherapies of the future will become one of the strongest bridges between East and West.

The rapidly changing geography of the world with its consequent changes in interpersonal relations takes man unawares in his habitual mode of behavior and demands greater resilience in his attitude towards himself and the world, which is not always easy to bring forth voluntarily. It, therefore, produces undue strain upon him. Such a constant demand does not leave much time to recollect, to take stock of things and carry his whole being in an integrated form to meet the need of the changing environment within and without. As a result man begins to live on his surface rather than from his depths. His life becomes flat and two dimensional without abiding staying power. Such a situation produces a

140

gradual split within him, between his depth and the surface, and lays the foundation for later mental disorders of minor or major kinds.

Man tends to forget what he essentially is and begins to believe himself to be a system of interactions with the environment. He thinks he is adjusting and adjusted to the world, but in fact, he is living by defenses. He is living a life of falsity, because it is merely reactive. Unless he comes to realize this and turns inward to recognize his depth and disidentify himself from the false wrappings of his adaptations, he cannot start building his natural personality and be the man he is. Almost all the systems of psychotherapy, beginning with Sigmund Freud, have striven as their initial step to do deeper analysis to make man aware of his defenses and discover his natural heritage. The neurotic or psychotic has begun to live in his fantasies at the cost of the realities of life. He sees the world from a wrong standpoint because he has learned to look upon himself wrongly. Unless he is prepared to discover himself, he cannot get free from the disorder. It becomes the task of the therapist to slash one by one the false wrappings with which he has covered himself. This is exactly parallel to the procedure a *guru* adopts with the seeker. The *guru's* first task is to cut assunder the bonds and the veils in which the seeker has shrouded himself and to let him gaze at his own naked self.

Freudian psychoanalysis aims to make the analysand conscious of the defenses he has been building since childhood against the Oedipus situation. His early emotional relations with parents and siblings have coloured the world view which he carries with himself as a means of adapting to the changing demands of the world. It leads him more and more into complications and away from the realities of the world. He thus begins to live in the world of his own imagination and fancy with a complete or partial break with reality.

The process of analysis brings self-awareness and the recognition of what he really is and the reality of life and teaches him to adapt his erotic drives in conformity with his environment.

Self-discovery, thus, becomes essential to correct living with Freud. One may not agree with him in the understanding of man as a bundle of libidinous strivings of erotic nature, but one has to acknowledge Freud's belief in the need of self-discovery as a means of correct living.

Not only that, it is to the credit of Freud that he discovered a correct method -- the method of Free Association -- a tool for everyone who wished to understand himself. All other previous methods of Abreaction and Hypnosis kept the man dependent upon the doctor, whereas the method of Free Association was a sort of torch in the hands of men to enable them to enter the hinterland of the mind. Though born and bred in the extraverted, scientifically oriented culture of the West, he initiated the way for introversion and meditation, a distinctly oriental approach towards the psyche. I think it was the first and most important step in the history of psychotherapy in the West. It gradually opened the way to the discovery of the depth and richness of the psyche. It is, however, a different question when one asks how far this method was used and developed by Freud and by the Freudians. The method of Free Association released man from the compulsion of external and internal demands of life and mind. It gave him the opportunity to look within and discover the inner dynamics of mind. The method of Free Association unconsciously follows a few steps of the Eightfold (*Astanga*) path of *Patanjali* which I have tried to point out elsewhere.

Freudian psychoanalysis also brought into relief another important aspect of therapy, the doctor-patient relationship -- the transference situation. The patient involved the doctor in the maelstrom of his conflict, which the doctor could rise above, to the extent he himself was free from those conflicts within. This situation led to the need of the analyst being analysed before undertaking treatment of any patient. Otherwise the analyst fell into the danger of becoming disturbed himself, or exaggerating the conflicts of the patient and spoiling the case. Thus, with unusual insight, Freud touched upon a problem of great importance in the process of self discovery. However, it was left to others to discern the delicacy and intricacy of this problem. The relationship between himself and the goal, or standing still, or undoing whatever kind of familial relationship. It is a relation between the two -- a more or less dispassionate guide who educates the other into correct living and a disturbed person. Again, the education given is not merely intellectual. It is based on experiencing, something very much akin to that found between master and disciple.

To summarize, Freudian Psychoanalysis evolved a method akin to oriental Yoga, a method of interpretation to gain understanding of the defenses with which man has covered his libidinous drives. It is a method which reveals the structure of personality in its depths of which man has remained ignorant. Freud also showed us the importance of the transference situation.

The onesided understanding of man according to Freud came to be recognized and criticised during his lifetime and one of his close associates evolved a different theory about man.

Adler, interested in organ inferiorities and observing the compensatory function in the living organism, applied it to the understanding of man. From childhood, according to Adler, a child was faced with an environment in which he felt inferior and powerless. The elders of the home ruled and were powerful and free. They could do what they liked. In every respect the child was unfree and unable to do anything he chose because he was handicapped by his relative lack of knowledge, strength and intelligence. This, along with other situations at home, viz. his placing in the family, and his own physical handicap if any, exaggerated his feeling of inferiority. Early interpretation of these situations paved the way for the style of life and later neurotic disorders. The exaggerated sense of inferiority moved him to compensate for it by setting up a goal of superiority -- a fictitious goal to be achieved in life. He turns away from the realities of life and imagines himself superior to others in certain respects. He therefore arranges his strivings in such a manner that he could never achieve the goal. Outwardly he seems to be sincerely striving for something superior, but unconsciously he ever tries to avoid it. He so arranges his life that he does not permit himself to be tested and the blame does not come to him but falls to the world or to the disease. But for this little thing or that, he would have achieved his goal. Poor me, he is blameless.

Therapy with the Adlerians consists in piercing through these arrangements and self-deceptions and making the patient aware of them so that he may recognize himself as he is and look at the world as it is and start afresh the task of adjustment in conformity with reality.

In spite of differences in viewpoints of what man's nature is, Adler understanding man to be governed by a power motive as against the erotic drive in the case of Freud, Adlerian and Freudian therapy seek the same result -- the recognition of man as he is.

According to Freud, after the false vestures are cast aside, man is revealed to be in constant conflict between instinctual drives of the Id and the social, moral and other cultural forces which themselves are not original to man but the sublimated aspects of the libidinous drives. The Adlerian analysis reveals man to be charged with a drive for power which, if utilized in conformity with the world, makes man live a normal life.

Having given a brief idea of the psychotherapies of Freud and Adler to illustrate the field and the problems covered by them I will now take another approach so that we are able to observe the progress which has been made in psychotherapy. I wish to make it clear that I use the terms psychotherapy and psychoanalysis interchangeably. I intend to take up three aspects of psychotherapy and their historical development. I shall deal with the method, the understanding of man, and the doctor-patient relation in different schools of psychotherapy.

In spite of all the criticism against Freud, he was the pioneer in this field. He initiated a method which revealed the hidden depths of the human mind, widened our scope of understanding of human nature and paved the way for further development in this field.

The method of Free Association is characteristically oriental in nature. The patient reclining, relaxed in the analytical couch, giving free reign to his associations, is diverted from the rationally directed thinking which is characteristically Western. He is asked to inwardise and to soak into whatever is coming from within. The freely directed association or thought trains man into a posture (*asana*) and a way of concentration which would lead him gradually to the path of *Non-action*. But this method was not perfected by Freud and the Freudians. The far-reaching implications of this method were brought out and utilized by the Horney school. Kelman in a paper on Free Association brings out these aspects clearly.

He shows how Free Association leads man to become aware of contradictions and paradoxes and enables him to reach spontaneity. "Freer and freer associating not as a method or technique but as a way of being is both manifestation and possibility for experiencing and resolving human paradoxes unique to each individual in his era, with the effect of there being more spontaneity and creativity."

In the early period with Freud this method was employed to understand symptoms and dreams. It became a valuable tool to pierce through the defenses and to uncover the falsities of man. Jung very correctly remarked that it is invaluable in revealing the shadow side of man.

In the Horney school with Kelman this method deepens and becomes a way of being. It makes man aware of paradoxes and becomes a way of communing -- a unitary process as opposed to a dichotomous process. This aspect of Free Association has deeper spiritual significance in so far as it revolutionizes the whole attitude and the way of thinking, the characteristic Western subject/object way of thinking which is detrimental to self-realization. It is a process, in which the subject gradually loses itself into a single unitary entity.

The analytical psychology of Jung neither made use of this method nor the couch of classical psychoanalysis. He believed in the face-to-face confrontation between the patient and the analyst. He called for association by the patient permitting ramification of thinking into available memories. He extended the scope of this method in his interpretations at the subjective level. Here the doctor helped the patient in associating the material by supplying from his own fund of knowledge. The face-to-face confrontation with the patient brings the personality of the doctor into prominence. The doctor is no more a passive listener to free associations who hints at interpretations when necessary, but an active cooperator in the process of healing. This change in associating was due to the discovery of archetypes and the objective psyche -- the unconscious of far deeper significance than what Freud had discovered.

Experiencing conflict honestly without any attempt to avoid it is recognized by Jungian psychotherapy. In the later stages of analysis and especially in solving the problems of the later half, Jung emphasised that it is by going through sufferings of being involved in the dualities of life that the transcendent function can be activated and the experiencing of higher unities made possible. In certain cases he advised active imagination so that the unconscious archetypal material might be assimilated. Suffering meaningfully undertaken is a kind of *Tapasya* which purifies man. The value of suffering and *Tapasya* is also recognized by the *Dasein* school. They believe that there is no escape from the misery of man's existential situation. He must face it squarely and boldly. Correct meaning of life comes from purified vision. If we go deeper into this process we shall find that active imagination also leads to *Non-action* and releases man from his compulsions and conditioning.

We shall now deal with the second aspect of therapy -- the nature of man.

One of the important contributions of Freud was his empirical demonstration of the unconscious and the use of this term in understanding human nature. Man is more than a mere ego, conscious only of its exterior strivings and behavior. He is determined to a great extent by a part of his being which he doesn't know about -- the unconscious.

It was left to Jung to discover the deeper layer of the unconscious and its implications. But Freud paved the way. Freud understood man to be ridden with libidinous drives from which he could not escape. Man's life can only be a compromise with these impulses because only a part of its energy can be channelised into higher forms. Horney has remarked that the conflict, for Freud, cannot be resolved. Man has to bear with his burden as he is caught in between the irreconcilable opposites.

According to Adler, analysis revealed man as a social being who can adjust himself to the environment and become a useful member of society if he can avoid becoming involved in compensatory drives to suppress imagined inferiorities. He does not explain why man is caught in this conflict. Adler says that normal man also lives by fictions, but they are workable and practical. A neurotic lives by fictions which are unattainable because they are totally unrealizable.

With Jung the picture of man changes. There is no self-deception practiced by the unconscious upon man. Here the unconscious is helpful, being more than a repository of repressed and forgotten material. The unconscious is the origin of consciousness and the rich soil from which man can draw all he needs to transform himself and reach selfhood.

The basic opposition between the conscious and the unconscious which gives rise to all other dualities and opposites which involve man in suffering and misery is not absolute. The *Dvandas* in life are two sides of an identical thing, hence relative to the standpoint of man. Such an understanding of man gives a different orientation to the ills of man. In the malady itself are contained the seeds for regeneration of man and of his creative possibilities. Jung found in these opposites a natural dynamic process which he called the individuation process. This is a process which man can utilize, if it is his destiny, and become a whole man. For Jung the unconscious becomes the source of spiritual life and deep mystical, religious experiences. It is man's onesided emphasis on partial personality systems within and without which involves him in all sorts of conflicts and absurdities in life. If man has the strength and capacity to go through the suffering of these identifications and consequent meaninglessness of life and relativity, the unconscious helps him to transcend all conflicts and lead him to the state beyond opposites. As man frees himself from the bonds of outer realities of the collective conscious and the inner realities of the collective unconscious, his horizon widens and he gets an opportunity to experience the self.

Freud disillusioned Western man from the misunderstanding and self-satisfiedness that he is the ego and it is everything. He showed a deeper side to his personality, the dreaming, the unconscious side. From the state of waking life he brought man to understand that he is also the dreamer of his dreams at night and it is an important part of his personality. Jung through his method of active imagination showed a still deeper side of the unconscious and confronted man with his *Sunyata* of the dreamless state. The analytical process, if pursued carefully and sincerely, led man to experience what he called the "Night Sea Journey." Jung never wrote about the Fourth State -- the *Turiya* -- in his books. He could not understand it till very late. One knows through personal communications that his last days were spent in unravelling the mystery of this state in which the study of Zen Buddhism played an important part. Of this I have referred in my Radio Talk from Jaipur in 1962.

Existential Psychotherapy with Victor Frankl especially tackles this situation directly. Existential Neurosis in modern man is a terrible experience of the meaningless void, a state of utterly helpless suffering from which he finds no escape. Man can come to new meaning in life only when he goes through this suffering sincerely. By accepting his destiny man can regenerate himself with vigor and enthusiasm for still richer hidden meaning. He has come to this state of affairs because he has reached the end of his one-sided game of reading meaning into life through an intellectual, positivistic approach. The other side of man reveals itself when man experiences the consequences of this undertaking to its full.

Karen Horney looks at man from a different angle. Man is neither ridden with irreconcilable conflicts between pleasure and reality principles nor with the drive for power, but he is involved in the strivings of opposed nature of his own making. Still there is within him the potential to realize his self. This can free him from neurotic conflicts.

Because of the basic anxiety arising out of feeling helpless and isolated in a potentially hostile world, man develops the neurotic trends of a contradictory nature. He turns towards submission, aggression or detachment compulsively to solve his basic anxiety. These contradictory trends lead him further into vicious circles of deeper conflicts between his imagined and real self. Man is thus led into greater falsity and further away from realizing his self. Horney calls this the process of self-alienation. By understanding his false attitude and behavior one can arrive at self-realization. There is always hope and redemption for man according to Horney. Man must be prepared for honest self-examination and go through the sufferings of giving up his false gains and imagined realities.

Recent developments in the Horney school make it quite clear that the therapeutic process tends to annul every kind of dichotomy and leads man to experience the total awareness of himself.

We shall now take up the last part of our discussion, the doctor-patient relationship. With the advance of knowledge, Freud became conscious of the peculiar relation developing between doctor and patient. He saw its immense importance in the therapeutic process. The remark he made to Jung when both were on a lecture tour in America in their early days of association makes the point clear. He meant to say that if one understood transference he understood psychoanalysis. Confidence and emotional rapport with the analyst is necessary for any successful analysis. The delicacy of the transference situation necessitated that the analyst be analysed before he undertook analysis. The image of the doctor as it emerged in the Freudian psychotherapy is that of a dispassionate guide who is more or less free from the conflicts he is supposed to treat. According to Freud the emotional situation in transference is centered round the Oedipal situation. And thus it was a sort of reactive behavior that developed between the two. The doctor-patient relationship with Freud did not go beyond the limited part of each one's personality. The relation remained formal and distant in spite of being intimate.

With Jung the transference situation took a deeper meaning. Jungian psychotherapy extended beyond the field of the so called abnormal patients. In solving the problems of the later half of life of normal man, it becomes a process of turning man to reach his centre -- the Self. With this, deeper spiritual meaning was discovered in this situation. It was not merely a situation in which one gave and the other received. It turned out to be an archetypal situation in which both were in the powerful grip of some numinous, transpersonal factor. This situation demanded as much self-examination on the part of the analyst as it did of the patient. It is an opportunity to further realization of the self, its depth and richness. Anything like cocksureness on the part of the analyst would be detrimental for both. Thus in Jungian psychotherapy the transference situation becomes a steady and constant opportunity for the demand of self-awareness, alertness lest one may fall into fossilized, static self-assurance. The same aspect of the transference situation and its importance is hinted at by Kelman when he says that if analysis does not change the doctor from what he was it is not an analysis. Continual self-knowledge and alertness are characteristic of a correct analytical procedure.

We thus see that the dichotomy of doctor-patient and that of the basic dichotomy of subject/object gets slowly dissolved with Jung in the transference situation and makes for the fusion of the two personalities and prepares for the experiencing of *Non-dual*, transcending the limited personalities of the two. The far-reaching spiritual significance of this situation comes to be understood here. Kelman has pointed out the same fact when he talks about communing in this context. He says, "Communing is essential to and the essence of being human. Communing is essential to self-realization, to realizing others and the world of which we are an aspect. While communing is obtaining, feeling and thinking in dualism cease. There is only oneness feeling. Communicating is not possible. There is only being silent."

Thus we have tried to trace the progress of the psychotherapies of Freud, Adler, Jung and Horney, taking into account three points for discussion, the therapeutic method, the understanding of man and the doctor-patient relationship. It is not possible for me to cover all other therapies for lack of sufficient knowledge.

From this brief review it should be evident to us that psychotherapies in the West have moved and progressed consciously and unconsciously towards those very methods and understanding of man which are close to the spiritual tradition of self knowledge in the East. What I tried to point out in a limited way in 1940 returns to be substantiated today, that psychotherapies if taken to their logical end must end in *Yoga*.

Eastern wisdom asserts that man cannot live well and usefully by practicing self-deception, by identifying himself with external as well as internal roles, one given to him by society and the other by his inner system of *Samskaras*. The life of compulsion and drivenness can only bring more misery and suffering. Every attempt to free oneself and gain his independence based on false attitudes towards others and compulsiveness to do something leads to greater involvement in the vicious circle. He has to become aware of his falsities in the first instance, difficult and full of suffering as it may be. This is what a *guru* does to a disciple. It is a cutting of his bonds, uncovering of false veils of ignorance. This makes him aware of his distinction from the body. Deeper dream analysis of archetypal contents leads a step further to the awareness of one's distinction from the dreaming state or the subtle body. Further deeper analysis and understanding confronts man with his emptiness -- *Sunyata*, the typical experiencing of the Night Sea Journey. It comes to be experienced otherwise also, as in the Existential Neurosis in the feeling of general meaninglessness of life and suffering caused by the feeling of utter loneliness in the dark and dreary world. Modern psychotherapies have recognized these experiences, their healthy and neurotic aspects, and have discerned the value of suffering with full sense of responsibility and consciousness.

It has become evident to all serious psychotherapists today that man is not what he appears to be, what he thinks himself to be. Behind the upper crust of ego, intellect and self-consciousness, there is a deeper man within, who is the life and origin of the upper structure. It is by turning to it that man can gain the necessary strength, knowledge and the wisdom to solve problems and live a decent civilized life. The key to the solution of human suffering is not outside but within him, he only needs to look within.

Though wisdom is within him, man needs to be directed by a guide, who must be dispassionate and already much advanced in self-knowledge and who does not sit in absolute judgment upon him, but is a co-worker and a co-sufferer in the struggle to be free. The guide, the doctor, is not merely a person but an image of something transpersonal, of which both he and the patient are equally authentic images. The one in whose wisdom and magic power of healing the patient has such confidence and to whom he devotedly surrenders and feels bound by strong emotional ties of strange, unqualified nature is not the doctor -- the man before him -- but the transpersonal archetype of Self or God, in terms of Jung and the *Guru* in our way of thinking. If the patient does not concretize his *guru* and god in the person of the doctor, he can discover the same within himself, and from then on his guide is always within him. Intimate disinterested personal relationship between the *guru* and *sisya* have from time immemorial been the steps to realize the transpersonal within.

The psychotherapies of the West have grown out of the treatment of human ills. The doctors who apply them humbly wish to remain psychotherapists at this juncture and if they do not make any statement about religion and spiritual discipline as an Eastern wise man does, it is their humility and honesty. It will not be long until the psychotherapists of today will play the part of *gurus* of the future.

Before I conclude, I have to make only one observation directed towards my colleagues in India, who are sincerely working for the redress of human ills. They have to grow out of the old scientific philosophies and advance shoulder to shoulder along with their co-workers in the West from whom they draw inspiration. It may be difficult for them to discover roots in their tradition directly because proper conceptual forms may not be available to them. Such a thing, however, is available with some schools of psychotherapy in the West. If the West has discovered the East through the empirical way, why can we not discover ourselves again and be effectively useful in our profession?

30. 12. 63   *New Delhi*

*Paper read to the International Academy of Philosophy.

COMMENTS

by

J. Marvin Spiegelman

Dr. Vasavada clearly and engagingly discusses the roots of western psychotherapies here: their basis in the discovery that psychological illness results from alienation from Self and/or world, the empirical realization of man as he is, and the methods of exploring the unconscious. Who of us in the West could characerize the diverse philosophies of India so intelligently and simply?

Of special value is the comparison between western therapy and yoga. One wonders if the reader was moved to question certain aspects further, such as, how did Freud's free association "follow a few steps of the eightfold (Astanga) path of Patanjali"? Or what more could one say about "suffering meaningfully undertaken is a kind of *tapasya* which purifies man"? And one wishes to see or hear the radio talk in Japur in 1962, in which "the fourth state" and Jung were compared. Finally, one would love to read of Dr. Vasavada's demonstration, in 1940, that "psychotherapies, if taken to their logical end, must end in yoga." These questions, alas, were not answered, but our appetites are whetted and perhaps our own thought processes can fill some of it in.

In this paper, Dr. Vasavada gives us an impression of one who has really looked at East and West. How many westerners, even, can quote Kelman and Horney so intelligently? It is, therefore, touching that he concludes with a plea to his own colleagues in India to embark upon self-discovery. For those of us in the West who have discovered the "lonely path" that analysis brings, think how it must be for a philosopher *cum* psychologist *cum* psychotherapist from India, first and only of his nation to have undertaken both an eastern yoga and a western one (Jung's) as well!

THE UNCONSCIOUS AND THE MYTH OF THE

DIVINE MOTHER (1971)

by

Arwind Vasavada

Lord Siva has just completed the dance of destruction, the *Tandava* dance, and all the colorful and fascinating forms alluring to the senses and mind have disappeared and returned to the womb of eternity and timelessness. Everything is enveloped in the twilight of darkness and deep calm has prevailed all over. Lord Vishnu, the protector of the three worlds and the sustainer of the Universe is taking his well earned rest on the coils of Sesa Serpent, floating on the deeps of the ocean. God Brahma, the creator of the Universe, is quietly meditating, seated on the lotus issuing from the navel of Vishnu. The thousand hoods of the Serpent Sesa has made a canopy over the resting head of Vishnu. It is all a vast and deep calm pervading everywhere.

In the course of time, two demons, Madhu and Kaitabha, are born out of the wax of the ears of Vishnu. As they grew under the depths of the ocean, frolicking in its vast expanse, they thought and wondered, "Who made this vast ocean? Who is the creator of this limitless expanse?" Thinking over it, they become convinced about the existence of such a power. At that time there came an enthralling sound -- a hum from the heavens. Listening to it they felt sure that it was the seed chant -- *Bija Mantra* -- of the creative power. Repeating it, they went into deep absorption -- *Samadhi*. At the end of five thousand years, they were awakened from their trance by a voice from heaven, "O Demon Twins! I am much pleased by your devotion and worship. Ask a boon from me of Your choice." The demon brothers were delighted to listen to the voice of the power and said, "O Unseen power! If you are pleased with our devotion, please grant us that we may become immortal." The unseen power replied, "Death is inevitable for anyone, hence you can choose your death. You cannot hope to be immortal." The demon twins then replied, "O Unseen power! If that is so, please grant us the boon that we may die only when we choose to die."

The demons having got the boon of immortality by a trick became proud and arrogant. Their mischiefs and pranks took a violent turn. They began exploring the surface of the ocean heedlessly and came upon the place where God Brahma, the creator, was contemplating seated on the lotus. They questioned Brahma, "Who are you? What is your business here? If you are powerful, prove your strength by defeating us or else be gone from here. This seat belongs to us now."

God Brahma was very scared seeing the two powerful and arrogant demons in their aggressive and quarrelsome mood. He looked towards Vishnu, the protector, and prayed for help, "O Lord Vishnu! O the protector of three worlds, these two demons are intimidating me to fight. I am weak before them and am sure to be killed by them. Please, awaken yourself from your sleep and help me."

In spite of repeated prayers, nothing stirred on the face of Vishnu. Brahma began to wonder, who is that power that has held even the Lord of the Universe under its control? For sure, that power seems to be even more powerful than Vishnu since it has made him so captive, lifeless and inactive. God Brahma, as he reflected over it, became aware of the power and began to pray, "O the Great Deluder! O the Deep Sleep of Yoga! Thou indeed are the most powerful of all the three Gods. Thou art the Enchantress and also the energy and power behind all Gods, including myself, Vishnu and Siva. We indeed are powerless without thee. Thou art indeed the mother of us all and everything. Please have pity on me. These two demons are harrassing me and I find myself unable to cope with them. Either awaken the Lord Vishnu from your power, or you yourself destroy these demons." At this the Divine Mother separated herself from the body of Vishnu and stood aside near him. Vishnu awoke from the deep sleep. Brahma apprised him of the situation. Thereupon, Vishnu challenged the demons and continued to fight with them for five thousand years without being able to defeat them. He became totally exhausted and asked for a respite. Vishnu began to wonder at the situation and could not understand as to how the demons could not be defeated. What could be the source of their strength. Accidentally, his eyes fell on the Divine Mother who was standing behind him watching the whole scene with a smile. Vishnu at once realized that the demons have a support from the Divine Mother. He appealed to her to help him destroy the demons. The Divine Mother, out of compassion for Vishnu, and also because it was time for the demons to die, having become arrogant, consented to help him. When Vishnu started to fight the demons the second time, the Divine Mother revealed her most beautiful maiden form to the demons. The demons got bewitched by this form and were transfixed. They ceased to fight with Vishnu. Vishnu, thereupon spoke to them that he was very much pleased to see their strength and that he would be pleased to grant any boon they might choose to ask of him. The demons bewildered by the glances of the Divine Mother retorted, "We are not beggars to ask any boon from you; moreover you are not our equal. Rather, we shall be pleased to grant you a boon." Vishnu took this opportunity and told them, "If that is so, please grant me that you may be killed by my hunt." The demons were taken aback realizing their mistake. They, however, said that since they can choose their death, they choose to die on a solid surface away from the waters of the ocean. Vishnu, thereupon, increased the size of his thighs to raise them above water and placed the demons upon them and killed them there.

The above account of the myth of the Divine Mother from *Devi Bhagawat-Purana*, clearly shows the nature of the unconscious according to Jung. Let us try to understand it.

The myth opens with a state of deep calm and stillness; all elements and the multiplicity of creation are dissolved into one homogenous whole. The darkness of deep sleep -- absence of self-consciousness -- prevails. In this state of nothingness and void, the energetic polarities and that which relates them are all submerged. Energetic activity presupposes the principle of excitement, i.e. that which disturbs the equilibrium; the principle which maintains and continues the activity going and that which resists and opposes the activity, i.e. the principle of inertia. These three elements are represented here by Brahma the creator, who is the principle of excitement or disturbance; Vishnu, the sustainer of the three worlds, is the principle of continuance, and the Divine Mother is the principle of inertia. All these three, necessary for activity and creation are held in equilibrium. It is also very beautifully pointed out that these three are all one and interdependent. These three principles are otherwise called *Rajas, Tamas* and *Satva*. The Divine Mother has overpowered Vishnu and thus she is unidentifiable with him. Vishnu is asleep. Brahma is depicted as seated on a lotus issuing from the navel of Vishnu. Thus Brahma, Vishnu and the Divine Mother form one whole and are shown to be in the state of equilibrium. There is no stir of activity, no movement. The serpent Sesa, who forms the bed for Vishnu and protects him with his thousand hoods making a canopy over his head, is again one with the Divine Mother, who is addressed as the Deep Sleep of Yoga or *Yoga-Nidra*. Sesa, floating over the oceanic waters is thus a container like a Mother's womb. The picture taken as a whole, in its unity, very clearly and impressively suggests the pre-natal state of creation -- the great womb. It is because of this that the name of Vishnu in this state is *Marayana*, one whose abode is water.

In this deep and profound stillness of the graveyard, since the Universe has just been destroyed by the Tandava dance of Siva, the spouse of the Divine Mother, the first movement begins with the birth of twin demons Madhu and Kaitabha, from out of the ear wax of Vishnu. It is as if polarities are created and motion is caused in the oceanic calm by the exploratory pranks of the demons. Since there is no opposition between the two, they both being brothers, it seems to represent the state of optimum tension in the undifferentiated state. It is a state of tension previous to creation, i.e. here the polarities do not conflict with each other, since ego-consciousness is not yet born to take sides. The conflict of polarities is possible only in relation to the ego, who begins to take sides with one or the other pole. This is identical with the state of deep sleep in man. In deep sleep all conflict and tensions ease and come to an end temporarily. This is the daily experience of each one of us. In deep sleep, ego-consciousness comes to an end. However, the deep sleep of the Divine Mother is on the cosmic level.

The two demons, during their childish pranks, listen to the humming, wordless sound of the Divine Mother and, meditating on it, they got the boon of immortality. Thus, they find their relatedness to the Divine Mother, who in the myth is represented as the main controlling power. Moreover, on account of their birth from the ears of Vishnu, they are one with the whole Vishnu enveloped by deep sleep, i.e. in the lap of the Divine Mother. This represents one whole of Cosmic masculine and feminine principles in unidentifiable unity.

The tension in the picture mounts rapidly after the boon of immortality is granted to the demons by the Divine Mother. The demons approach and confront Brahma, the principle of disturbance, and he is thus activated. He tries to rouse Vishnu from his sleep. When he is unable to rouse Vishnu, he realizes the immense power of the Divine Mother, who has held all the Gods in her power. The Divine Mother, in other words, has held the energetic activity in balance. She is, therefore, invoked by different names by Brahma. She is called the Deep Sleep of Yoga, or *Yoga Nidra*, the Infinite Power and the Enchantress.

It would be interesting to understand the invocation *Yoga Nidra*. The Divine Mother is not called the deep sleep of ordinary human beings but the deep sleep of yoga. The sleep of ordinary human beings is the sleep of ignorance, in which one is unaware of anything. *Yoga Nidra* is called also *Samadhi*, a state of mind achieved through meditation and absorption following yoga practice. This state brings man to the experience of pure awareness without consciousness of an object. In *Yoga Nidra*, one has the experience of oneself as pure awareness -- the Self. The sleep of human beings and *Yoga Nidra* represent the state of optimum tension, with the difference that ordinary sleep, which is ignorance, eases the tensions and conflicts temporarily without transforming human personality, whereas the sleep of yoga transforms man totally. The Divine Mother represents this primal state of man's being. It can be called Unconscious only from the point of view of individual ego-consciousness, because mind and intellect do not and cannot teach it. It transcends them both. Mind and intellect are rather illumined by it and only as so illumined can they function. Thus, the Divine Mother or the Unconscious is truly the mother, the progenitor of all psychological functions and through them, also of the objective world experienced by them. Jung seems to give the nearest expression to what I have just said in the *Archetypes and the Collective Unconscious:*

> It is quite impossible to conceive how 'experience' in the widest sense, or, for that matter, anything psychic could originate exclusively in the outside world ... The structure is something given, the precondition that is found to be present in every case. And this is the *Mother*, the matrix -- the form into which all experience is poured. (C.W.9)

Brahma invoked the Divine Mother. She, being pleased, leaves her hold of Vishnu, the protector of the three worlds, and stands aside. Vishnu is awakened from his sleep and is now ready to kill the demons so that the act of creation of the new world gets started.

What is the meaning of killing the demons? Creation is based on destruction; the two activities represent the phases of an identical movement. In order that creation of a new universe may begin, the optimum tension has been broken so that the dynamism of polarities may come into play. Just as sleep has come to an end in order that the ego may begin to experience the polarities, so that the unfinished task of life may be completed, likewise *Yoga-Nidra* has come to an end so that the universe may come into existence and give opportunity to souls to complete their unfinished journey towards the Self. The killing of the twin demons would then mean separating the two energic poles into their natural tension so that their dynamism starts the work of creation.

It might be interesting to pay attention to another aspect of this mythic organic relation between the various figures and their unity in spite of differences. The myth starts with wholeness: Brahma is connected with Vishnu through the umbilical cord of the lotus and the Divine Mother is one with Vishnu in so far as she has enveloped him in sleep. Hence, they both are in unity. This is the completely undifferentiated state of the human personality — it is the Great Beyond — the Self.

The two demons are born from the ear wax of Vishnu, who is one with all. In so far as they are born of the Vishnu unity, they form a part of the whole, though differentiated. The two demons are supported and nourished by the Divine Mother and lastly also killed by her. They are thus assimilated into the whole. The Divine Mother reveals her anima aspect as the temptress and enchantress, when the time for the demons to die comes. The demons get inflated by the boon of immortality which brings the excess of *libido* on them and crushes them to death. Thus, their death in this manner is their return to the source and origin. In fact, the Divine Mother has done nothing; the demons brought about their destruction through their own doing. Or to speak in another language, they returned to the source from which they originated. All this movement was part of the whole. So, in spite of everything happening as it happened, nothing actually happened. Zero added to zero is zero, and zero subtracted from zero is zero. And zero is everything and nothing.

I wish to draw attention to another point, that the Unconscious and the Self are two different names for an identical experience. This holds true for Jung. In *Memories, Dreams and Reflections,* he says, "Hence, I prefer the term The Unconscious knowing that I might equally well speak of God or Daimon, if I wished to express myself in mythic language." (p. 335-337) The Unconscious is the Self. And the Self is pure awareness, light and illumination, the fulfillment of one's destiny. It is not the state of unconsciousness of a stone or matter. That is why the Divine Mother is called *Yoga-Nidra.* It is not a metaphysical concept or a hypothesis of science, but a matter of experience, supported by all the mystics and prophets of the world. In this aspect, the Divine Mother is all compassion, infinite bliss, love and power. This is the goal of individuation, the end and aim of the journey of life.

This is one aspect of the Divine Mother. She presents a different side when creation has come into existence and the individual human beings begin to perceive differences and distinctions. In this aspect, the Divine Mother is the source of all our psychological functions, emotions and objects of experience. This side is seen by ego–consciousness. In this aspect, she plays varying roles according to the predilections of individuals, with the sole aim that they may realize their true being through tension and conflict. In this aspect, she is known as *Prakriti,* Nature, the name of all energic tension, full of the dynamism of instinct and emotion. She creates out of herself the psychological functions, ego–consciousness and the colourful alluring objects fascinating to all the senses, and enchants man into her snares. We find a similar echo in Jung's works. He says "She (Mother) makes us believe in incredible things, that life may be lived. She is full of snares and traps in order that man should fall, should reach the earth, entangle himself there and stay caught so that life should be lived." (C.W. 9, p. 26-27)

In one of the prayers to the Divine Mother in this aspect, she is invoked as Mother, intelligence, sleep, hunger, shadow, craving, patience, sex, modesty, peace, faith, loveliness, wealth and prosperity, mercy, memory, contentment, delusion and error. These aspects of the Divine Mother are experienced by each one of us in our lifetime according to our specific state of mind and development. The prayer reads, "YA DEVI SARVA BHUTESU MATRI, LAJJA, SRADDHA etc. RUPENA SAMSTHITA, NAMASTASYAI, NAMASTASYAI, NAMONAMAH." I bow down again and again to the Divine Mother, who is present in every being as modesty, patience, hunger, etc. In terms of Jungian psychology, this aspect of the Divine Mother comes very close to the anima aspect of the mother goddess, who is alluring, tempting and draws back human beings in regression to the inactive state in the womb. She disturbs man from his state of ease and comfort, rouses his emotions and all the baser instinctual shadow side of his life, drags him into the open battleground of life so that he may fulfill his destiny, but from which he always fights shy. She appears both as positive and negative mother, compassionate as well as cruel, according to the developmental stage of each individual. There can be nothing more severe and exacting and disciplining than the Divine Mother in this aspect. She spares no one, whether old or young, child or adolescent. She goads him on and does not allow him to rest in peace and comfort with one's imagined, self-satisfying goals, till he has reached the final destination of identity with the Divine Mother. It is normal and natural for youth and the adolescent to feel tempted, because it is the age for it; but has she even spared so-called mature persons? She disturbs them out of their rigid habits, goals and beliefs, bringing them into open conflict so that they may become whole.

Jung, when he talks about the Dual Mother, in *Symbols of Transformation*, seems to have in mind these two aspects of the Divine Mother. An individual, in his life, whether he wills it to cooperate with his natural goal of individuation or not, has to experience, first of all, the struggle to be free from the Divine Mother as Nature -- his dark and instinctive side, his passions, greed and cupidity, his laziness and regressive tendency to go back to the comforts of Mother's breast and womb. It is only when he first sacrifices his childhood dependence that he confronts this anima or animus. The confrontation with anima or animus is an ordeal by itself.

How many of us are really able to sacrifice our projections; how many of us wish to remain satisfied in succumbing to the fascination of his anima or animus aspect of the Divine Mother and what untold suffering and sorrow do we continue to endure? There is no peace and rest for man, whether he follows the path of individuation or his instinctive desire. To be individuated is to be completely naked; stripping oneself completely of all the false vestures he has adorned himself with. Becoming whole, becoming individuated, is to realize what one in fact is; it is to detach oneself completely from all the foreign trappings. It is going through a fiery ordeal. But to succumb to natural instincts and to the fascination of the Divine Mother as anima or animus is no less than writhing in hell-fire or being burnt alive on a funeral pyre. Suffering on this road multiplies, till it deadens a man to the insensitivity of a stone. Suffering and pain on one side becomes penance and purification, leading to illumination; whereas it leads to insensitivity, dullness and torpor of a stone in the other case. It is only when one has gone through this fiery ordeal of penance and purification that man is reborn of the Great Mother, the second aspect of the dual Mother.

It seems necessary for us, the students of Jung, to realize the distinction between the unconscious as the Great Mother, the source and origin of all archetypes, and the unconscious as the ego experiences it. The ego's experience of the unconscious is the projection of ignorance. It could be easily equated with the concept of *Avidya*, or ignorance, according to Vedanta. The Unconscious as the source of all, as Great Mother, can be called unconscious only metaphorically. And Jung used it only for the purpose of making himself understood to scientifically minded people. In fact, it is pure consciousness. It is the light which illumines all the psychological functions, including the ego. The ego and its functions are conscious only by borrowing the light of Great Mother. Jung seems to be aware of it when he said the following in *Symbols of Transformation*, when he discusses the hero's longing for the mother:

> Always he (Hero) imagines his worst enemy in front of him, yet he carries the enemy within himself -- a deadly longing for the abyss, a longing to drown in his own source, to be sucked down to the realm of the Mothers. His life is a constant struggle against extinction, a violent yet fleeting deliverance from ever-lurking night. This death is no external enemy, it is his own inner longing for the stillness and profound peace of all-knowing non-existence, for all-seeing sleep in the ocean of coming-to-be and passing away.
>
> (C.W. 5, pages 355-6)

How accurately the last sentence of Jung echoes with *Yoga-Nidra*, "the all-seeing sleep of coming to be and passing away." The longing for the Divine Mother is man's longing to reach the Self, which is pure consciousness. In the same book, Jung says, "It seems to us rather that he (the wandering hero) is first and foremost a self-representation of the longing of the Unconscious, of its unquenched and unquenchable desire for the light of consciousness." (C.W. 5, p. 205)

Another point that I would like to bring to our attention is the danger for the analyst and the analysand to get caught up in the archetypal realm of the Unconscious, since the Great Mother is infinitely creative. There is no end to the fascinations of the creative, alluring side of the Divine Mother. One can and does easily get caught up in the fascinating game of intellectual interpretations, since it bolsters the ego. It is more important to feel and experience the archetype and surrender one's understanding to reach the goal of Selfhood. Such an attitude of mind brings a natural intuitive understanding. Jung has emphasized this point more than once in his books; to quote only one from the *Archetypes and the Collective Unconscious*, "Only when all props and crutches are broken and no cover from the rear offers the slightest hope of security, does it become possible for us to experience an archetype that up till then had lain hidden behind meaningful nonsense played out by the anima." (C.W. 9, p. 32) It is probably because of this that there is no attempt to interpret and intellectually understand the innumerable myths available in the Indian tradition. They are religiously recited in temples and homes and listened to by the simple folk. They believe literally what is recited, since it gives each listener a time and space within to feel and experience it.

Commenting on the myth of the Divine Mother, I pointed out the organic unity of the story in which each figure is a part of the whole and how, in spite of differences, all events form a unity of purpose. The Divine Mother going forth into creative activity and returning to the original calm after destruction are two sides of the same movement. The outer world of objectivity and the inner world of archetypes make up the whole. These distinctions do not exist in reality, since it is the same pure consciousness which pervades both movements. They are different expressions of an identical thing, like waves of the ocean. Jung also tried to bring this point home, to the extent to which it was possible for him to communicate with people of his time. In his monumental paper, *On the Nature of the Psyche*, and in other books also, he has shown how futile it is to distinguish between matter and mind and between spirit and instinct, since man's knowledge at this stage of his development cannot say exactly what the nature of matter is. It also cannot fathom the mystery of mind and spirit.

All our deepest experiences are in the realm of the psyche. Man, therefore, cannot oppose the outer world to the inner world. I feel that what Jung seems to suggest here is to make us aware of the dichotomy which man in the West so naturally makes and gets involved in.

In bringing this discussion to a close I do not find a better description of the relation between man and the Divine Mother as Nature than that given by the author of *Samkhya Karika*. In a poetic language, he compares the creation and life of man in this world to the dance of *Prakriti* -- Nature. He compares Nature to a bashful and coy dancer who, while performing her dance, never appears before the audience. Soon she knows that the audience has recognized her identity. Elaborating on this theme further, the author very clearly brings out the attitudes of both towards each other. The man from the audience says, "I have now known her true identity as to who she is," and becomes detached and calm. The dancer, as a coy and bashful maiden says, "I have been recogized," and retires from the stage. She feels as if she has become bare before the public and never returns to dance. For a man who understands the true nature of the world, the alluring dance in terms of tension and conflict, ceases for all time.

COMMENTS

by

J. Marvin Spiegelman

In this lovely presentation and interpretation of an Indian myth, Dr. Vasavada reveals to us his own poetic and deeply Asian psyche, one in which the feminine origin of God, the universe and the psyche is fully understood and revered. A seamless whole is presented and one which can only be apprehended by a person who has experienced it. Dr. Vasavada makes judicious use of quotes from Jung, showing the parallel understanding of east and west, yet the quotes themselves echo a difference between the two. The images and interpretation are similar, yet Jung's words refer to "enemy," struggle, "sucked down," whereas Vasavada's words betoken submission and adoration. One can easily see Dr. Vasavada in full obeisance before the Great Mother, whereas Jung, in his *Memoirs*, could not fully touch his head to the floor in such a gesture, he tells us. Yet both views are needed, and both battle and surrender are part of the process itself. Are not the demons, Madhu and Kaitabha, like the precursors of the ego? They are the ones who ask questions, they long for greater consciousness. And, it must be noted, they rise out of the ear wax of Vishnu Himself. We, poor mortal egos, born of the detritus of God, raise questions. We, too are part of that longing, in the unconscious itself, for greater consciousness.

We westerners are privileged to hear and read this contribution of Dr. Vasavada, who came to our world and helps us understand both his and ours so much better. Moreover, he does so, like the Divine Mother whom he serves, with beauty. We, in our feminist dilemma of the modern day, could do well to absorb this deep reverence.

DR. JUNG, A PSYCHOLOGIST OR A GURU? (1971)

by

Arwind Vasavada

In a previous lecture, I have tried to compare the process of individuation with that of self-realization according to Indian thought. I would like to elaborate this with the aim of clarifying the ultimate experience of Self so that statements of Jung concerning this experience may be understood.

It should be clear that the Indian standpoint is holistic; there is no division or split between spirit and instinct, mind and matter, between man and his environment. The non-dual, formless, undefinable, and unnameable manifests or expresses itself out of its creative play into this universe at different levels of mind or psyche, life and matter. There is the unnameable, unmanifest, primordial state from which the manifestation takes place, at three different levels, the stage of the purity of universe or creation, comparable to the prenatal stage of creation. This is called the state of deep sleep. Just as in deep sleep, we exist, but we are not conscious, either of ourselves or the world. Likewise, in this unmanifest stage of spirit -- which may be comparable to the Unconscious according to Jung -- differentiation into multiplicity does not exist. In Alchemical terms, this may be called *Unus Mundus*.

The next stage is that of the dream, the manifestation of spirit at a psychic or psychological level. Lastly, comes the waking state with consciousness of material objectivity. Thus, one spirit manifests itself at these different levels; it alone exists and, even in its manifest state, it is one organic whole in spite of differentiations.

Man as an individual, like a wave in an ocean, out of ignorance of his correct identity, considers himself separate and different from others and the world. This ignorance is the cause of man's identification with his body, mind and the ten thousand things of the world. This ignorance of his correct identity is the veil of Maya, which acts as a screen between him and the world, and upon which projections of mind and imagination are made, thus preventing the correct picture of himself and the world.

163

The work of a guru consists in removing this veil of ignorance from the disciple so that he may see himself correctly and the world as it is. The process of the gradual removal of veils of ignorance, which consists in withdrawal of projections in Jungian terms or disidentification from attachments to mind and body according to Indian thought, aims to lift the aspirant beyond the polarities of life this polarization of the ego has brought about. The vision of the individual is limited by the ego's identification with things. Both the removal of veils and the limitation of ego-consciousness are effected and one is flooded with the light of the Self, which is pure Consciousness or awareness. This experience of dissolution of the ego, or the ego's recognition of its identity as Self, is described in different ways by all mystical cults and religions. It is called harmony, bliss, illumination or realization, identity between the individual and the Self, or God. It should become clear that one can function in a natural way only when attaining the correct identity.

All that I have stated so far appears to be more philosophic than psychological. This, however, is so because an experience gets stated in philosophic terms when it is based on and supported by a living tradition. We might anticipate that Jungian Psychology might state this in a similar manner in the course of a few hundred years, if this tradition continues.

In the living tradition of Self-realization, the guru plays a classless role. He belongs to no institution, class or sect and lives under no bondage to society, except the one he willingly chooses for his work of awakening people to the realization of Self.

The tradition of Psychotherapy is a very recent one in the West. It has, however, arisen under conditions similar to those in which any mystical religion originates. For Dr. Jung, at least, it fulfills the same need which mystico-religious traditions of the East fulfill, i.e. attainment of Selfhood.

Since it is a recent development, however, it has not yet found its proper place in the scheme of Knowledge and Sciences. The history of medical psychology tells us of its struggle for freedom within medical science and, lately, within psychology proper. Naturally, this situation puts psychotherapists in a very precarious position. Jung found himself in such a situation when he discovered and experienced for himself the realm of archetypes. Trying to understand the function of mind and Consciousness and passing through the dark and illuminating realm of the Unconscious, he landed himself in the realm of the Spirit. The realm of Spirit is beyond mind and intellect; however, it illumines all the psychological functions. Naturally, the product or the effect cannot know or comprehend the producer, the father.

Jung, therefore, had an immensely difficult task, to communicate and pass on his experiences and wisdom to the people of his time. In the West, as we know so well, every aspect of knowledge and science is well defined as is the role of experts. The knowledge about mind was the concern of the science of Psychology and the knowledge and wisdom about God and spirit was the concern of churches and priests, the custodians of institutional religions.

Whatever Jung discovered and experienced grew out of the study of mind, but it transcended mind and psychology; naturally, therefore, it cannot easily fit in with the science of psychology. Since religious tradition in the West has almost ceased to be a living tradition, Jung had no one from this fold to whom he could talk meaningfully. Jung, therefore, found himself in a no man's land -- which is exactly the position of a guru in any living religious tradition. Where such a tradition is still living, this unique roleless role of the guru is understood and recognized.

Jung, therefore, had the task of making himself understood to the scientist as well as to the theologian and the priest. He had to speak to scientific-minded psychologists in their language and yet to show where the deeper experiences reached beyond mind and intellect, since they are subjective and wordless. In order to be intelligible to theologians, he had to speak to them in their language and yet show them that the deeper experiences are religious but are not the same as theologians are wont to interpret them. The only available realms Jung had access to were Alchemy and the mystical traditions of East and West, through which he could make himself understood. Naturally, therefore, he has drawn so much from these traditions in order to bring home the experience of Self to the scientist and the priest.

From among his listeners, a few came closer to him and the relation of master and disciple developed between them. This is really what happens in a mystical tradition. It is transmitted directly to those who care to live up to it and experience it.

On one side, Jung could not confine himself strictly to scientific standards and on the other side he overstepped the bounds of a priest. It was only a role that a guru plays. But unfortunately, such a role does not exist in the Western tradition where each man must fill a specific role and never overstep the boundaries assigned.

Jung cannot be called a psychotherapist in the sense in which it is commonly used. Since he was interested in resolving human problems, he touched the realm of spirit, which gave him the understanding of the total man. Thus, the realm of the spirit became his prime concern. Though only a few would and could undertake the journey of individuation, he undoubtedly felt that it is the natural goal of human life. A psychotherapist tends to remain on the psychological level and is concerned with his research of the observable. Since Jung reaches deeper religious, experiential levels of human life, he has no place among the psychologists, because he is more than a psychologist.

However, we can see the struggle of Jung to free himself from psychological stands in his work. Let us examine this journey of a struggle.

By drawing parallels between Eastern and Jungian ways of self-realization in my earlier lecture, I tried to show that Jungian analysis leads to the goal of selfhood or individuation comparable to that of Vedanta. It is implied that there is identity in the final experience. It is widely held that this stage is beyond the domain of words and any kind of rational communication. It is a 'communing,' where all dualities cease. It is true that psychic functions lead to it, but there they end also. At this stage, a doctor or for that matter, the seeker, must, I contend, transcend his vocation and become a guru in the true sense of the term, the illuminator of the darkness of Ignorance, and thereby a true healer.

In the psychic realm, we have to distinguish between two different kinds of representations of the self: one in which the self appears as the wise old man and, alternatively, as the black magician and such other figures in contradictory attributes. These experiences compare with those in the Eastern tradition when one works with a guru. The images are projected on the person of the guru and create complications.

This is still a stage of duality, since the archetypes appear with contradictory qualities, invoking similar emotional responses in the analysand. These experiences reflect, on the one hand, the tremendous dynamism and infinite richness of the source of archetype and its utter ungraspability with the rational means at our disposal and, on the other hand, the lack of maturity in the analysand in so far as he is caught in his own duality -- the quality of a particular archetype being an index of his own attitude toward it. Thus, these experiences are relative to the development of the seeker or an analysand.

It is only when he has matured enough neither to be possessed by, nor to be identified with, the archetype that he enters the stage of experiencing mandala symbols. If we examine what has happened in the person when he has learnt to keep clear of the two pitfalls, we shall find that he has abandoned the personal or ego-attitude which was producing the compensatory archetypes. His last sacrifice of the ego-attitude leads him to the goal of individuation.

The second kind of self experience met with is mandala symbols. The very differing forms of mandala symbolism reveal that they are emblems of the *conjunctio oppositorium* par excellence. These symbolic experiences are accompanied by intense emotional significance, including pure joy and utter freedom and spontaneity, in which all inhibitions are overcome. As long as this experience lasts, one feels dissolved and transcended beyond all psychic activities. The mandala symbols can be meditated upon, as in Tantra Yoga, in order to constellate the archetypal experience or they may appear in dream, fantasy or active imagination to indicate the advent of similar developmental stages in the person in the course of the individuation process. The task of an analyst, then, lies in amplifying the symbols from such sources that the analysand is enabled to understand them. The result is identical.

Thus it becomes clear that the process of individuation leads ultimately to the experience of the self, which is a complete integration of the personality. And since it is a wordless experiencing of wholeness -- union of all opposites -- it is identical with the experience of the Non-dual according to Vedanta.

> Just as the lapis Philosophorum, with its miraculous powers, was never produced, so psychic wholeness will never be attained empirically, as consciousness is too narrow and too one-sided to comprehend the full inventory of the psyche (*Mysterium Coniunctionis*, p. 533.)

In certain contexts, statements made by Jung concerning the self show his despair, whereas, in certain other contexts, they show him purposely keeping the standpoint of an outsider or an onlooker, with the definite aim of making people understand the psychic quality of these experiences and their inscrutability in order to talk to them at their own level.

> It therefore seems to me, on the most conservative estimate, to be wiser not to drag the supreme metaphysical factor into our calculations, at all events not at once, but, more modestly, to make an unknown psychic or perhaps psychoid factor in the human realm responsible for inspirations and suchlike happenings (*ibid.*, p. 550.)

Statements of this sort bring man to utter hopelessness with regard to his endeavour to know the source of the archetype; they reflect man's utter despair, an experience obtained by reading such books as those written by Kafka. Jung's statements of other sorts, however, fill us with the experience of *mysterium tremendum*.

I have been bothered by several questions concerning Jung: Why does he seem to waver? Why does he cling to the roles of doctor and scientist when to all purposes he seems to transcend all such roles?

> As a doctor I cannot demand anything of my patients in this respect; also I lack Church's means of grace (*Psychology and Alchemy*, p. 27.)

This is how it appears to an Easterner. Why does he theorize about the source of archetype? (*Ibid*, p. 14.). Has the experience of totality left him deficient in anything? If individuation is reaching the consummation of one's fateful call, what more remains to be achieved?

Such statements need to be properly understood. Discussing the source of the archetype and the imprinter of the god-image, Jung says,

> The religious-minded man is free to accept whatever metaphysical explanations he pleases about the origin of these images; not so the intellect, which must keep strictly to the principles of scientific interpretation and avoid trespassing beyond the bounds of what can be known ... The scientist is a scrupulous worker; he cannot take heaven by storm. Should he allow himself to be seduced into such an extravagance he would be sawing off the branch on which he sits (*Ibid.*, p. 14).

In the light of the present state of religion, which does not inspire living faith in man, where God and the kingdom of heaven is either understood to be outside oneself or among us (not within us), Jung very correctly shows that his psychology opens a way through which one can experience God within himself and that the soul of man contains within itself'... the equivalents of everything that has been formulated in dogma and a good deal more' (*ibid.*, p. 13). Thus taking issue with dogmatic religion and the Church, he shows how his psychology is an art of seeing the truth. 'It is high time we realized that it is pointless to praise the light and preach it if nobody can see it. It is much more needful to teach the people the art of seeing ... In order to facilitate this inner vision we must first clear the way for the faculty of seeing' (*ibid.*, p. 13).

This makes sufficiently clear to an aspirant from the East that Jung is talking about giving divine sight by clearing the mist of illusion from before one's eyes. It is often said in India that the dialectical discussion between a guru and a disciple is applying the collyrium of knowledge to the disciple's eyes which gives him divine sight.

In *Psychology and Alchemy*, Jung takes up the roles of scientist and doctor, wishing to avoid any metaphysical conclusion about the essence of archetypes or the imprinter of the god image *vis-a-vis* a dogmatic priest, who may talk about God out of faith but not from conviction born of personal experience. In all this, what he is actually trying to do is to prevent the experience of the transcendent being contaminated by hollow metaphysical statements. That which one experiences can only be pointed to by the intellect. Correctly, therefore, the Upanisads say, 'whence words return along with the mind not attaining it. He who knows that bliss of Brahman fears not from anything at all' (*Taittariya Upanisad*, p. 552). However, in the same breath it should be pointed out, that to an aspirant from the East, the standpoint to which Jung sticks and which he does not wish to overstep, i.e. of scientist and a doctor, can be called scientific in the sense that it goes beyond the affiliation to any creed, dogma, or cult. Since countless people feel satisfied about the forms and rituals of the religious cult and the safety of the creed, the temple and the Church, one of the main tasks of a guru comes to be to free the aspirant from the bondage of creed and cult.

How many of us cling to dead ceremonies and pointless austerities in the name of religion? The work of a guru, therefore, opens a way for everyone to find the true meaning in what he does: 'I can corroborate this from countless experiences: people belonging to creeds of all imaginable kinds, who had played the apostate or cooled off in their faith, have found a new approach to their old truths, . . . not a few Catholics among them. Even a Parsee found the way back to the Zoroastrian fire-temple, which should bear witness to the objectivity of my point of view' (*Psychology and Alchemy*, p. 15).

It now becomes quite evident that when Jung refuses to make any metaphysical statements about the transcendent, it is only because of the inadequate means at our disposal and, secondly, that words like god have meaning contaminated by history which do not liberate us to have a total response to total reality (*Mysterium Coniuntionis*, p. 548). But this should not mean that one did not have the experience of the transcendent. There is knowledge of it in experience which is far more profound and richer than our rational knowledge. In all humility and truth, should one say he does now 'know' the transcendent? A rational formulation of such an experience may be very helpful for communication, and such formulations have always been made, time and again, by saints and mystics.

Jung himself says: 'If he can formulate it more or less, then he can more easily integrate it with consciousness, talk about it more reasonably and explain its meaning a bit more rationally. But he does not possess it more or in a more perfect way than the man who cannot formulate his possession' (*ibid.*, p. 524).

In the East, rational formulation is, however, an esoteric knowledge to be given to the aspirant only when he comes nearer to the guru and follows the path. One often hears a guru telling his disciple not to read any scripture until he has realized the Self. The sacred texts are called revelations because they reveal their true meaning only in the close proximity of the guru, i.e. only when one has experienced the Self are the texts clear in meaning. The very meaning of Upanisad is 'that which is given when the seeker sits close to the guru.' 'I discovered myself within myself, when the guru unravelled the mystery. Every word then became illumined' (Surdas, a saint-poet of India). Let us examine a similar statement of Jung from the *Mysterium Coniunctionis*.

Interpreting alchemistic symbols from the standpoint of analytical psychology, Jung rightly says that Dorn was speaking of the self when he was talking about the stone or *caelum*. It is a 'third thing' in which the opposites unite, '. . . a transcendental entity that could be described only in paradoxes. . . . For the psychologist it is the self -- man as he is, and the indescribable and super-empirical totality of that same man' (p. 536).

This experience and its symbolization in terms of the mandala is confirmed in the history of religions and lives of mystics and prophets all over the world. 'We could compare this only with the ineffable mystery of the *unio mystica*, or *tao*, or the content of *samadhi*, or the experience of *satori* in Zen, which would bring us to the realm of the ineffable and of extreme subjectivity where all the criteria of reason fail. Remarkably enough this experience is an empirical one in so far as there are unanimous testimonies from the East and West alike, both from the present and from the distant past, which confirm its unsurpassable and subjective significance' (*ibid.*, p. 540).

It is not, surely, subjective experience in a narrow sense that is meant. It is certainly personal but psychologically objective, hence universal. Jung, however, creates difficulty in understanding his meaning a few lines later and becomes an enigma to an aspirant from the East when he says: 'This totality is a mere postulate, but a necessary one, because no man can assert that he has complete knowledge of man as he is' (*ibid.*, p. 536). He goes on to elaborate this point at length in subsequent pages.

One who has gone through the indescribable and ineffable experience will surely understand the difference between statements of a seer after the experience of the Self and statements about the Self without such an experience: a sort of an intellectual wrestling game to understand the Self. In the former, one struggles to exhaust the richness of it; one evinces fullness of experience. Whereas the latter shows despair and ignorance. Jung, at least in this portion of this work, regresses to the level of duality. The man of experience does not speculate about the nature of the transcendent, because he knows it through his being, and would not bother even if he were unable to formulate it rationally.

Jung himself believes in the inadequacy of rational formulations and their ineffectiveness in bringing about the experience. 'The intense emotion that is always associated with the vitality an archetypal idea conveys even though only a minimum of rational understanding may be present -- a premonitory experience of wholeness to which a subsequently differentiated understanding can add nothing essential, at least as regards the totality of the experience' (*ibid.*, pp. 544-45). They enable one to communicate easily but verbal discourse is not the only sort of communication. The man of experience radiates knowledge and wisdom — there is a wordless communion.

If we take this trend of Jung's thought seriously, we are completely abjured to make any rational statements about the transcendent because they are all one-sided and false. Such a state of affairs will imprison one in the psychic world; but in spite of it, saints and sages have spoken effortlessly and spontaneously and the tradition has been handed down to all mankind. This has been the source of inspiration and testimony for all such experiences. In the Indian tradition they serve a valuable purpose, as one of the threefold testimonies, viz. the experience of the seeker, that of the guru and the revealed text.

It is only natural for an Easterner to wonder: why does Jung talk like this? Why does he remain on the other side of the gate and talk about it? Why does he not talk about the Experience itself, its richness — its transforming effect upon the seeker?

It cannot be said that Jung remained outside the gate and that he felt and touched only its fringe and was overpowered by the mystery. It evidently is not so. He could not have carried out the immense task of unearthing and interpreting the history of Christian religion in *Aion* and of dispelling the darkness of ignorance surrounding alchemy. He could not have interpreted so masterfully and with such authority the hidden spiritual current in these institutions and brought them into relation with modern man's understanding of his personal and deeply religious experiences. Such work cannot be done by a mere Pandit, a so-called learned man, since there is no dearth of learned theologians in the West and nothing has changed the people in spite of them.

He clearly understands that the process of individuation or self-realization takes one beyond ego personality on all sides and that '*the experience of self is always a defeat for the ego*' (*Mysterium Coniunctionis*, p. 546; see further, p. 499). The experience of wholeness and totality is the consummation of man's search; it is the end of all polarities. Evidently such an experience transcends the psychic field and no problem arises as to one's being imprisoned in it. One can feel imprisoned only when an attempt is made to formulate the nature of the transcendent from the standpoint of an outsider. In the wholeness, there is no division into outside and inside; it is one whole, as much transcendent and unknown as anything, yet nearest to oneself. That is why it is called Atman, one's own Self, and is also Brahman because it is the whole of what appears before us including the seeker, a unity in difference and multiplicity of the psychic and physical field, personal as well as collective.

We can understand this enigma only when we take into consideration the time and the people to whom Jung was himself addressing. In this situation, he had to reckon with two types of person in the West, the scientist and the priest — one the repository and trustee of all worldly knowledge, and the other the trustee of all religious and other-worldly knowledge. Both of them wield immense influence and power, so Jung was obliged to talk to the scientists in their own language. This was the only way through which man in the West could be made to experiment with his depth and know his origin. It was the only way through which Jung could dispel the mystery with which religion and religious experience had been surrounded for ages and show that man's soul has a religious function within it. It is an empirical fact and can be experienced; it is not opposed to science in the true sense of the term.

At the same time Jung could also not help talking about religious experience, which he came upon naturally in the course of his struggle to understand his depth. From the standpoint of dogmatic religion, he encountered the privileged field in an unauthorized manner. In the West, a healer of the mentally ill has no business stepping outside his domain and saying anything about god and god-experience. Opposition from the trustees of dogmatic religion is naturally to be expected here. As a matter of fact, these trustees of religion have stifled the religious function in man's soul and brought about a state of religious stagnation.

Jung, through his psychology, actually emerges as a helper to them in their mission, yet it is only natural that Jung should take up cudgels with priests whenever there was an opportunity for it, and become involved. Whenever he says that no metaphysical statements can be made about the transcendent, he has in his mind the priest who, having made absolute statements about god and given his own meaning to them, has prevented self-discovery. To them Jung presents a *tu quoque* argument, for his statements about self-experience may be misunderstood in the narrow religious sense and thus be coloured; he keeps to a scientific standpoint and uses its language so that the priest is left without any temptation to interfere with them.

Jung could not, it seems, express himself openly about this integral experience in a richer way only because then he would not have been understood and the destiny of his work would have remained unfulfiled; he would have been labelled as another religious fanatic. He had to talk to people in their language, and science is the only way of knowledge in the West. It is because of this that he uses terms like postulate and hypothesis, etc., and purposely does not give up the standpoint of an outsider. His main task throughout life had been to lead man to the psychic realm of archetypes and the experience of them. He left them alone afterwards, to make of this experience what they liked.

In spite of being a deeply religious man, surcharged all over, and suffused with the richness of experience, he donned the robe of a psychologist and a doctor. He would not have done this had he been in the East. To people who have grown highly intellectual and for whom religion is a fixed dogma away from one's inner life, confrontation with the irrational was the surest way to open their eyes. In order to keep company with the scientist and man in the West, he went all the way with the scientific procedure and showed how these experiences could be understood scientifically.

At times I feel that Jung, the shrewd and consummate guru, was playing meaningfully with his people with a cunning in his eyes, so that religious people, as well as those scientifically minded, might each experience an intense struggle to understand the transcendent in their own way and experience the complete futility of their procedure so that consequently they may find release by being awakened from the illusion of knowing the transcendent in their own way.

A scientifically-minded inquirer going through the individuation process is drawn into the mystery of archetypal experiences which are evidently highly emotional and dynamic in nature. Such a person is required to be neutral and colourless in the face of experiences of a highly affective nature. Can he manage to be? The utter futility of this attempt will bring him to the wordless experience about which Jung has said nothing in his books -- except in his autobiography, and then only in a personal statement.

A similar experience, but with a different approach, comes to the religious-minded person. None of his conceptions about god are fulfilled by the transcendent experience. It does not fall into any category known to him. The experience of utter futility of the way opens his eyes.

Why Jung did not expose the transcendental experience and often got involved in quarrels with the priest and a friendship with the scientist seems non-understandable.

Those who follow Jung should not avoid making statements about the transcendent experience because Jung did not make any, for this would be misunderstanding him. No statement can be made about it, and yet all statements are all about it. It is generally said in Eastern tradition that whatever Vedas have expressed about the Self is false and whatever has remained unexpressed is the truth. Consciousness in the West has grown since Jung wrote his books, trained his associates and died in 1961. Enormous progress in understanding Eastern ways of thinking, feeling and experiencing has come about recently. We should not hesitate to take the decree of fate when it comes, otherwise we shall be mere imitators of Jung.

Jung generally kept to the role of doctor and scientist, and rarely did he speak about the transcendent in the way that saints and mystics have, but there are fragments of evidence in some of his works that show that he knew and he spoke profound, practically useful, wisdom. However, in his autobiography he gives up this role in the end and he speaks of Love, giving up the way of Jnana or knowledge.

> At this point the fact forces itself on my attention that beside the field of reflection there is another equally broad if not broader area in which rational understanding and rational modes of representation find scarcely anything they are able to grasp. This is the realm of Eros. . . . I falter before the task of finding the language which might adequately express the incalculable paradoxes of love. Eros is *kosmogonos*, a reactor and father-mother of all higher consciousness. . . . Here is the greatest and smallest, the remotest and nearest, the highest and lowest, and we cannot discuss one side of it without also discussing the other. No language is adequate to this paradox. Whatever one can say, no words express the whole. . . . Love 'bears all things' and 'endures all things' (I Cor. 13, 7).

> These words say all there is to be said; nothing can be added to them. For we are in the deepest sense the victims of and the instruments of cosmogonic 'love.' I put the word in quotation marks to indicate that I do not use it in its connotation of desiring, preferring, favouring, wishing, and similar feelings, but something superior to the individual, a unified and undivided whole. . . . Man may try to name love, showering himself in endless self-deceptions. If he possesses a grain of wisdom, he will lay down his arms and name the unknown by more unknown, *ignotum per ignotius*, that is by the name of god (*Memories, Dreams, Reflections*, p. 353-4).

COMMENTS

by

J. Marvin Spiegelman

In this hard-hitting, closely reasoned, excellent paper, Dr. Vasavada takes up some central questions about Jung and Eastern thought which are exactly to the point and merit this exchange between us.

First of all, neither I nor Dr. Vasavada can be certain as to just what Jung's intention was, other than what is stated directly in his writings. We can only rely on that, or conjecture, or reason further. Dr. Vasavada reasons that Jung's remarks about science and religion are somehow to convey his message better to a world hostile to the depth of his insight, and that he had truly transcended and was no longer psychologist nor scholar. I don't think so. He surely wanted to convey his views, but I think that he meant what he said. My reasoning follows.

Jung, I believe, was deeply committed, both in role and attitude, to the scientific point-of-view. He took to heart Kant's remarks about reason and the limits of science, and, so often, made it clear that he could not, as a scientist, go beyond its limits. He also cautioned theologians not to transgress their limits either, just as Dr. Vasavada shows. Jung certainly transcended psychology, science, theology, and all other categories in his own experience — as is shown in the profound accounts given in his *Memoirs* — but he made a clear distinction between what one experiences or "knows" (a favorite and controversial word he used in an interview when asked if he "believed" God exists) and what he could *demonstrate*. Dr. Vasavada, or Jung, or I, may "know" truths for ourselves, and have such conviction that it is unshakeable, but we may not be able to demonstrate these to others. Such was Jung's place, especially when we consider those profound experiences of mystical union he describes in the autobiography. A man who dreams of Kabbalistic, Greek and Christian mystical union on successive nights, achieves the "bliss" that the Eastern viewpoint speaks of, who sees himself (in a dream) as meditating upon himself as a Yogi —all this is clearly one who has "transcended." He could be seen as Jew, Christian, Pagan and Hindu, just because of these dreams, yet has transcended them. Thus far, Vasavada is correct. But Jung is also a Westerner, a scientist, deeply wants to advance knowledge, and not be known as a "mystic."

The difficulty can be resolved, I believe, if we make a contrast between the *individuation* advanced by Jung as a concept fitting into psychological science, and *enlightenment*, or *liberation* of Eastern thought. Jung clearly studied and demonstrated the former, while he merely attempted to understand — from the scientific point of view — the latter. Individuation is an empirical fact, demonstrated in every psyche. Its general process is enhanced by conscious participation in this event, and then occur those processes (mandalas, etc.) about which Vasavada writes and Jung spends so much time. Most patients — and this is where Jung gets his data — do not arrive at those specialized places, yet they often show material which is indicative of such events or states and both the facts of Tantra and Alchemy are demonstrated in our everyday work.

Individuation, furthermore, is a process aiming at the realization of the self in everyday life, not only as a mystical event, but as a particularity, as a uniqueness. This latter is not stressed in eastern thought, as far as I know, nor even mentioned very much. The accent on liberation, transcendence, leads to the image of the guru, a kind of saint or type-condition which is far from individuation. Hence Jung's lack of interest in visiting holy men.

He found the same thing in just an ordinary Indian man as he mentions in his paper on that topic. Individuation, in addition, leads to the experience of opposites in life and, rather then bliss, just as much suffering and pain occurs as one continues on this life-long path, ending only with death, not with enlightenment.

So, the difference between enlightenment and individuation may also shed light on the rejection by Jung of the "guru role." The guru, as Vasavada says, may be a special category of transcendence in India, but it is still an accepted and honored role. There is no such role in the West. A saint, for example, is a particularly good person, or generous, not necessarily "individuated" in the conscious sense. Jung, then, both transcended his culture and was contained in it. He was certainly a "guru" for many of us, but rejected the role, as a role.

To summarize, Jung lived the paradox, rather than only transcend it. That is very western, since we want to improve life, make "paradise on earth," etc., even though we know this is foolish illusion, even *maya*. There is a commitment to *consciousness, individuality,* rather than to the Eastern categories. As Vasavada points out, anyone who goes deeply into the soul is bound to come up with those events and conditions so richly described in Vedanta, Tantra, etc. That is why Jung used such information for comparative purposes. That is why he experienced what he experienced. But was he a guru, in the Indian sense? No.

Dr. Vasavada ends his paper with Jung's comments about eros or love. There the traditions meet, since love transcends all. Yet Jung speaks about love not as the Great Mother, or the ever-kind guru, but as it carrying the "lowest" as well as the highest. This is not apparent in the Indian conception, certainly not as an outcome.

What Dr. Vasavada is imaging, I believe, is the "seamless whole," the experience and condition of the unity of the opposites. This, I believe, Jung experienced, as have many others. How this is lived is the significant difference between East and West. It is just the gradual meeting of the two forms of consciousness which is so exciting for us all, since we have the image of the Earth itself as a "seamless whole." We, in my opinion, are only in the beginning of the world-wide process and the resolution of differences, and the integration longed-for is still quite a ways off. Indeed, I think that Jung was a most important "prophet" of this event (to use another category he would reject!), and that many of us, including Dr. Vasavada and myself, are advancing on the way. This very book, in my opinion, is an expression of that process.

FEE-LESS PRACTICE AND "SOUL WORK" (1980)

by

Arwind Vasavada

When I started to work in this country in the 1970s as a Jungian analyst, it was difficult to talk about fees when an analysand enquired about them. It felt strange to equate a certain fixed sum of money with whatever happened in the session. What was the fee for? That hour? My person? His need to pay? Was he buying something? Was he exchanging money for work done? If it was an exchange of money for work, then what is the criterion for deciding the amount of money? Is it merely time on the clock? Is it the quality of work? If it is the quality of work, then the fee must be different each hour, and must be assessed according to the value of the hours. This is what one does when buying goods. Oftentimes the sessions were less than illuminating and helpful to me and I was left with depression, which I could see in the face of the client as well. Then I was unhappy at receiving the fee. Of course it was different when the sessions seemed successful.

Can payment for our work be looked at as an installment purchase? If so, then it belongs to a long-term contract for work that is supposed to be done. But can one guarantee in advance the quality of work according to an agreed upon fee.?

Perhaps the criterion for payment is biological security; a fee simply takes care of human needs. Once again the problem gets complicated. How much do I need? I see no limit to what I can want. I want all the comforts and luxuries others have, and I feel I deserve them as others do.

While living in India on a fixed salary from the University, it was a simple matter. I adjusted my needs and wants to fit within that sum. Here I became aware of my greed, and I liked it. I said, "That is how I have to live here. In Rome do as the Romans do." I soon became comfortable with this idea. This continued until 1972 when I was making good progress money-wise and with work. It was naturally reflected in the way I was living. I could rent a reasonably good apartment and have a car. I visited India that year for the first time since being in America. I visited my Guru, the blind saint.

177

He must have become aware of whatever was going on in my life through letters I had written and our talks when we met. He asked me how long I would be working and if I could see a time when it would not be possible for me to work. If I could not work, then what would I do? He put it very clearly. "To this day your mind and body are healthy, and you can work. There will be a time when the mind will not be sharp because of age, and the body will probably be too weak also. What will you do then? How would you feel without work?

"Remember the time when you were an infant, helpless in every way? Were you not cared for? You will be cared for always if you can feel into the trust you had then as an infant. Helpless and without work, you will not feel lost. Just be Nothing, and in order to be really Nothing, be free from all ambitions and desires. You worked as long as you were in India --until your age of retirement. Naturally you would not have worked anymore if you had stayed. So do not work there, but serve instead. Don't ask any fixed fee; accept what is given freely and happily."

I listened to all of this and to all the doubts that were surfacing within me. I was quite unclear as to how I could follow this guidance, even though it appealed to me. I promised myself that I would try it out. He was after all my Guru.

This person had been blind since the age of ten and was uneducated. He was more than sixty, perhaps more than seventy; none knew his age. He had no house of his own and no bags and baggages to carry whenever he was called to go to different parts of India.

This conversation served to remind me of my experiences with my first Guru. I had received and had not paid.

My first Guru was a family man. However, he did not have any kind of work to support himself; His only income was whatever persons offered him. Yet he came some 1500 miles from his home to see me whenever I asked, and also spent sums of money in entertaining me adequately whenever I visited his home. I know I paid him hardly any money.

By the time I had come to this country, I had fully realised that the way of Jung and the tradition of my Gurus were alike. The work was "Soul Work," "Soul-making." This country gave me the opportunity to fulfill this possibility within myself and to do "Soul Work" with others. However, it was only when I visited my Guru in 1972 and he spoke to me about abandoning fees did I become aware of the lacuna in my practice, that it was not a professional work for money. It was indeed "Soul Work." Hence the title of this paper.

When I returned to the United States, I began to change. Whenever a client asked about my fee, I told him that I will be happy to receive whatever is given happily. "Give me happily and freely whatever you can conveniently, without any constraint." If he asked me about the fees charged by my colleagues, I informed him about the present rate of fees.

The discussion with my Guru put me again to my Soul Work, and it felt truly in line with the way of Jung. If the way of Jung is to explore the Unknown and live with the uncertainty and unpredictability of the Unconscious, then not depending on a fixed sum of money as a fee and living with this uncertainty in daily life seems to be the correct way to experience what Jung said and taught. What is the relation of money to soul? What exactly is this uncertainty and fear of it?

During this period people paid what they felt happy about. A few could not pay; a few paid five or ten dollars, and some the full fee. A few offered to do work, such as cleaning, altering my clothes and making a book case.

The experiment with the above kind of fee-less practice opened many dark corners of my psyche, and the process is still continuing. I have my practice as a Jungian Analyst and occasionally teaching Indian Philosophy and Psychology in a small suburban college.

As one might expect, there is a rise and fall in the number of clients as well as in the income. One month is not the same as the other, nor one year like the next. I began to feel the impact of the rise and fall of the income and work, or what we might call "no work," most acutely. The fluctuation in income and the depletion of my small savings, whenever it should occur, was felt in dread. My stomach felt hollow. A sense of insecurity pounded at my heart. It was with pain that I drew sums of money from savings to pay the I.R.S. and other bills. The sense of insecurity intensified when these periods came regularly, every two years, or even more frequently, whenever I returned from a long visit to India.

Although some years were bad, the savings balance gradually returned to its previous level. I felt very happy and even secure, and as my habits are, I became a spendthrift. This was a period of intensely interesting experiences of ups and downs. From today's distance I can say I enjoyed it, but I didn't then. This continued until 1977, when the sense of insecurity due to the instability of my income and my aging took all my attention.

In the summer of 1977 another and more interesting phase of life came up; it had remained unnoticed and neglected until then. In the late part of August 1977 I returned from India after discharging the last responsibility to my family -- seeing my youngest daughter married. A great burden was lifted from my shoulders. Since the time of my wife's death I had felt keenly the responsibility to see that our pet child be married happily. During this period and two years before, I had to go to India three times. Naturally it had effects on the bank balance and the clientele.

Curiously enough, the sense of relief at her marriage and at the corresponding reduction of my financial burden was not long lasting. In its place, surreptitiously, a sense of worthlessness, meaninglessness, came to be experienced. I had done all I had to do for the family; it was all over. Where was the purpose in living? Not only that, but I began once more (I had felt it earlier, but the feeling went away unnoticed) to see that what I so far knew, whether in terms of what I had learned from Jung or from my Gurus, was hackneyed, stale and useless. I did not feel like repeating these words and feelings in the analytic hours or in the Friday or Monday group meetings. I did not really know anything new. All I knew left me feeling quite cold. I was out-of-date, good-for-nothing. There was a sense of total futility in my existence as it was then. "Why is this life not ending?" I had done all I wanted to do and experience: I had realised my life goals. I was happy to see that the way of Jung and the path of Self-realisation of the East are similar, that the basis of any kind of psychotherapy is the knowledge and awareness of who I am. I saw that without this basic awareness no help really comes to us in our work. Yet the soul was going through agony. It seems like a classical depression.

If I knew nothing because all knowledge had left me, how should I work and live? This total uncertainty scared me. No knowledge ... no work ... no money ... what then?

During this period something happened. Sri Shunyata (Mr. Nobody) came to stay with me for a month. He is today ninety, comes from Denmark, and has been living in a small hut in the foothills of the Himalayas on a small stipend of fifty Rs. per month. In 1930, when he came to India at the invitation of Dr. Rabindranath Tagore to teach silence to his countrymen, he met Raman Maharshi. Raman Maharshi gazed into the eyes of Mr. Sorensen (his original name) and called him a born mystic. He said, "We are always aware, Shunya." Thus he was named Shunyata by Raman Maharshi.

Sri Shunyata's unobtrusive and powerfully silent personality had an unknown effect on me. After he left, I saw some light in what had happened earlier — the classical depression.

Am I nothing if I cannot work? Am I nothing if all the acquired knowledge leaves me? What is work? Is it doing Jungian analysis and getting money, or is it what happens to the soul through living in interaction with clients and the world? Then the effacement of the one who could work only with acquired knowledge scared me through and through.

The fear of insecurity was experienced in different situations, and that fear was the test of the fearless experiment, the path I had embarked upon. It opened innumerable fears in me. Ultimately it led me to inquire into the root of insecurity itself. Let me explain: it had become natural for me to forget myself in the process of doing what we call therapy. Once I was involved, the hour of the session progressed spontaneously and generally to the satisfaction of us both. There was security while working.

I became aware of the fact that I was identified with knowledge, which had become the basis of the work and had paralysed it. When knowledge and work had gone, had left me, where was I? I was nothing. I was mightily scared by this face of Nothingness. I was unable to stay wholly with that experience, and could only see the nothingness of myself. While Mr. Nobody, Sri Shunyata, presented himself as a person based in Nothingness, and whose work on my soul emerged not from knowledge, not even from work, but from soul itself. I found a new basis for Soul Work.

Let me divert and cite an experience with my client during the periods of ups and downs of income and work. This shows how freedom from money (not charging fees) gives inner strength. Therapy happens between two souls when they meet honestly and sincerely. This discovery is a relief and freedom.

This client had been working with me for the last seven years. When he retired, he reduced the number of his appointments to half. He was a very greedy man in the sense that he wanted a return on all the benefits of his past payments to me, now that he had retired. However, he was not at peace with himself, and as he was now all alone and without work, he became impatient. He did not have his salary, only his pension and social security. He started remarking, first in a veiled manner and later plainly, that he had paid so much, not only to me but to many others like me, and had not yet gotten what he really wanted. It was my duty to give him that now.

Once in a session, he got angry and made no bones of telling me how he had been robbed. He ought to have peace of mind now in his retirement, he told me. His anger did not disturb me. I could honestly tell him that I had never entered into a contract with him to give him this peace of mind in return for money. I calmly told him that I never claimed to be a therapist, although therapy happened every time we met. His anger, nonetheless, was justified. He had invested so much for the goal, and he ought to get a return for that. However, he was getting angry with the wrong person. I could make him see the Healer within him that he was projecting onto me. This Healer was the right person with whom to be angry. If he really placed his complaints before him clearly and openly, an answer was sure to come.

This short autobiography seems to present two problems of the journey in Soul Work clearly. Whether we call our work "the way to wholeness" or "a spiritual journey" or "individuation" or "Soul-making," every encounter in our work with people is a learning opportunity for us and leaves us transformed. Dark corners of the Psyche are illumin⟨...⟩ It is always a two-way process -- receiving and giving. Is this receivi⟨...⟩ giving the same exchange in a money sense? There is a superc⟨...⟩ factor at work which encompasses us both, the therapist and the⟨...⟩ does the thing if we are open to it. In this case "who" gets paid a⟨...⟩ pays?

What is true of therapeutic work is perhaps true of all kinds of⟨...⟩ work is Soul-making, since the problems which surface in th⟨...⟩ problems of every man. These problems do not belong to ⟨...⟩ simply because of the economic ramifications, but because ⟨...⟩ Work involved.

Two issues here seem important to me: my uncertainty in the world, and my fear of being without work. Perhaps both meet at a common point and have a common root. Let us see.

It is a fact that as a biological being I am quite insecure. I need shelter, food and clothing to protect me. We all need this, but it is also true that my life can be terminated any time without notice. In spite of all care, it is beyond my control. If I worry about security in any way, it is a neurotic and unhealthy fear. I have to live with this insecurity. I cannot but yield to the moment of death when it comes. But while alive, I need money to live.

When I go back to the periods when there was no work, no money coming and savings depleted by paying bills, I discovered the fear came from the spectre of not being able to maintain a certain standard of living. What is this attachment? Is it fear of poverty? If so, what kind of poverty? Is it fear of poverty or love of creature comforts?

Can I not be what I am without these comforts? Why am I here in this country doing whatever it is I am doing? Is it not because it supports my love of comforts? I can see that I can be what I really am in spite of these comforts, yet there is a fear lurking behind it all. Take away these comforts, and I face what is called poverty. I cannot and do not want to face it.

It seems the fear of poverty does not allow me to discover something important. I do not trust something within me which prevents me from finding out who really supports us all and everyone. I remember the words of the blind saint, "When you were an infant you were cared for. Have trust."

Could it be that the discovery of man's need for this trust in order to live correctly resulted in all religions asking their Priests to choose poverty? God's work and poverty were supposed to go together. A Brahmin was honored and respected because he lived a spiritual life; he did not "work," but did Soul Work for himself and others. He was thus dependent on the community for his support. Both of my Gurus and Mr. Nobody lived in that manner. They did not "work" in order to live. They lived in order to do Soul Work.

So what is this experience of facing poverty? It opens before me my total dependence for everything on others. I would not like a beggarly place in society. If I have money, I can be independent and not have to stand as a beggar to have my needs met.

Could it be that choosing poverty makes me feel only in an intellectual sense dependent and as a beggar? In fact, it could help me discover the basic trust within me and my interdependence with the universe.

Thus I see that in facing insecurity in the right way I am confronted with soul. I want money for my creaturely comforts; it leads me to *insecurity* and *uncertainty* because I cannot control my income. I look within and listen to what goes on within — the *Soul Work*.

Let us now see what this fear of being without work is.

I have my status as a Jungian Analyst, which allows me to charge so much money for my hour's work in order to feel secure materially, and to support my image as a Jungian Analyst. But I am never really secure. My security is based on something outside of me which is always fluctuating, and worry and anxiety hovers over me for not having enough.

It seems my separating the world into I and the other are the root cause of my insecurity. This act does not only separate me from the world, but from my wholeness. The split is in me first, then outside.

The outside is a reflection of the inner schism. I am better qualified . . . my work is more important than that of others . . . I have special needs . . . all of which serves to isolate me. Of course I do not see that when I am functioning as an analyst. I try to fortify certainty and security by clinging to and controlling whatever makes me feel important and secure. I have fragmented the world, both inner and outer, by this self-importance; then I feel my uncertainty, which is another face of isolation. I try to make that isolated part appear whole by adding different parts of the same world to feel safe and secure. This kind of isolation makes me identify with my work; I have no identity if I have no work.

Let us see what this work is. I am overvaluing it. Whatever kind of work I do, I do it when I'm awake. This waking period is comparatively smaller than other periods of dreaming and deep sleep, which also belong to me. The whole of I AM includes all of them. The absurdity of my identification with work is apparent. I am telling myself that I am the whole of me when I am working. Have I not cramped my Self into a very narrow hole? Should I not then feel uncomfortable in so many ways?

Soul Work is valuable in itself; it cannot be equated with money. If I equate it with money I create a hierarchy of values, distinctions, separations, and divisions within me and the world. I forget the unique worth of each individual and myself. In the giving and receiving of each individual's worth, the soul is lost in an exchange of dead matter — money.

Further, this work I do is based on acquired knowledge; it can be destroyed at any time, for example, by brain damage. It can leave me in old age. A stroke of paralysis can make me totally helpless.

Reflections like these — Soul Work — slowly brings me nearer to face my Nothingness. Perhaps in facing this "No-thingness" one finds the real answer. Perhaps the root cause of the sense of insecurity and the fear of No Work exists because I do not really see "who" is so worried about security . . . who I AM.

COMMENTS

by

J. Marvin Spiegelman

I was privileged to listen to this paper, presented by Dr. Vasavada at the meeting of the International Association of Analytical Psychology in San Francisco in 1980, and was deeply moved by it. I sat next to a colleague, a psychiatrist and analyst from San Francisco, and, at the end, we each noticed that the other had tears in his eyes. We smiled and nodded, for here was a deeply moving work, an honest, sincere, and Self-revealing work in every sense.

Dr. Vasavada, in my opinion, clearly shows a deep struggle and union between East and West. Just as, in previous papers, he contrasted one with the other, seemed to long for the East then the West, and vice-versa, here he not only unites them in an *individual* way, he transcends them. I love this quote: "I began . . . to see that what I so far knew, whether in terms of what I had learned from Jung or my gurus, was hackneyed, stale and useless . . . I did not really know anything new. All I knew left me feeling quite cold."

The man who says those words is deeply involved in what in the west we call the "dark night of the soul." In that, he must transcend not only all of his old teachers, but even his own knowledge and experience. And Dr.

Vasavada does this. His reflections are very much the path of western individuation, his content is very Eastern, and he ends with "Nothingness" and even not knowing. Just as Jung ended his life, as he said in his autobiography. After a lifetime spent in becoming conscious of himself, he did not know who he was! My God, my God, how Thou dost transcend us, wheresoever we go, whatsoever we do!

It is instructive to me that the process of East and West continues in Dr. Vasavada, even as he entertains the great guru "Mr. Nobody," who was himself a Dane from Europe! And so we watch this process in Dr. Vasavada, struggling deeply with a great western symbol, Money, and coming to his individual place with it. I salute him, as colleague, friend, fellow seeker on the path to Enlightenment and Individuation.

MEETING JUNG

by

Arwind Vasavada

Note: Dr. Vasavada wrote the following remembrance, Meeting Jung, at my request. He told the story of this experience at a weekend's visit to our house, in the fall of 1986, at a moment of mutual warmth and sharing of our memories of Zurich. My wife and I were so moved by his recounting of this experience, that I asked him to write it for inclusion here. In its brevity and clarity, it speaks volumes about the meeting of East and West, of therapist and guru, of scientist and philosopher, and, finally, of person and person. It is an honor to include it in our book.

J. Marvin Spiegelman

Soon after arriving in Zurich, I wrote to Jung expressing my desire to work with him or Mrs. Jung. He wrote back that it was not possible as they did not take any new clients. I wrote back that I would like to pay my respects to him, which he granted.

I went to his house on Seestrasse and waited in a room below. I heard some steps coming down the stairs after some time. The door of the waiting room opened. I had expected the same person to take me to Jung who brought me to this room; instead, I saw Jung at the door. It was a surprise and joy to see the guru in person for whose Darshana (visit) I had travelled thousands of miles, leaving my home and children. I involuntarily fell flat at his feet. He lifted me and led me to his study upstairs.

In the course of the conversation, I asked him the first question, "Why do you call yourself a psychologist, a scientist, as you have said in *Psychology and Alchemy.* You are a guru leading man to experience the truth of life beyond all 'isms." I then recalled what he said about a Parsee returning to his Fire Temple. I added, "This is what a guru does." Jung was humble and did not accept it.

A couple of months after that, I received a letter from my State Government that they miscalculated the educational expenses and that I would have to sign for an additional loan. (The scholarship I had was such that half the expenses were to be covered by the Federal and half by the State Governments. Since the State had refused to do so, they had given me a loan before I left India.) I wrote back to my State that I could not take on any additional burden. I and my analysts, Drs. Meier and L. Frey, were disturbed and I was very sad. I was expecting the call back home anytime. I felt like a starved man deprived of a meal just after having been offered it. When Jung learned of my misfortune, he called me. I met him with heavy heart and intense yearning. I had taken a small crystal of Camphor with

186

me to perform the Arati (a ritual before god and guru, signifying one's yearning).

Jung received me at the door and led me to the garden. He sat on a bench and I squatted on the lawn facing him. Jung was silent and I remained in depression and yearning. I said to Jung that perhaps it was not fated for me to learn from him and, knowing that, I would like to perform a ritual before him. I took out the piece of Camphor from my pocket, placed it on a leaf and lighted it. The Camphor burnt up, leaving no ashes, as it does. Jung asked me the significance of the ritual. I said that at the end of every prayer in the morning and evening, the ritual signifies that the devotee wishes to dissolve into god or guru, not leaving even the trace of ashes (ego).

I took my final examination in the spring of 1956, as the scholarship was only for two years. I failed in Psychiatry. The question "What is depression?" sank me into depression and I could not answer. It is not easy to face the world and your home across the distant waters with failure when one has done his best. There was anger and disappointment within. I fantasied saying to the Curatorium, "I did not come here to study Psychiatry. I wanted to learn Jung's Psychology. I have passed that examination." It felt like having been betrayed. I was to return home within a month or so and was waiting for my passage from the Indian Consulate in Berne.

One day I received a letter from Jung telling me that I did not understand his Psychology and that I had learnt nothing. It was a long and very nasty letter. It devastated me. Nothing worse could have happened to me. For a Hindu, the anger of his guru is like hell fire, unbearable, especially when he sees that he has done nothing to hurt him. I searched my heart and found that I held him in the same reverence as I did my guru. I could not stand it. I wrote to him at once telling him that I did not deserve that. I, a Hindu Brahmin, cannot return home burning like fire without explanation and an understanding of what caused his anger.

On Jan. 26, 1956, the Indian Embassy invited Jung to the celebration of India's Republic Day. The Ambassador asked me to be in Berne to entertain Jung.

That day in Berne, I told Jung that my dissertation was a comparison between Jung's Psychology and an old Sanskrit text. I asked him if he would like to read it. He readily agreed. I sent him a copy of the dissertation "Tripura Rahasya" in the beginning of February '56. In the synopsis of the thesis I said, "A Jungian Analyst charges Sw. Fr. 30 or 40 for an hour of analysis, a guru's fee is the ego of the disciple." Perhaps this may have annoyed Jung.

After writing the above letter I waited for a week or so to hear from Jung. There was no reply and the days were drawing near for my departure. I spoke to Dr. Meier and requested him to intercede with Jung so that I could explain my situation. Dr. Meier told me that Jung was in Bollingen. No one can reach him there. "Your letter may be waiting there. He will open it only when the Unconscious will tell him." It was terribly frustrating to know this. A couple of days afterwards, I heard from Jung. He asked me to see him in Bollingen on a certain day and time. I was very happy and reported it to Dr. Meier, who said he would drive me to Bollingen on that day and leave me some distance from Jung's home.

I walked to Jung's home. There was a heavy wooden door with an iron ring on it. It was a cloudy and rainy cold day. I tapped the ring. Jung opened the door and led me to the fire place. The fire was burning and on a tripod water was boiling for coffee. There was something to eat also. After partaking of coffee, he started lashing out at me, saying that I did not understand his Psychology. His Psychology was a science and not a philosophy, he said, and I was trying to compare the head of one with the tail of the other. I do not recall how long it lasted. It was almost two hours when I left him. I listened to every word of Jung attentively and with all humility. I had had similar experiences with my first guru in India. I knew how to respond to such a fire.

When he had finished, I calmly told Jung that even though I had a Doctoral Degree in philosophy and had learned that subject from an internationally known person like Dr. S. Radhakrishnan, I really had not understood the heart of the wisdom of the Upanishads. The texts revealed their meaning only after I worked with my first guru. He asked me to throw away the books and to listen to him. I further reminded Jung that he had called me from time to time, at a critical period of my analysis, and had followed my progress. I told him that I had learnt his psychology to the best of my capacity. Then I told him a dream I had after my failure in Psychiatry:

July 19, '56.
I am going to Junagadh (an ancient town where my family belongs) and have to change the train at Viramgam, a border town between British India and the native state of Junagadh. The train comes on the platform and goes up a siding on a small hill where the rail lines are in circles. The train for Junagadh comes near the siding and runs parallel to our train and then halts at the platform. I go to the train to find a place for myself. It is very crowded. Looking for a place, I come across an open carriage where a man is selling betel-nuts (a green leaf we chew after meals and the one also used in the worship of deity). It is an exhibition carriage on the train.

This one is not crowded. I start placing my luggage there to reserve the seat. The man says, "Do you not see that this is meant for exhibition and not for ordinary passengers?" I am disappointed but still stand before him and look into his face. He seems to change and asks me if there are many people with me. I say we are only four (in fact, we are five). I tell him that I am much concerned about my old mother, she will die in such a crowd. He allows me to keep the luggage in the compartment and I go to bring my mother and the others. I see them coming down the slope of the hill.

(Dream changes)

I find myself in a waiting hall of a rail station. Near me is an oval table. Either on this table or on my arm lies a small baby child, like a balloon. It is Dr. Jung. He points towards a wall. There is an iron ring that strikes on the wall every moment and makes a round impression on it, then the wall moves (recedes). One sees series of round impressions receding as the ring strikes and the wall moves. Dr. Jung says, "Like this ring I am making impressions in the past. I am thus in the past, in the future and in the present."

I exclaim, "This is the ancient wisdom you speak. Why do you then contradict yourself so often?" He replies, "This is to bring you to utter despair so that you may speak." End of Dream.

Everything changed the moment I mentioned to Jung about having this dream. He was eager to hear it: "What is it? Tell me the dream," he said.

The dream made it clear that I was going back to India, to my native state, passing through the custom post of British India, the foreign rule, with the child Jung with me in my arms.

The whole atmosphere changed when I told him the dream. I then requested him to give me a testimonial if he felt convinced that I had learnt his Psychology, since I was going away without a Diploma. He agreed and sent it to me later.

I got my Diploma still later, having passed the examination in Psychiatry in India with a Swiss Psychiatrist, Dr. Erna Hoch.

AFTERWORD: A LETTER FROM C.G. JUNG

Introduction

by

J. Marvin Spiegelman

Having made the voyage through Hinduism and Jungian Psychology — at least that part of the great sea which was navigable by Spiegelman and Vasavada — the reader may have deepened his understanding, but is still unreconciled as to how these two areas finally come together. If so, he is in much the same "boat" as the authors, who, having travelled the same route, arrive at where they came in: East and West. This may not be a loss at all, however, since our path is truly a circle, the world is a sphere, and, in the travelling, we have deepened both our experience and our understanding of it. In the end, we face the paradox of the soul, which is, perhaps, just like our polarization of East and West: one looks at the ego or the particle or one looks at the whole or the Self. And one may be looking at the whole from the point of view of the particle or from the whole. Yet, as Jung rightly maintains and is evident, as long as we are in a mortal frame, we are limited, we can never grasp the whole. This has the advantage of material realisation but the disadvantage of lack of final wholeness. Perhaps we have glimpses of the final condition, and thereby, with Christmas Humphreys, can speak of ego (our own little particle) and Self (our own experience of the totality) and SELF, that which includes us all and is beyond us all but which we can only glimpse. In any case, the authors are grateful to Jung for being the one to truly begin the unification in this very modern process, and to lead us, individually, on our path, coming as we do, from East and West.

It seems only fair, however, to let Jung have the last word. His late words, in his *Memories, Dreams, Reflections* and in those marvellous East-West dreams and visions, are known to us all. Not known, perhaps, is the letter he addressed to one of the present authors, Vasavada, in response to just the kind of question that the latter has posed in the course of this book. It is with pleasure that we close with Jung's beautiful answer, hoping that the reader will let this paradox work on him/her and, in so doing, further the dialogue of East and West as it emerges in our individual souls.

To Arvind U. Vasavada

(Original in English)

Dear friend,   22 November 1954

Thank you for your kind letter and the beautiful "salutation to the perfect Master." In the guru, I perceive, you greet the infinitesimal God whose light becomes visible wherever a man's consciousness has made even the smallest step forward and beyond one's own horizon. The light of the Dawn praised by our medieval thinkers as the *Aurora consurgens*, the rising morning light, is awe-inspiring, it fills your heart with joy and admiration or with irritation and fear and even with hatred, according to the nature of whatever it reveals to you.

The ego receives the light from the self. Though we know of the self, yet it is not known. You may see a big town and know its name and geographical position, yet you do not know a single one of its inhabitants. You may even know a man through daily intercourse, yet you can be entirely ignorant of his real character. The ego is contained in the self as it is contained in the universe of which we know only the tiniest section. A man of greater insight and intelligence than mine can know myself, but I could not know him as long as my consciousness is inferior to his. Although we receive the light of consciousness from the self and although we know it to be the source of our illumination, we do not know whether it possesses anything we would call consciousness. However beautiful and profound the sayings of your Wisdom are, they are essentially outbursts of admiration and enthusiastic attempts at formulating the overwhelming impressions an ego-consciousness has received from the impact of a superior subject. Even if the ego should be (as I think) the supreme point of the self, a mountain infinitely higher than Mt. Everest, it would be nothing but a little grain of rock or ice, never the whole mountain. Even if the grain recognizes itself as being part of the mountain and understands the mountain as an immense agglomeration of particles like itself, it does not know their ultimate nature, because all the others are, like itself, *individuals*, incomparable and incomprehensible in the last resort.

If the self could be wholly experienced, it would be a limited experience whereas in reality its experience is unlimited and endless. It is our ego-consciousness that is capable only of limited experience. We can only *say* that the self is limitless, but we cannot *experience* its infinity. I can *say* that my consciousness is the same as that of the self, but it is nothing but words, since there is not the slightest evidence that I participate more or further in the self than my ego-consciousness reaches. What does the grain know of the whole mountain, although it is visibly a part of it? If I were one with the self, I would have knowledge of everything, I would speak Sanskrit, read cuneiform script, know the events that took place in prehistory, be acquainted with the life of other planets, etc. There is unfortunately nothing of the kind.

You should not mix up your own enlightenment with the self-revelation of the self. When you recognize yourself, you have not necessarily recognized the self but perhaps only an infinitesimal part of it, though the self has given you the light.

Your standpoint seems to coincide with that of our medieval mystics, who tried to dissolve themselves in God. You all seem to be interested in how to get back to the self, instead of looking for what the self wants you to do in the world, where -- for the time being at least -- we are located, presumably for a certain purpose. The universe does not seem to exist for the sole purpose of man denying or escaping it. Nobody can be more convinced of the importance of the self than me. But as a young man does not stay in his father's house but goes out into the world, so I don't look back to the self but collect it out of manifold experiences and put it together again. What I have left behind, seemingly lost, I meet in everything that comes my way and I collect it, reassembling it as it were. In order to get rid of opposites, I needs must accept them first, but this leads away from the self. I must also learn how opposites can be united, and not how they can be avoided. As long as I am on the first part of the road I have to forget the self in order to get properly into the mill of the opposites, otherwise I live only fragmentarily and conditionally. Although the self is my origin, it is also the goal of my quest. When it was my origin, I did not know myself, and when I did learn about myself, I did not know the self. I have to discover it in my actions, where first it reappears under strange masks. That is one of the reasons why I must study symbolism, otherwise I risk not recognizing my own father and mother when I meet them again after the many years of my absence.

Hoping I have answered your questions, I remain,

Yours sincerely, C.G. Jung

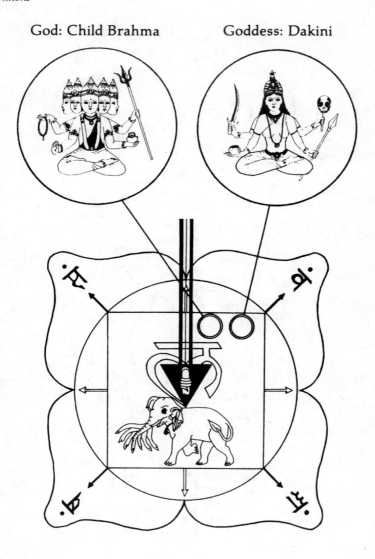

God: Child Brahma   Goddess: Dakini

Muladhara: The First Chakra

God: Visnu   Goddess: Sakti Rakini

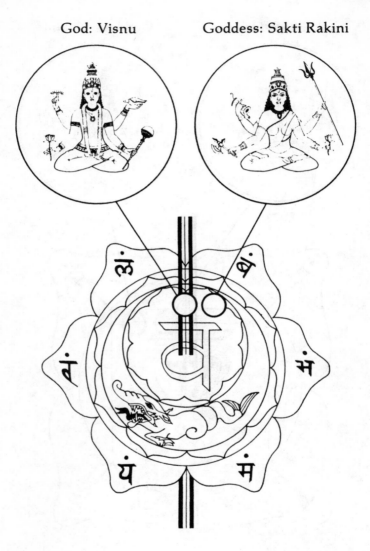

Svadhisthana: The Second Chakra

God: Visnu   Goddess: Lakini

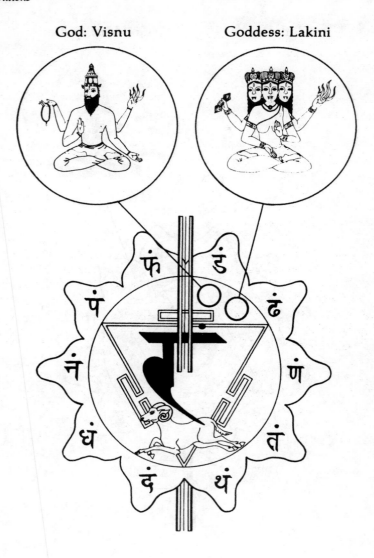

Manipura: The Third Chakra

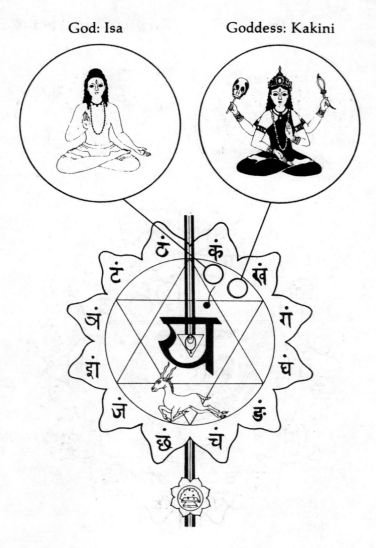

Anahata: The Fourth Chakra

God: Sadasiva   Goddess: Gauri (Eternal)

Vishuddha: The Fifth Chakra

God/Goddess: Sakti Hakini

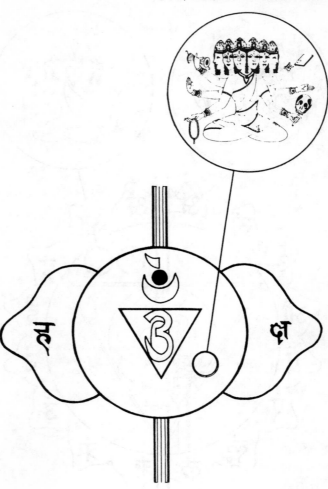

Ajna: The Sixth Chakra

Sahasrara: The Seventh Chakra

Whipping Men

The Tree

Holding up the Goat's Eye

Dance of the Moon Goddess

Books of Lives

Six Headed Goddess

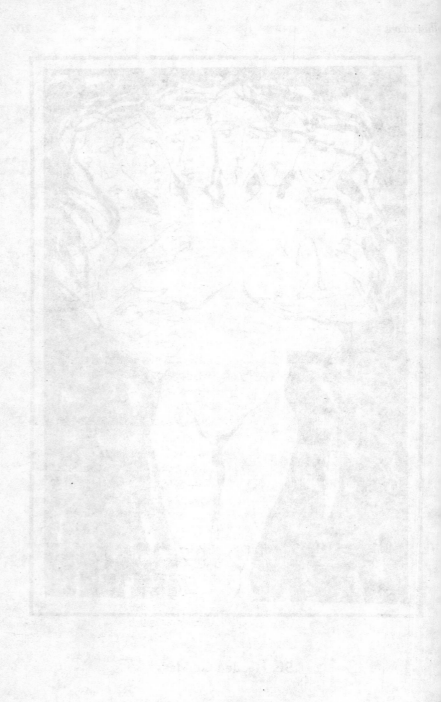